Black Africa 1945~80

Economic Decolonization & Arrested Development

Black Africa 1945~80

Economic Decolonization & Arrested Development

D. K. Fieldhouse

Jesus College, Cambridge

London
ALLEN & UNWIN
BOSTON   SYDNEY

Allen & Unwin (Publishers) Ltd,
40 Museum Street, London WC1A 1LU, UK

Allen & Unwin (Publishers) Ltd,
Park Lane, Hemel Hempstead, Herts HP2 4TE, UK

Allen & Unwin, Inc.,
8 Winchester Place, Winchester, Mass. 01890, USA

Allen & Unwin (Australia) Ltd,
8 Napier Street, North Sydney, NSW 2060, Australia

First published in 1986

British Library Cataloguing in Publication Data

Fieldhouse, David
    Black Africa 1945–1980.
    Economic Decolonization and arrested development.
1. Africa – Economic conditions – 1945–.
I. Title
330.96'032   HC502
ISBN 0-04-325017-3

Library of Congress Cataloging-in-Publication Data

Fieldhouse, D. K. (David Kenneth), 1925–
    Black Africa 1945–1980.
    Economic Decolonization and arrested development.
Bibliography: p.
Includes index.
1. Africa, Sub-Saharan – Economic policy. 2. Africa,
Sub-Saharan – Economic policy – Case studies. 3. Decolon-
ization – Africa, Sub-Saharan – History. 4. Great
Britain – Colonies – Africa – History. 5. France –
Colonies – Africa – History. I. Title.
HC800.F54 1986   338.967   85–32067
ISBN 0-04-325017-3 (alk. paper)

Set in 10 on 11 point Plantin by Grove Graphics, Tring, Hertfordshire
and printed in Great Britain by Billing and Son Ltd,
London and Worcester

For Sheila Fieldhouse,
who read it first

Contents

List of Tables and Figure   *page*   xi

List of Abbreviations   xiii

Preface   xv

PART ONE: The End of the Colonial Period   1

1   *The Economic Dimensions of British and French Decolonization in Black Africa*   3

    Great Britain   6
    France   12

2   *The Colonial Inheritance*   27

    The Late-Colonial Economies, *c.*1945–*c.*1960   32
    The Nature of the Late-Colonial State   55
    Post-Colonial Economic Relations between African States and One-Time Metropolises   58

PART TWO: Economic Performance and Explanations, 1960–1980   67

3   *Performance, Expectations and the 'Policy' Approach*   69

    General Trends in Black Africa, 1960–1980 – an Overview   71
    False Expectations and their Origins   85
    Weakness at the Centre: African Governments as a Prime Cause of Limited Development   90

4   *'Non-Policy' Explanations of Limited Development*   101

    Africa and the International Economy   101
    Endogenous African Influences on Development   122

PART THREE: The 'Policy' Explanation in Six
    African States   137

5 *Anglophone West Africa: Ghana and Nigeria*   139
   Ghana   139
   Nigeria   150

6 *Anglophone East Africa: Kenya and Tanzania*   163
   Kenya   163
   Tanzania   173

7 *Francophone West Africa: Ivory Coast*   187

8 *Francophone West Africa: Senegal*   207

9 *Summary and Conclusions. Economic Decolonization
    and 'Arrested Development'*   231

Bibliography of Works Cited in the Text   247

Index   255

List of Tables and Figure

Tables

page

2.1 Fixed Capital Formation as a Percentage of GNP for Selected African Countries, 1950–1964   39

2.2 Gross Domestic Investment, Gross Domestic Saving and Resource Balance as a Percentage of Gross Domestic Product in Selected African Territories, 1960   40

2.3 Population, Income and Manufacturing Output in Selected African Countries, 1960   43

2.4 International Liquidity of Selected African Colonies at or about the Time of Independence, Compared with their Position in 1982   50

2.5 The Public Debt of Selected British Colonies at or about the Date of Independence, Showing its Relationship to Public Revenue and GNP   52

2.6 Public Debt as a Percentage of Public Revenue and GNP of Selected Colonies and Other Countries at or about the Time of Independence   53

2.7 External Public Debt Service Ratio of Selected African Countries, 1965, 1970, 1982   54

3.1 Black Africa, 1960–1982: Basic Indicators   72

3.2 Black Africa, 1960–1982: Growth of Production   74

3.3 Black Africa, 1960–1982: Structure of Production   76

3.4 Black Africa, 1960–1982: Growth of Consumption and Investment   78

3.5 Black Africa, 1960–1982: Structure of Demand   80

3.6 Black Africa, 1960–1982: Growth of Merchandise Trade   82

4.1 Capital Flows to Black Africa, 1965–1977   107

4.2 The Burden of Interest and Repayment on External Public Debt for Selected African Countries, 1970 and 1982   109

4.3 Debt Service as a Percentage of GNP and the Export of Goods and Services for Selected African and Other Countries, 1970 and 1982   110

4.4 Average Terms of Borrowing for Sub-Saharan Africa, 1970–1982   111

4.5 Third World Indebtedness, 1970–1980: Total External Public Debt by Creditor Source, and Private Non-Guaranteed Debt   112

4.6 Growth Rates of Third World Indebtedness, 1970–1980: External Public Debt by Creditor Source, and Private Non-Guaranteed Debt   114

4.7 Sources of Third World External Debts, 1970–1980: External Public Debt by Creditor Source, and Private Non-Guaranteed Debt   116

5.1 Ghana's Public Debt, 1959–1964   148

5.2 Ghana's External Debt and Debt Service, 1967–1982   148

5.3 The Relationship between Ghana's External Public Debt and GDP, 1960–1979   149

5.4 Nigeria's External Public Debt and Debt Service, 1959–1982   160

6.1 Kenya's External Public Debt and Debt Service, 1959–1982   172

6.2 Tanzania's External Public Debt and Debt Service, 1962–1982   183

7.1 Ivory Coast's External Public Debt and Debt Service, 1967–1982   203

8.1 Senegal's External Public Debt and Debt Service, 1967–1982   210

Figure

9.1 Continuities and Discontinuities between Colonial and Post-Colonial Practice   240

List of Abbreviations

Only those abbreviations which occur more than once, other than in the same paragraph, are listed.

BDS	Bloc Démocratique Sénégalais
BNDS	Banque Nationale de Développement Sénégalaise
CD&W	Colonial Development and Welfare (Acts)
CFAO	Compagnie Française de l'Afrique Occidentale
CJAS	*Canadian Journal of African Studies*
CPE	centrally planned economy
CRADs	Centres Régionaux de l'Assistance au Développement
DAC	Development Advisory Committee (of the OECD)
EEC	European Economic Community
EGS	export of goods and services
FIDES	Fonds d'Investissement pour le Développement Economique et Social
GATT	General Agreement on Tariffs and Trade
GDP	gross domestic product
GNP	gross national product
IBRD	International Bank for Reconstruction and Development (World Bank)
IDA	International Development Association (of the World Bank)
IMF	International Monetary Fund
JMAS	*Journal of Modern African Studies*
OCA	Office de Commercialisation Africain
OECD	Organization for Economic Co-operation and Development
OEEC	Organization for European Economic Co-operation
OPEC	Organization of Oil-Exporting Countries
PDCI	Parti Démocratique de Côte d'Ivoire
RAPE	*Review of African Political Economy*
SC	Service de la Coopération
SCOA	Société Commerciale de l'Ouest Africain
UAC	United Africa Company
UN	United Nations
UPS	Union Progressiste Sénégalaise
WDR	World Development Report

Note on the Use of Measures

All measures of size, length and weight are metric throughout, including 'ton'. Billion (abbreviated b.) is one thousand million (1,000,000,000), as in American usage, not one million million, as in official British and French usage.

Preface

The genesis of this book helps to explain its character. It began as a paper I was asked to write for the conference on 'African Independence: Origins and Consequences of the Transfer of Power, 1956–1980', which was held at the University of Zimbabwe, Harare, in January 1985. The organizers, Prosser Gifford and Roger Louis, asked me to write a paper on 'The Economic Dimensions of Decolonization and Independence in Anglophone Black Africa' to balance a paper by Catherine Coquery-Vidrovitch on Francophone Africa. I found it quite impossible to deal with so large a subject briefly: the result was not an essay but about half a book. The organizers tolerantly distributed this aberration to the conference and I later boiled down the core of the argument to chapter length for eventual publication as part of the proceedings of the conference. But having got so far, I decided to complete my half-book by adding material on France and Francophone African states and filling structural gaps pointed to by friends and colleagues. The result is the book in its present form.

These origins help to explain some obvious features and limitations of the book. First, this is not the result of original research over many years but an attempt to absorb and assess a large amount of published material in the course of about three years. Secondly, it is restricted to Black Africa because that was the focus of the conference; but in fact this has the advantage of imposing greater unity of place and theme. Thirdly, because these were the twin themes of the conference, it deals, though at unequal length, with two related but distinct questions. On the one hand, what relative importance had economic considerations in the decision of the metropolitan powers (here limited mainly to Britain and France for reasons of length) to decolonize? On the other hand, to what extent and for what reasons was economic development in Black Africa unsatisfactory after independence? These are quite distinct issues and each would rate a book. Their combination here suggests that there may have been some causal or sequential relationship between them, and this possibility will be explored in the final section of the last chapter.

The book is intended primarily to provide a critical introduction to large and controversial issues. Few of the questions it poses can yet be answered with any confidence since no primary sources are open after the mid-1950s and insufficient research has yet been published on economic development in the two decades after 1960. The footnotes make it obvious that I, in common with most other writers on modern African economic history, have relied very heavily on statistical data collected and published by the International Bank for Reconstruction and Development (IBRD: usually referred to as the World Bank), United Nations (UN) and International Monetary Fund (IMF), particularly the World Bank's *World Tables* (1976 and 1980), *Accelerated Development in Sub-Saharan Africa* (the Berg Report, 1981) and *Toward Sustained Development in Sub-Saharan Africa* (1984). They are used because there is in most cases no alternative source of statistics; but it must be said that, quite apart from the fact that all represent fairly conservative standpoints on Third World problems, they have significant limitations. Four seem worth a short comment.

First, these agencies depend on information provided by reporting governments. This is not invariably given and what is available is not necessarily accurate nor comparable as between one state and another. Precise figures are, therefore, almost certainly misleading, even though I have necessarily reproduced them. It is broad trends, not exact percentages or totals, that count.

Secondly, few of these publications contain statistics before about 1960 which are comparable in concept and detail with those for later periods. This makes it difficult to treat the late-colonial period and the first decades of independence as the economic continuum they of course were and as I have tried to describe them in this book.

Thirdly, in these sources values are either published in local currencies or converted from them into dollars at the prevailing official exchange rate. For some states whose currencies were tied to foreign currencies (as were most of the Francophone states) this may be realistic; but for many others, which maintained heavily over-priced currencies, it gives an exaggerated and non-comparable impression of achievement.

Finally, I had difficulties with the tables showing the growing burden of African indebtedness, which is necessarily an important part of the story. Modern analysis tends to concentrate on the debt service ratio, that is, the proportion of the export of goods and services of a state which is absorbed by interest and repayment of principal on external debts. Before the early 1960s these concepts were not generally used and I have had to make do with other measures of colonial indebtedness. From the early 1960s to 1977 one can work out an internally consistent series from the World Bank's *World Tables* published in 1976 and 1980. But for the years 1979–82, important here because they represent a crisis period for independent Africa, I have found difficulty. *Accelerated Development* and *Toward Sustained Development* give figures for total external debt, the amount of debt service and the debt service ratio as a percentage of export of goods and services for 1979 and 1982 respectively. They give the total value of the export of merchandise but no figure for export of goods and services itself, which is, of course, larger than that for these visible exports. One could derive such a figure from other data on export of goods and services as a percentage of the gross domestic product (GDP) given in these publications; I have in fact taken it from the IMF *International Financial Statistics Yearbook*. In neither case did the debt service ratio consistently work out the same as in *Accelerated Development* and *Toward Sustained Development*. Unable to explain these variations, I have, therefore, in these tables shown my own calculation of this ratio and given the World Bank's ratio in brackets. The trends are always the same but the figures are sometimes different.

Two other obvious limitations of the book are that it deals in any detail only with Francophone and Anglophone African countries and that there are only six studies of individual states, four of them in West Africa. There is no detailed material on Zaire or the Lusophone countries. By a different measure, there is not enough on mineral-exporting as contrasted with agricultural-exporting economies. For these limitations there are several reasons. The aim of Parts Two and Three of the book is to examine those common factors which seem to have determined the economic fortunes of African states. Since the Lusophone states became independent only in 1974–5, the evidence does not cover a sufficient time period to provide a useful guide to longer-term trends. Moreover, the state of endemic internal conflict in Angola and Mozambique makes it impossible to measure the operation of purely economic factors. For the rest I chose countries on which the best research seems to have been done and which could also be said to present different but characteristic features of recent African economic development.

Ghana was an inevitable choice as the state which was the first in Black Africa to become independent, was then one of the most affluent, was first to undertake development based on huge foreign borrowing and industrialization, and later became an economic casualty. Nigeria, the most populous and rich Black African state, had to be included to study the effects of sudden wealth from oil. Kenya earned a place by virtue of its importance in the current debate over the evolution of an indigenous bourgeoisie in an open capitalist economy; Tanzania because of the unique character of its experiments in rural social engineering and state socialism. The two Francophone states, Ivory Coast and Senegal, had to be included because they appear to represent two contrasting consequences of continued dependence on commodity production and export: Ivory Coast because of its well-publicized 'economic miracle', Senegal for its allegedly disastrous record. These are dealt with at rather greater length than the Anglophone states because much of the material is unfamiliar to English-speaking students. I do not regret including any of these countries; I can only

regret that there was no space for more individual studies. I have tried
to compensate for this by including statistical data on a wider range of
states and by broadening the scope of the discussion in the general
chapters in Part Two.

Most contemporary studies of Third World history are replete with
terms of art, and I have been unable to avoid using some of this
terminology. Among the terms used here are the following, with the
meaning commonly attributed to them. 'Growth' implies a quantita-
tive increase in production, either in national or per capita terms.
'Development' indicates a qualitative or 'structural' change in an
economy and society which enables it to undertake sustained growth.
'Arrested development' presents more serious conceptual difficulties.
I have used it in the title as evocative short-hand but it needs careful
qualification. In the radical terminology of dependency and Marxist
literature it has a specific meaning, suggesting that an economy has
reached a stage at which exogenous or endogenous obstacles absolutely
bar further development until and unless there is fundamental
economic and political reconstruction. Samir Amin has used 'blocked'
in the same sense. In this usage 'arrested', therefore, poses an implicit
question: did the economies of Black Africa in fact reach such a static
and immobile condition during this period? This book is not primarily
concerned to answer such a question; indeed, for the empirical
economic historian it is unanswerable because, even if (using the
standard measurements of growth) an economy ceased to grow at a
particular time, this would not necessarily imply that it could not
resume development thereafter. Its development might simply have
been checked. My aim, therefore, is more general: to consider in the
loosest terms how and for what reasons economic development in Black
Africa seems to have been unsatisfactory or to have gone wrong after
decolonization, leading to the critical situation of many countries in the
early 1980s. Going wrong has many possible dimensions and may be
indicated by different words. Decelerating would imply that rates of
growth, however measured, became slower over time; limited that
development went less far than was or might have been hoped for;
checked or arrested (in a non-technical sense) that, at least for the time
being, growth had reached a statistical standstill. In the text 'arrested'
will, therefore, only be used in the radical sense when in quotation
marks. The other terms are used less specifically; but in the final
chapter an attempt will be made to decide which of them most
accurately describes what went wrong with Black African economies
after decolonization.

Finally 'the transfer of power', 'independence' and 'decolonization'
are used synonymously to indicate the handing over of sovereignty by
an imperial power to a colonial dependency. 'Economic
decolonization', therefore, suggests the emancipation of a colonial

economy from formal constraints imposed by an imperial economic system as a result of the transfer of political sovereignty; and the title of the book can be translated as 'The end of imperial economic control over Black Africa and the check to or blocking of sustained economic growth there during the next two decades'.

In a preface one can never thank all the people who have helped in the making of a book by reading drafts or discussing its themes. I am particularly obliged to two colleagues in Cambridge who are far more expert in African history than I, John Iliffe and John Lonsdale; to Martin Knight and Steven Bell of Morgan Grenfell & Co. Ltd., who sent me valuable material and gave expert advice on African indebtedness; and to Maurice Scott of Nuffield College, Oxford, on whom I rely for advice and correction on economic matters. I am also grateful to Hilary Walford, who did the copy-editing and picked up innumerable errors and inconsistencies. None of these or my many other advisers is, of course, in any way responsible for what I have written.

Jesus College, Cambridge   D. K. Fieldhouse
November 1985

PART ONE

The End of the Colonial Period

1

The Economic Dimensions of British and French Decolonization in Black Africa

It has long been a problem for those who hold that the colonial empires were a successful device by which advanced capitalism in the West could extract wealth from the dependencies to explain why these milch-cows should have been set loose. The problem was not peculiar to the mid-twentieth century. Adam Smith stated bluntly in 1776 that: 'To propose that Great Britain should voluntarily give up all authority over her colonies . . . would be to propose such a measure as never was and never will be adopted, by any nation in the world.'[1]

For nearly two centuries his prediction proved correct; the only colonies any European state lost permanently before 1931 (when the white settler Dominions were enabled to become sovereign states within the Empire–Commonwealth) were the result of successful rebellion or international war and diplomacy. A comparable problem, however, was posed by the end of the slave trade and the emancipation of slaves by Britain between 1807 and 1834; and the way this has been treated provides an interesting rehearsal of arguments later used to explain the apparently inexplicable benevolence of the capitalist states in liberating Africa.

In each of these cases the official rhetoric originally stressed the benevolence of the liberating state. In the case of slavery the conventional account was that an altruistic Britain destroyed the economic foundations of its most valuable overseas possessions simply to clear its conscience. It was only with the publication of Eric Williams's *Capitalism and Slavery*[2] that an explanation compatible with the assumption that capitalist states act only in self-interest became widely accepted. Williams argued that Britain ended the slave trade and subsequently slavery only when and because the sugar industry had ceased to be critical for its own economy. This ingenious and initially persuasive proposition, though much criticized by specialists on the slave trade,[3] led naturally to a still more ingenious suggestion that Britain ended the slave trade when it became less profitable to transport African labour overseas than to use the same labour in its homelands to serve the great new commodity trades of the nineteenth century – vegetable oils and other West African products.[4]

Right or wrong, this revisionist approach provides a key to the standard radical explanation of European decolonization after 1945. Europe transferred political power when and because it no longer needed to govern the colonies in order to ensure opportunity and security for metropolitan capital there.[5]

The common argument, in brief, is as follows. Historically the main function of colonialism was to restructure the economies of the Third World countries so that they would fit into their allotted slots in the newly emergent world system. This process had three main aspects. First, types of production had to be moulded so that the colonies produced commodities needed by the capitalist states (mostly raw materials and foodstuffs) and ceased to produce those manufactures which the metropolitan countries wished to sell to them. Secondly, modes of production had to be articulated with capitalist modes of production; for example, compulsory growing of cotton, groundnuts, palm oil, etc., by peasants had to be organized so as to provide materials for capitalist processing and export. Thirdly, it was necessary to create physical, political and juridical structures which were well adapted to the needs of foreign capital; that is, so that capitalism could operate as efficiently in Africa as it could in Europe or North America.

Applying this scheme to the chronology of African history, the process began in most parts of Africa in the later nineteenth century. It was well advanced by about 1929, but the Depression and the Second World War slowed up the process: things were little if at all more advanced in 1945 than they had been in 1929. Hence the main thrust of post-1945 colonial schemes for economic, social and political 'development' was to resume the momentum of transformation. By the later 1950s much progress had been made, particularly in those parts of Africa which had the longest exposure to the international economy. In these at least, notably France's North African protectorates and British West Africa, progress was so advanced by the mid-1950s that these powers felt that they could safely transfer formal political power. Many other territories had clearly not reached that stage by 1957–60, when the Gold Coast and Nigeria received independence, and the imperialists had then to face the need to establish a timetable for the remaining territories.

Until perhaps 1957–8 it had been assumed in London, Paris and Brussels (with Portugal still committed to permanent integration of her African territories with the fatherland) that each colony must be treated as a special case; decolonization would come only when certain 'objective' conditions had been met.[6] By the later 1950s, however, two factors stimulated the powers to speed up the process. On the one hand the experience of the Gold Coast and Nigeria during their semi-independent apprenticeship in the 1950s suggested that the successor African rulers were not only more competent than had been expected (with the aid of continuing European administrative support) to run their countries efficiently, but also that they were eager to safeguard and promote foreign capitalist enterprises. Secondly, the evolution of political organizations pledged to work for independence in the colonies not only caused inconvenience (hardly more − there were no 'freedom' fighters in sub-Saharan Africa except in the Portuguese territories) to colonial governments but suggested that the best policy for the imperialists was to establish good relations with their assumed successors before they became embittered by years of friction and waiting. Even the interests of white settlers in East and Central Africa would have to be sacrificed to these overriding considerations.

The result was the quite unpredicted transfer of power to virtually all African colonies, other than those of Portugal, between 1957 and 1965. In many places the transfer constituted a gamble on the part of the imperialists that the process of restructuring had gone far enough to be irreversible. In a few places, at least superficially, it later seemed that the gamble had failed: Guinea, Guinea-Bissau, Angola and Mozambique claimed, in different ways, to have destroyed their links with the imperialist West and cut the umbilical cord of capitalism. Most other new states proclaimed themselves to be 'socialist' and, in varying degrees, altered the rules of the economic game as they affected foreigners. Yet, so the argument goes, this was largely rhetoric. The essential dependence of virtually all these new states on Western aid, combined with the interest of the new dominant groups in each state, ensured that in reality all remained embedded within the international economic system in the roles originally allotted to them. Indeed, the policies of rapid social and industrial development they adopted provided an unprecedented opportunity to foreign investors, particularly, the multinationals (MNCs), which, it is important to note, had shown remarkably little interest in industrial investment in tropical Africa before independence. 'Neo-colonialism', 'dependence', or whatever one calls it, was thus the intended result of decolonization, just as the cultivation of groundnuts, palm oil and cocoa had been the planned consequence of ceasing to transfer Africans to the New World in the nineteenth century.

This scenario is attractive because it seems inherently likely. It is, moreover, very similar to the arguments produced by B. R. Tomlinson, among others, to explain why Britain was increasingly ready to leave India by the 1940s, but not earlier.[7] But it may not be true, or be only partly true, of Africa. Such large hypotheses always tend to argue backwards from *ex post* situations. Many of those in Britain who, after decolonization, proclaimed that liberating the colonies had all along been Britain's intention and that the Commonwealth fully justified her liberality would, from the 1920s to the early 1940s, vehemently have opposed rapid devolution of power to India or the African colonies. In the same way, the fact that economic links between the one-time metropolises and the new states of Africa remained close after independence, and that private capital often found much better opportunities than before, may suggest that such results were expected and that these expectations encouraged officials and capitalists to look forward to decolonization without fear and possibly with enthusiasm. Let us treat all such assumptions with suspicion. It may have been so, but equally it may not.

We are, then, faced with a basic question: was political power transferred to the Black African countries during the decade from 1957 primarily for economic reasons? It may in fact by impossible to answer so large a question with any precision, but at least the attempt can be made. What is the evidence?

In all matters connected with overseas possessions the historian has to deal with at least two collective attitudes: that of the offical mind and that of private interests. Let us investigate briefly how much is known about the attitudes of each of these in Britain and France to the economic dimensions of decolonization before it happened.

Great Britain

The Official Mind

The great irony of decolonization in Africa is that it came almost immediately after the post-1945 period when officialdom in the metropolitan states had regarded their colonies as an essential economic foundation for their own recovery and future development.[8] By means of a complex network of administrative controls (currency pools to channel all colonial dollar earnings to London, Paris or Brussels, bulk purchase of commodities to keep down prices in the metropolis, limitation of the export to colonies of manufactures which might earn hard currency elsewhere, building up credits representing the surpluses of marketing boards, hard currency earnings converted into sterling balances or francs, and so on), these metropolitan states squeezed and exploited their colonies in Africa (and also in South-East Asia) in ways never seen before. A rough calculation suggests that between 1945 and 1951 Britain extracted some £140m. from its colonies, putting in only about £40m. under the Colonial Development and Welfare (CD&W) Acts.[9] Under such conditions it would have seemed suicidal for any European government to transfer political power over the dependencies and so give them the opportunity to break out of this economic cage. Or, to put it another way, it is inconceivable that full decolonization could have occurred in any European possession in Africa during the post-1945 economic crisis.

But by about 1952 that crisis was over. At least temporarily the dollar shortage was past, European economic recovery was well advanced, international trade was moving freely and European currencies were becoming increasingly convertible. Conversely, and most significantly, from about 1952, as the Korean War boom ended, commodity prices dropped. From that year British colonies as a whole began to run a deficit with the dollar area, so that, instead of providing support for the pound sterling, they became a burden which became increasingly heavy as these currencies weakened later in the decade. Thus the most important new economic fact of the 1950s was that, with the end of war and postwar shortages, it was no longer necessary or useful to keep political control over African dependencies in order to harness them to the bogged-down imperial economies.

Once this was so, a number of economic or political factors began to support the case for decolonization. None was a sufficient motive in isolation, but collectively they not only neutralized the perceived benefits of political control but, on balance, probably encouraged the politicians to act.

One significant factor was experience in several colonies of the difficulty of mobilizing sufficient public support for what were perceived to be essential development projects of many kinds: for example, measures against soil erosion in Kenya. Deeply committed now to the concept of restructuring colonial economies, officials were coming round to the view that only elected indigenous governments, provided they were of the right kind, could carry their peoples with them into modernization. From the British side a number of economic and financial arguments for giving up the huge responsibilities undertaken since about 1940 were being aired in the mid-1950s. Colonial demands on the London capital market were tending to increase interest rates. The cost of aid under the CD&W Acts was escalating, and it was still believed in the mid-1950s that such aid would cease when colonies became independent. The cost of bulk purchase of sugar from the British West Indies (one of the few residual bulk purchase agreements) seemed too high now that world prices had fallen below the contract price. There was even some fear that imperial preference would enable newly industrializing colonies to compete unfairly with British manufactures.

By January 1957 such fears had induced Harold Macmillan, newly appointed as Prime Minister, to ask officialdom what was probably an unprecedented question: what costs and benefits might result for

Britain if the remaining colonies were given independence in the near future? As summarized by the official historian of colonial development, D. J. Morgan, the collective official reply was ambiguous:

> Taking this consideration along with the most likely effect on the flow of investment funds from the United Kingdom, on the use of sterling balances, on the sterling area balance of payments and on the trade of the United Kingdom, the conclusion was drawn that the economic considerations were fairly evenly matched [because, while Britain might save on some types of expenditure, there might be costs resulting from reduction of special commercial advantages it enjoyed in the colonies]. Consequently it was felt that the economic interests in the United Kingdom were unlikely in themselves to be decisive in determining whether or not a territory should become independent. Nor was it believed that strategic considerations should be uppermost, as the maintenance of bases against the will of the local Government and people would seriously limit their usefulness.[10]

This neutral reply may not have given Macmillan much help in deciding future policy but it did at least suggest that the official mind in Britain did not now regard economic factors as being decisive either way. Indeed, the current consensus was that the essential aim must now be to secure the goodwill of those who would eventually succeed to political power in the colonies. In the words of an African Committee of the Cabinet in 1959, as paraphrased by Morgan, 'It was taken for granted that Africa would continue to be an important market and that, whatever the political future, Africans would continue to desire to trade with us'.[11] Indeed, political and strategic considerations were far more significant. As Sir Roger Stevens put it in 1961, 'in spite of our substantial commercial and other interests in Africa, the latter's chief political importance for the West derived from the Cold War'.[12]

For British officials, at least, it therefore seems clear that willingness to transfer complete political power to colonies as soon as the transfer could be made decently – that is, to a democratically elected government which could reasonably be held to represent a 'national will' – was not in any direct sense the outcome of economic considerations. Rather one might say that the mid- and late-1950s, when general decolonization became an established British policy aim, were, in economic terms, a slack tide. Before about 1951 Britain's dependence on colonial currency earnings and commodity exports would have made such a policy inconceivable; indeed, it has been argued that the primary aim of the first tentative steps towards giving self-government in West Africa in the later 1940s was to extend the period of imperial control by keeping ahead of nascent nationalist demands before they became unmanageable.[13] After about 1960 the inconvenience of controlling these movements might well have forced Britain to evacuate in indecent haste, without the satisfaction of going through the now established rituals and, above all, at the risk of losing goodwill and therefore future economic opportunities.

The 1950s were, therefore, a decade in which economic considerations were virtually neutralized. Britain was free to decolonize because, for the moment, it did not depend on colonial economic support, though there were, of course, still countervailing non-economic influences, notably the strategic factor, which linked airfields and military bases in Kenya and Uganda to the problems of the Middle East. Conversely, the official mind never consciously decided that British economic and investment interests would do better under independent African regimes. On the assumption that independence was bound to come sooner or later, policy was to make it sooner, in the hope that a friendly parting would have the fewest possible bad effects on British political and also economic interests in Africa.

Non-Official Attitudes: British Business

It is far more difficult to know what attitudes British business as a whole took towards the prospect of decolonization in Africa than to know what the officials thought. On the one hand it is not the concern of businessmen to state their attitudes publicly on this sort of issue and their records seldom spell out their views on general principles. On the other hand very little work has been done or published on what these men said within their board rooms. Indeed, I know of only one study which deliberately set out to analyse such attitudes, J. E. Milburn's *British Business and Ghanaian Independence*;[14] and in many ways this book provides disappointingly little hard evidence. Milburn probably had the same experience as I had when researching on Unilever's overseas enterprises – that the records are remarkably silent.

The general impression, however, is that British business firms never thought very clearly about the prospects of decolonization. Certainly they did not regard it as the logical consequence of a process of restructuring colonial economies to the point at which political control was no longer necessary or desirable. For the Gold Coast, Milburn shows that the main British firms – United Africa Company (UAC) and John Holts in the import–export trade; Barclays DCO in banking; Cadburys in cocoa purchasing; and the mining companies, Consolidated African Selection Trust and Ashanti Gold Fields – had begun the process of Africanizing management well before the 1950s. But, significantly, all were following the logic of costs rather than political prevision. The process was conditioned by the nature of the work required and the limited stock of sufficiently educated Africans. As a proportion of the total management, however, African managers in UAC changed hardly at all between 1949 and 1957; the big change came after independence, and from 1957 to 1964 the percentage nearly doubled.[15] None of these firms seems to have played an active role in supporting or initiating proposals for political development. As Milburn puts it, 'the firms did not oppose political changes, nor did they try to arrest the increased political activity of the Ghanaians. They waited until changes took place and then attempted to cooperate with the new political leaders'; though there is some suggestion that one mining magnate was less unconcerned. In support of this argument Sir Alan Burns remarked that most companies in the transitional 1950s contributed funds to all parties but that none of the companies took any part in pressing for or against independence.[16]

The same cautious but not pessimistic attitude was adopted by Unilever in its various manufacturing and plantation enterprises in different parts of Africa. In Nigeria the small soap factory established near Lagos in 1923 had been a very limited enterprise until 1940. The war acted as a stimulus: soap sales rose from a peak of 4,400 tons in 1937 to 10,643 tons in 1946, the range of products was greatly expanded and profits were high from 1941 to 1956. This generated optimism. But for Unilever the first impact of political change came in 1954 when the three previous regions were made into semi-autonomous states whose assemblies controlled economic policy. The company's response was positive. A marketing expert advised in that year that it was now essential, for 'overwhelmingly political reasons', to expand by building a second factory in the new Eastern Region, since it seemed likely that, if Unilever did not get there first, the new regional government might set up its own factory. Moreover, he thought, 'the new form of government might be more co-operative [than the British authorities had been] and more anxious to attract industrial capital and encourage industrial products'. The London management accepted the proposal in December 1954 on the following grounds:

> In considering the whole project it was necessary to take account of the probable future political development of the country. Although it was possible to have doubts in this respect, having regard to the rapid transition from colonial status to self-government as elsewhere within the Commonwealth, there seemed no reason to have any special doubts about Nigeria.[17]

The factory was duly built at Aba. It proved a commercial disaster, because the market did not in fact justify a second production unit. But political considerations remained paramount. In 1965 the managing director of the whole West African business suggested that 'it would be extremely dangerous from a political point of view' to close the Aba factory; indeed, the same considerations might make it necessary to build a third factory in the Northern Region.

Unilever, in fact, saw Nigerian independence as a challenge rather than a threat or an advantage. Its main effect was to speed up changes in company policy already under way: the replacement of expatriate by Nigerian managers and the complete transformation of UAC from a trading to a manufacturing and retailing enterprise. Ghana provides a clearer example of the potentially stimulating effect of the prospect of independence.[18] Until the mid-1950s there had never been any serious possibility of Unilever making soap in the Gold Coast; the market was too small, there was no tariff protection (a 5 per cent revenue duty on imported soap was balanced by a duty on imported raw materials) and there was inadequate local production of raw materials. But when Kwame Nkrumah became Prime Minister in 1952 it became clear that he proposed to use every possible device to stimulate import-substituting industries; and from that moment Unilever was both forced to consider local manufacture in order to safeguard its large import market, and also attracted by the prospect of good profits behind a predictable wall of tariffs and import controls. It took nine years of negotiations from 1954 before their new factory at Tema came into operation; but at no time did Unilever show either fear of or positive enthusiasm for the prospect of Ghanaian independence. The import trade was eminently satisfactory and carried minimum risks, so the company saw no positive advantage in independence. But equally, since decolonization was now clearly becoming a fact of life, one had simply to adjust policy to meet the new situation.

Such limited evidence can prove no general hypothesis. But it does suggest that British capitalism did not play a positive role in the decolonization of Black Africa. For this there were many reasons. Few, if any, British firms actually stood to gain from a transfer of power; the dangers for foreign capital had already been demonstrated in South and South-East Asia by the later 1950s, and capital was accustomed to dealing with the certainties of colonial government. Again, few businessmen seem to have foreseen the speed the process would gather in the later 1950s, as indeed few politicians did; all expected a much longer period of transition. They therefore made no short-term plans. Conversely, the evidence available from British West Africa before the early 1960s suggested that there was no great cause for concern, that the new regimes would positively welcome continuing foreign capitalist activity and might actively promote its interests in their drive for import-substituting industrialization. Big companies were confident that they could cope with changing situations by adapting their methods and activities; it was the small men – the white settlers of Kenya, the Rhodesias and the Congo, Syrians in West Africa and Asians in East Africa – who had cause for fear that decolonization would destroy their world.

It is, therefore, reasonable to surmise that, as more evidence becomes available, it will become clear that decolonization was primarily a political rather than an economic phenomenon so far as British officials and businessmen were concerned. Their common ground was that, if the transfer of power had to come, the primary need was to establish good relations with the rulers of the successor states. This, in their different ways, is precisely what both groups attempted to do in the 1950s and early 1960s.

France

The evidence available on French attitudes to the economics of decolonization is in most respects less even than for Britain. There seem to be few detailed studies of either official or private assessments of the economic advantages of retaining or devolving political power, so that all conclusions must be provisional. Nevertheless recently published work makes it possible to provide at least tentative answers to the questions posed above, and these seem to bring France broadly into line with Britain.

The French case presents the same basic paradox. After 1945 the metropolis regarded the colonies as essential to its economic recovery and, like Britain, invested more capital and showed greater interest, particularly public interest, than ever before. Jacques Marseille, in a recent and very important study, calculated that in the period 1940–58 total new metropolitan investment in the empire as a whole (in 1914 gold francs) amounted to some 11.9m. francs – nearly half the cumulative total of 25.7m. for the whole French colonial period.[19] What proportion of this went to Black African territories is less clear. Bloch-Lainé estimated that between 1947 and 1955 some 350b. francs (current values) of public funds went to French sub-Saharan Africa, of which 271.4b. went to French West and Equatorial Africa, Togo and Cameroun. Since Poquin's figure for these last territories was 245b., this is probably about right.[20] It is true that much of this huge amount was used to pay the salaries of French 'technicians' and 'advisers', and that much of the money flowed back to France as repatriated salaries and payment for goods and services provided by France. Nevertheless, so large and unprecedented a transfer from metropolis to colonies must indicate French belief after 1945 that the empire was of critical importance and must be developed and retained for the indefinite future.

In order to understand French decolonization, however, it is important to discover who in France thought the colonies so important that it was worth while for a France attempting to modernize itself after the war to be prepared to put so much into them. The critical point made by Marseille and others is that, in marked contrast with most periods before 1939, the great bulk of metropolitan investment in this period came from the state through the Fonds d'Investissement pour le Développement Economique et Social (FIDES), not from private investors. His figures for 1940–58 (1914 francs) are 1,989.8m. for issues by French private companies operating mainly in the colonies, against 10,000.5m. for public funds contributed to colonial government investment budgets, a ratio of about 1:5. By contrast, the figures for investment before 1914 show the private/government sector ratio at 1:1.23, for 1915–29 at 7:1 and for 1930–9 at 1.48:1, though these earlier ratios exclude colonial government borrowing in Paris, which they did not need to do after 1940.[21] As a cross-check, Poquin's estimate for new public share issues by French companies primarily active in the sub-Saharan colonies between 1945 and 1955 was 63.5b. francs, giving a private/government investment ratio of 1:4.3.[22] However crude, these estimates suggest that most of the post-war enthusiasm for investment in French Black Africa came from the government rather than from private capital and that this was the first time in French colonial history that this was so. The starting-point for understanding economic factors in French decolonization is, therefore, the reason for this reversal of roles and, in particular, the predominant role now played by the state.

The basic reason for French public investment in Black Africa (as in North Africa) after 1945 was the same as that for accelerated British colonial investment – desire to maximize intra-imperial trade at a time when hard currencies were in very short supply.[23] French Africa was treated as an integral part of the metropolitan economy and its development integrated with that of France in the two main plans for the overseas empire of 1946–52 and 1953–7. The first of these, deriving from the decisions of the Brazzaville Conference of 1944, envisaged a radical transformation of the colonial economies by creating an adequate infrastructure, including hydroelectric power, mechanization of agricultural production, and the construction of industrial enterprises. The results were a huge increase both of imports from France, which rose by 100 per cent between 1949 and 1955, and of exports to France, which increased even more, by 115 per cent in the same period. As in the British case, a considerable part of the French funds credited to the colonies was spent on unsuccessful grandiose projects to increase the supply of raw materials otherwise needing dollars, notably the notorious Office du Niger, intended to increase raw cotton production. By 1961 this had resulted in only 48,000 ha under cultivation at a total cost of 44b. francs, or about a million francs a

hectare. It had absorbed 56 per cent of total allocations to agriculture
in French West Africa and had produced only 1,000 of the projected
300,000 tons of raw cotton.[24] Agriculture, the main staple of the
French colonial economies, changed very little; there was limited
success in developing mineral production (in the later 1950s minerals
amounted only to about 3 per cent of AOF exports); and the main
achievement was the creation of the first central hydroelectric
production.

What, in fact, was becoming evident by the mid-1950s was that the
main function of French public investment in the colonies was to
enable them to run enormous deficits in their balance of payments.
Although exports from French Black Africa (including Madagascar)
increased rapidly – from a total US$291.1m. in 1948 to $484.0m. in
1953[25] – these could not cover the adverse balance on private
transfers, consisting initially mainly of visible trade, but, from 1955,
increasingly of 'invisibles', including payment of interest and
repatriation of capital and profits. Thus, for the franc zone as a whole,
the overseas countries had an adverse balance with France of 257.8b.
francs in 1952, which was more than offset by French public transfers
of 287.5b. In every year from then until 1958 French public transfers
filled the same function, and in 1958 the figures had risen to 621.1b.
colonial deficits as against public transfers of 666.7b.[26] This is the
essential background to changing official and private attitudes to the
future of the French colonial empire in the 1950s.

The French Official Mind

The key to changing official attitudes to the possibility of decolonization lies in the question of what benefits this huge commitment of
metropolitan subsidies – far greater than those of Britain to its
colonies – was seen to offer to France. Had these subsidies been short
term, a temporary help to enable the colonies to modernize their
economies to the point at which they could once again be financially
autonomous and able to meet the cost of further modernization from
budget savings or overseas loans, France might well have accepted the
burden. But this was clearly not so: the absolute size of these
metropolitan subsidies increased rather than diminished during the
1950s, despite not unfavourable terms of trade for colonial exports and
the artificially high prices paid for selected colonial staples in France.
What, then, it was increasingly asked, was the benefit to France and
who were the beneficiaries of this massive aid? Was it the metropolis
as a whole or only sectional interests? Marseille has analysed this
problem in detail and has suggested the following answers.

First, it is clear that, except for the period of intense international commodity shortages between 1945 and 1950, the French economy obtained little benefit from the 'resource base' notionally offered by the colonies. In 1958 the colonies collectively provided over 70 per cent of French imports of a wide range of edible agricultural products, ranging from 72.1 per cent for fruit to 95.4 per cent for rice; but none of these was in short supply by the 1950s, all could have been bought more cheaply in the world market, and some were in competition with the same or substitutable French products. Conversely, apart from phosphates, the colonial share of imported industrial raw materials was very small: 11.1 per cent of minerals and metals, 18 per cent of raw cotton, 0.8 per cent of linen, 0.0 per cent of raw silk, 30.9 per cent of rubber and 40.5 per cent of timber.[27] Clearly in time of peace and ample international commodity supplies the colonies provided no special benefit to the metropolis as a consumer; in fact, because of the protection provided for key colonial commodities, French costs were being raised above those of its Western competitors. The main beneficiaries of this protection were metropolitan-owned firms which traded in these colonial goods in Africa and industries in France which processed coffee, cocoa, groundnuts and sugar – all of them part of an earlier phase of French industrialization. By contrast, colonial products were of no significance for the new, developing industries such as electronics and chemicals.

Reversing the standpoint, which French industries found important markets in these highly protected colonies? Again, the contrast between old-established, often internationally uncompetitive, industries and the more modern enterprises, which increasingly looked to markets in Europe and the developed world, was obvious. Among the first group were vegetable oil manufacturers for whom in 1958 the colonies consumed 95 per cent of total exports, sugar refiners 85.5 per cent, and manufacturers of cotton textiles 83.6 per cent, clothing 78.8 per cent and soap 92.2 per cent. Cement, metal and engineering producers, chemicals and car manufacturers also found the colonies valuable, though not to the same extent as these older industries.[28] Clearly the colonies were most important for the least modern French industries and were of decreasing value according to the modernity and international competitiveness of the rest. For the high technology industry they were irrelevant.

To the historian at least, the conclusion seems clear. The essential feature of the post-1945 French imperial economy was that the French government, maintaining autarkic assumptions that stemmed from the later nineteenth century and had been reinforced during the 1930s and again after 1945, was using the power of the state to enable the colonies to buy a range of French consumer goods for which there would have been no alternative overseas market, and also capital goods which they could probably have bought more cheaply elsewhere. This was done in two ways: by massive injections of French money to correct the adverse colonial balance of payments and by artificially increasing the price colonial producers could get in France to enable them to pay the equally inflated price of French exports. In the last resort this was a most expensive way of keeping officiously alive metropolitan enterprises which might otherwise have been forced to modernize or go out of business. It also constituted a massive burden on an economy in the process of modernization. So much is obvious to the historian; the questions are when it became evident to the French official mind and whether recognition of the situation was a major factor in the decision to decolonize.

The evidence suggests that realization of the need for radical change came gradually, but was far advanced in French government circles by the early 1950s. Marseille traces proposals for liberalization of the economy back to at least the early 1930s, when a few enlightened men realized that a favourable metropolitan balance of payments with the colonies did nothing to help France's international settlements and that over-dependence on an empire which provided mainly unneeded agricultural products and took low-quality French manufactures was not an economic asset.[29] But such ideas made little impact at the time and it was not until the immediate postwar crisis was over that the liberal argument gained momentum. Within France there was growing concern at the refusal of heavily protected traditional industries, such as cotton textiles, to concentrate and modernize. Externally, the example of Holland, flourishing industrially despite Indonesian independence, and of continuing British economic activity in the first independent colonies, stimulated belief that France also might retain economic advantage in its colonies once it no longer had the responsibility for financing and ruling them. By the mid-1950s even the Comité Central de la France d'Outre-Mer, the guardian of all French interests in the colonies, was divided over the future of the empire; and Marseille suggests that the split corresponded roughly with that between French financial interests, who saw the need for moving the colonies towards self-government, and others who remained wedded to traditional economic and political relationships. By 1953 Claude Cheysson, a future member of the Mendès France cabinet, could write to Paul Reynaud, vice-president of the Conseil, advising that the components of Indo-China should be given their independence, on condition that close monetary links and tariff preferences were maintained and that French investments were secured. These were the essential elements in the Evian Agreement of 1962, negotiated by de Gaulle with the new independent state of Algeria.

It is still impossible to document this change of the official mind in the 1950s, though it seems virtually certain that calculations of this sort were increasingly dominant. But, if so, why did France fight on in

Indo-China until 1954 and in Algeria until 1962? Why, conversely, did de Gaulle concede independence to Black Africa in 1960 and to Algeria in 1962? Two answers emerge from the literature. In general terms, as Marseille argues, the majority of Frenchmen of all political parties continued to believe in the importance of the colonies and in France's beneficial effects on them well into the 1950s: in 1948 a sample poll showed that 81 per cent thought it was in France's interests to hold the colonies; in 1956 49 per cent thought that Algeria should remain a department of the metropolis. As in the British case, such beliefs were the product of half a century of propaganda which had, ironically, converted a people initially extremely dubious about the value of colonies, irrespective of their political connections. Only a man with the unique authority of de Gaulle could decide, as he did, and as he put it in the case of Algeria in April 1961, that 'the least one can say is that Africa costs us more than it benefits us . . . Our own progress has now become our great national ambition and is the real source of our power and influence. It is a fact that decolonization is in our own interest and is therefore our policy.'[30] Probably in France it required the acute political dangers to the Republic of the period 1958–61 to enable such a rationalization to become the basis of policy.

The Non-Official Mind in France

As for Britain, too little is known of the attitudes of particular enterprises and interest groups to justify any firm conclusions yet, but some rough generalizations can be made, distinguishing business firms and organizations operating mainly in the metropolis from those with a predominantly colonial base.

Within France it is clear that, as one would have expected, it was those industries for which the protected colonial market was critical that were most strongly opposed to decolonization in any form. The most important of these was the cotton textile industry, employing some 220,000 in the early 1950s, still dominated by family firms and small units of production, inefficient by international standards but reluctant to undergo the trauma of reconstruction and modernization. Marcel Boussac, as a leading member of the cotton textile industry and founder of the Comptoir de l'Industrie Cotonnière, of whose products 35 per cent were exported to the colonial empire in 1948 as against a mere 15 per cent sold in France, used his paper, *L'Aurore*, to publicize his case against political devolution and was particularly opposed to independence for Morocco in which he had commercial ambitions. In the 1955 electoral campaign he was supported on this issue by Pierre Poujade, who linked the decline of the Vosges textile industry with the decline of the empire in the East.[31] It seems likely that other French industrialists, who had a substantial stake in the colonies – sugar and groundnut refiners, soap makers, clothing manufacturers, producers of engineering and chemical goods – also saw the loss of colonies as a potential disaster.[32] On the other hand, because French agriculture and viticulture were in general competition with a number of colonial imports, notably wheat, wine and raw sugar, there was no alliance between the powerful metropolitan farming lobby and these colonial producers. Moreover, there were many French industries, particularly the more modern and technically advanced, for whom the colonies were of no significance as markets or sources of inputs.

If metropolitan industries were divided according to their dependence on protected colonial markets, so also were French enterprises which operated in the colonies and had investments there. Kahler divides these (as he does those of Britain) into two main 'waves', according to the period in which their initial investment was made.[33] The first wave, mostly established before 1939, included land concessionary companies, agriculturalists, primary producers, mining companies, public utility operators, the larger trading companies and commercial banks. Of the concessionary companies, originally so important in some territories (notably the French Congo) few survived into the 1950s. Only the Banque de Paris et des Pays-Bas, with a large holding in Morocco and dominating many sectors of the Moroccan economy, could compare in scale with the one remaining large British one-time chartered company, British South Africa Company. Significantly the BPPB made no opposition to Moroccan independence, probably because the range of its interests, there and in Europe, was so wide that it rightly felt confident that it could make satisfactory terms with any successor regime, so long at least as that was reasonably conservative. Predictably, the main hostility to decolonization among agricultural interests came from resident French producers, particularly those in North Africa: from the *grands colons* and small wine producers of Algeria and the settlers in Morocco, though not, surprisingly, on any large scale from the big land investment companies of Tunisia. In Black Africa there were fewer resident French agricultural interests, and the white planters of Ivory Coast do not seem to have played a significant role. There were few large private mining enterprises in French Africa: the new oil and gas enterprises of Algeria were state-owned, with some supporting private investment, and the issue that eventually held up Algerian independence (over the Sahara) had nothing to do with private French capital.

The case of the big French trading companies in West Africa – Société Commerciale de l'Ouest Africain (SCOA) and Compagnie Française de l'Afrique Occidentale (CFAO) – is more interesting.[34] Both were late-nineteenth-century enterprises which, like the big British firms, UAC and John Holt, dominated both the buying and the export of peasant crops and also the import and sale of trade goods.

Neither of these companies had a large fixed investment in the colonies; their investment was in credit to producers and the goods they traded. Given their general unpopularity with African producers, who widely believed that they were swindled both as producers and consumers, one might have expected that these companies would fear and oppose political decolonization. In fact they did not; rather they adapted their activities to meet changing conditions and prospects. The years 1947–51 were the apogee of their postwar trade of the traditional kind, helped by the huge increase in demand for tropical commodities, the inflow of French goods as part of the development programme and the fact that there were then no marketing boards of the British type to restrict their activities and profits. But from 1952 the golden age of the companies as traders was beginning to end. Commodity prices fell after the Korean War, local taxes rose to meet the higher costs of government, and African wages rose as unions in the towns increased their bargaining power. From 1956 and the Loi Cadre, which provided for greatly increased African self-government and decentralized the West and Equatorial African Federations, the probability was that African-dominated governments would control or take over the commodity trade.

The two companies responded in different ways. CFAO virtually stopped new investment in Africa from 1955 and ten years later began to withdraw capital to France. SCOA, however, adopted the same policy as UAC in the British territories: it moved out of trading into modern industrial activity, often in alliance with specialist foreign firms or with local private or public partners. In the last years of colonial rule 1954/5–1960/1, the proportion of its turnover that came from construction increased from 11.5 to 23 per cent; that from technical and industrial enterprises from 3 to 10 per cent; and from chain stores from 0 to 7 per cent. Meantime its general trade declined from 53 to 40 per cent and its buying of African products from 23.3 to 15 per cent. After 1960 SCOA concentrated mainly on its non-trading activities, though it still acted as agent for the new state marketing organizations in exporting commodities and continued to import and sell consumer goods, increasingly through modern chain stores rather than through the old system of wholesaling to African middlemen. Significantly, however, SCOA balanced its bets by establishing a firm base in France, with the supermarket chain, Prisunic, and industrial investments. By 1963/4 SCOA had invested 47m. NF in France as compared with 43m. NF in Africa.

These were all relatively old French colonial interests. In his 'second wave' of enterprises, most of which developed their modern form or were first established after 1945, Kahler includes banking and manufacturing as well as commerce.[35] The banking sector developed fast after 1945. The banks, with interests in Europe as well as in the colonies, and confident that they would been needed as much by self-governing or independent African states as by colonies, seem to have made no attempt to oppose devolution of political power. Industrial investors were equally confident in the future. The two essential points here are, first, that most new industrial enterprises in French territories were owned by large companies – often in alliance with local private or state capital – and that they could treat their colonial branches as a relatively high-risk gamble which offered potentially high profits; secondly, that they were mostly engaged in providing new consumer or intermediate products whose local production was strongly favoured by the incoming indigenous nationalist politicians. Such firms accepted the risk that individual enterprises might be less profitable under an independent regime or might even be forced to close, as did the Verreries de l'Afrique du Nord in Oran (a subsidiary of Saint-Gobain Industries) which decided to close in 1962 when the new government insisted on what the company regarded as unacceptable overmanning. That was a bad bet. But most French companies, particularly those in West Africa, seem to have responded to the prospect of self-government and the probability of highly protectionist post-independence regimes with great confidence, the more so after 1958 when all the sub-Saharan colonies except Guinea showed their desire to remain within the franc zone and the French economic and political orbit by their 'yes' vote in de Gaulle's referendum.

It seems likely, then, that the role of French private traders and capital in the process of French decolonization was similar in general terms to that of the British. Economic interest groups were divided over the prospective benefits and dangers associated with political decolonization, though there was probably greater fear and hostility in French circles than in Britain because of the greater importance to France than to Britain of colonial markets and the much larger influence of the North African settlers on metropolitan emotions. There is also an important time contrast here. The British analogue to the resistance put up by French industrial interests, particularly cotton, to colonial autonomy was the long fight made by the Lancashire cotton industry against any form of protection in India from the 1870s to the 1920s and the battle was long lost by 1945. It is interesting also that British industrial, financial and commercial interests were divided over the proposed introduction of protection and imperial preference in the 1920s in roughly the same way as those of France after 1945. Reacting to similar problems a generation later, the more modern and flexible French capitalist interests adopted a 'wait and see' attitude to the possible end of the integrated imperial economy, neither pressing nor opposing political devolution but constantly modifying their activities to take account of changing situations and prospects.

This suggests that the French metropolitan state was eventually left with a substantially free hand in forming its colonial policy. In the metropolis it was critical that the Comité Central de la France d'Outre-mer, once so influential, was divided and in decline. There was no strong *parti colonial* in politics and colonial issues did not divide one main party from another. The state could, therefore, take an increasingly rational view of the costs and benefits of the colonial empire. Although the trade to French Africa remained relatively important to France, taking 29.6 per cent of French exports in 1951, 28.2 per cent in 1959 and providing 14.5 per cent and 20.3 per cent of French imports in the same years,[36] French exports came largely from areas of French industrial decline, not from the new, dynamic industries. Most imports from the colonies were, as has been seen, those which France did not need. These factors were bound, sooner or later, to incline French governments, which were anxious to modernize the metropolitan economy and to prepare it for entry into a European common market, to see the colonies as an economic as well as a fiscal and military handicap. In the last resort France, like Britain, did not decolonize for simple economic reasons; but by the later 1950s the growing realization that the costs of the old autarkic economic system now exceeded its marginal benefits almost certainly weighed heavily in the French decision to end direct political control.

To what extent, then, should French and British decolonization be seen as primarily an economic phenomenon and how much truth is there in the argument that the imperial states ended political control when and because this was no longer a necessary or profitable basis for economic exploitation? The limited evidence surveyed above does not justify a clear-cut answer, especially as it has largely ignored non-economic factors. Some tentative suggestions on the balance of probability can, however, be attempted.

It is clear, in the first place, that in neither Britain nor France was there any deliberate scheme to end imperial rule in order to replace it by some form of neo-colonialist domination. It would have been surprising if there had been. Colonialism offered unique advantages to the imperial powers, above all certainty based on power. In a colony one could impose whatever economic regime the metropolis thought best for itself; an ex-colony had the freedom to make whatever arrangements it chose and would probably, if it could, attempt to turn the balance of advantage in its own direction. In the long term the new state was likely to escape from the domination of its one-time metropolis, either becoming an autonomous and eventually dominant economic force (as the United States had done) or, like many Latin-American states, moving from the orbit of one great power to that of another. More to the point, Latin American evidence from the 1930s onwards suggested that, despite the overwhelming dominance of the

United States in the region, such states might ignore the established conventions concerning international investments and expropriate foreign enterprises without immediate or complete compensation.[37] Even under continuing imperial rule India had adopted protectionist policies which virtually destroyed the British market there for a wide range of consumer goods and heavy iron and steel products by 1939. In short, no one in these metropolitan countries could – or, so far as one can judge, did – believe that the end of colonial rule would make no difference to the economic position of the imperial state in the ex-colonies. Neo-colonialism was not a synonym for empire and was not a planned and preferred condition.

That said, it nevertheless seems clear that decolonization involved a calculus in which economic factors played a significant role. The most important new consideration after about 1945 was that the undoubted benefits provided by imperial rule had now to be balanced against increasing costs in most colonies. These varied greatly from one territory to another. In Indo-China and later Algeria the main cost was what proved to be unwinnable wars which put an unacceptable strain on French military manpower and finances and, in the case of Algeria, eventually threatened the very existence of a civilian regime at home. In South Asia the British after 1945 had to accept that the cost of imposing a chosen timetable and form of decolonization on the Congress and League was beyond them. Similar extreme pressures deriving from the need to fight increasingly expensive wars to maintain colonial rule were critical in Palestine, Indonesia and later in Portuguese Africa. Such pressures never became intense in the bulk of British and French Africa, but fear that they might do so if preventive action was not taken undoubtedly had a formative influence on metropolitan attitudes from about 1947.

International influences were undoubtedly very important. From 1940 United States disapproval of the colonial regimes of others, particularly their economic exclusivism, had a significant impact on the now second-rate powers who held colonies: in the cases of Indonesia in 1949 and Egypt in 1956, American pressures become decisive. Yet the USA supported France in Indo-China in the early 1950s and did not play an active part in Africa. A more important influence on imperial attitudes towards that continent was (as was seen above in the case of the post-1945 Attlee government of Britain) fear that ill-judged resistance to nationalistic or xenophobic movements in the colonies might give Russia the opportunity to become influential or even dominant there. Fear of communism thus forced the imperial powers to buy the goodwill of their subject peoples. This did not, of course, necessarily imply political withdrawal. There was a strong belief, particularly on the moderate left in Britain and French politics, that extended colonial acquiescence in alien rule could best be bought by providing dramatic evidence of social and economic development; hence the great increase in the flow of grants and soft loans under the British CD&W Acts and the French FIDES programme. Both countries, though on different time scales, also believed that a controlled devolution of political functions to colonial elites would assuage their hunger for the fruits of politics and sustain their belief in democracy as their own ultimate objective.

The trouble with this formula was both that its economic elements took too long to mature, so allowing colonial dissidents to capitalize on discontent, and also that, when the aid programmes really got under way in the 1950s, they were found to be too expensive to sustain. No one had any idea of how much imperial aid would be needed for how long a period, or for what purposes it should be used, in order to raise the African colonies to an acceptable level of affluence; indeed, the target itself was not capable of definition. It should, of course, have come as no surprise that it was beyond the economic capacity of either Britain or France, both seriously weakened by the war, to transfer sufficient real resources to the colonies to enable them to modernize their economies quickly, and so pre-empt the claim of most nationalist leaders that affluence would begin with independence. Yet it was not until the later 1950s that the two imperial governments came to recognize that they were unable, without demanding unacceptable sacrifices from their own electorates, to give enough to the colonies to fulfil the rhetoric of 'colonial development' and so buy off demands that Africans should be able to do the developing themselves. The only way out of their self-created dilemma was to substitute rapid political advance for rapid economic advance: to give independence and then be free to restrict the flow of aid to manageable levels on the reasonable ground that independent states did not have the same claims as colonies. Or, to put it another way, the postwar substitution of expensive reformist empire for empire on the cheap made colonialism unattractive to those in Britain and France who might otherwise have clung indefinitely to established belief in the imperial mission and the rewards of empire.

Put in these terms, the strictly economic aspects of decolonization must play a minor role. Had the imperial equilibrium of the pre-1945 era continued, it is inconceivable that the main economic interests in Britain or France would have seen any need or advantage in transferring political power to indigenous elites. In the event the choice was not theirs. Those who stood to lose most by decolonization fought as hard as they could to check or slow up the process. Those who had the option of restructuring their interests – the bankers, investors, large industrial concerns, trading companies – did so as well as they could. The fact that many of them were highly successful, so that it later seemed to some that neo-colonialism was a complete and satisfactory substitute for and successor to colonialism, is misleading. There were many casualties: many of the white settlers of North, East and Central Africa; the weaker metropolitan industries that had depended on colonial markets; even large international enterprises whose assets were wholly or partly expropriated. Such difficulties were predictable and were predicted. The fact that many metropolitan firms put a brave face on it and decided to make the best of a bad job must not obscure the fact that at the time most of them regarded the change as bad, or at least not as good as the colonial status quo. In short, there were important economic elements in the process of decolonization; but the colonies were not set free simply because continued political control by Britain, France or Belgium offered them no economic advantages, or even because the difference was not thought important.

Notes

1 *Wealth of Nations* (1776; London, 1966), Vol. II, pp. 112–13.
2 Chapel Hill, 1944.
3 For example, Roger Anstey, *The Atlantic Slave Trade and British Abolition, 1760–1810* (London, 1975).
4 For example, see E. Sik, *The History of Black Africa* (Budapest, 1966), Vol. II, pp. 191–4. I am not sure where Sik got this idea, possibly from standard Marxist–Leninist doctrine. See also Walter Rodney, *How Europe Underdeveloped Africa* (London, 1972).
5 P. A. Baran, *The Political Economy of Growth* (New York, 1957); G. Arrighi and J. Saul, *Essays on the Political Economy of Africa* (New York, 1973); H. Bernstein (ed.), *Underdevelopment and Development* (Harmondsworth, 1973); P. Gutkind and I. Wallerstein (eds), *The Political Economy of Contemporary Africa* (London, 1976); G. Kay, *Development and Underdevelopment: A Marxist Analysis* (London, 1975); C. Leys, *Underdevelopment in Kenya* (London, 1975).
6 For evidence on this see in particular J. M. Lee, *Colonial Development and Good Government, 1939–64* (Oxford, 1967); J. M. Lee and M. Petter, *The Colonial Office, War and Development Policy* (London, 1982); W. R. Louis, *Imperialism at Bay* (Oxford, 1977).
7 In *The Political Economy of the Raj, 1914–47* (Cambridge, 1979) Tomlinson argues that each of the three earlier reasons which induced Britain to hang on to control of India as long as possible – the army, the market and control of a range of financial matters (currency, payment of home charges, etc.) – had lost much of its force by 1937. The Second World War completed the process, so that Britain had little left to lose and much, it was hoped, to gain by an amicable transfer of power. This hypothesis seems to be supported by recent detailed studies of the British decision-making process after 1945.
8 This section owes a great deal to a number of unpublished papers by Dr N. J. Westcott and to discussions with him about them: notably 'Sterling and Empire: the British Imperial Economy, 1939–1951'; 'The Politics of

Planning and the Planning of Politics: Colonialism and Development in British Africa, 1930–1960'; and, with M. P. Cowen, 'British Imperial Economic Policy During the War'.

9 D. K. Fieldhouse, 'The Labour Governments and the Empire–Commonwealth, 1945–51', in R. Ovendale (ed.), *The Foreign Policy of the Labour Governments, 1945–1951* (London, 1984), p. 98.

10 D. J. Morgan, *The Official History of Colonial Development* (5 vols, London, 1980), Vol. V, p. 102.

11 Morgan, Vol. III, pp. 87–8.

12 ibid., p. 90.

13 See in particular R. E. Robinson, 'Andrew Cohen and the Transfer of Power in Tropical Africa, 1940–1951', in W. H. Morris-Jones and G. Fischer (eds), *Decolonization and After: the British and French Experience* (London, 1978).

14 London, 1977. See also Miles Kahler, *Decolonization in Britain and France* (Princeton, N.J., 1984), ch. 4, for a general survey which provides little primary evidence on the attitudes of British and French business but supports the argument of this section.

15 Milburn, table 1, pp. 79–80.

16 ibid., n. 46 p. 144; p. 94.

17 D. K. Fieldhouse, *Unilever Overseas. The Anatomy of a Multinational, 1895–1965* (London, 1978), p. 362. Developments in Nigeria are outlined on pp. 345–79.

18 ibid., pp. 412–17.

19 J. Marseille, *Empire colonial et capitalisme français. Histoire d'un divorce* (Paris, 1984), p. 105.

20 F. Bloch-Lainé, *La Zone franc* (Paris, 1956), pp. 117, 136; J.-J. Poquin, *Les Relations économiques extérieure des Pays d'Afrique de l'Union française, 1925–1955* (Paris, 1957), pp. 195–6.

21 Marseille, p. 105.

22 Poquin, p. 195.

23 The following account relies partly on a paper by Catherine Coquery-Vidrovitch, 'Economic Decolonization in French Africa' which, in first draft, was given at the conference on 'African Independence', University of Zimbabwe, Harare, January 1985.

24 ibid., p. 6.

25 Organization for European Economic Co-operation (OEEC), *Foreign Trade Statistical Bulletin*, Series 1 (Paris, 1954).

26 Marseille, p. 134.

27 ibid., p. 55.

28 ibid., p. 54.

29 ibid., pp. 353–5.

30 Quoted ibid., p. 373; trans. by author.

31 Kahler, pp. 274–5.

32 Marseille, p. 53.

33 See Kahler, pp. 279–88.

34 The account of these trading companies is based mainly on C.Coquery-Vidrovitch, 'SCOA et CFAO dans l'Quest African, 1910–1965', *Journal of African History*, Vol. 16, no. 4 (1975), pp. 595–621. For the background

to these and other trading companies in West Africa see also P. T. Bauer, *West African Trade* (Cambridge, 1954) and A. G. Hopkins, *An Economic History of West Africa* (London, 1973).

35   Kahler, pp. 288–315.

36   *Annuaire statistique de la France* (Paris, 1966).

37   For a detailed study of this question, with material on Latin America, see Charles Lipson, *Standing Guard. Protecting Foreign Capital in the Nineteenth and Twentieth Centuries* (Berkeley, Los Angeles, and London, 1985), esp. chs. 3–5.

2

The Colonial Inheritance

Perhaps the most intractable question concerning the economic performance of Black Africa after independence is the relative importance of the colonial past. It is not proposed here to attempt even the most abbreviated history of colonialism in Africa, still less to pass judgement on it; but rather to describe some of the main features of African countries during the last years of the colonial period as they may have affected subsequent economic development. This will be done under three main heads: the character and prospects of the African economies between *c.*1945 and *c.*1960; the nature of the late-colonial state as it was likely to affect successor regimes and their management to the economy; and the framework provided by the metropolitan states for post-colonial economic relations between African states and their one-time metropolises after independence. But before doing this it is necessary briefly to outline three standard ways of seeing the impact of colonialism on Black Africa which may be described very loosely as from the left, the right and the centre. The left and the right share a common belief that colonialism fundamentally restructured African economies. Those in the centre argue that the colonial impact was limited and its effects confused.

From the standpoint commonly adopted by the left, including Marxists and dependency theorists, the central assumption is that, as colonies, the African territories ceased to be autonomous economies and were transformed into peripheral extensions of the metropolitan and international capitalist economy. For decades the stated aim of the imperial powers had been to 'develop' the colonies; but by this they meant only such forms of development as were compatible with their own needs. Since they were for the most part industrialized, the colonies must be non-industrial sectors of the metropolitan economy, consumers of manufactures and providers of agricultural, sylvan and mineral commodities. The general result was that the colonial economies were hopelessly 'skewed': over-specialized in one or a very few main cash crops, highly vulnerable to fluctuations in commodity prices which they could not influence, suffering from a secular deterioration in their terms of trade which made a mockery of the principle of comparative advantage.

The effect of this pattern of production was to cauterize whatever development potential these societies may have had before they were incorporated into the imperial and world economy. Specialization in cash crops had destroyed their ability to feed themselves and supply their other needs internally. Most domestic industries had died from competition with cheaper and probably better imported manufactures. Because foreign firms with their greater resources and knowledge of the international economy had replaced indigenous traders, bankers and entrepreneurs in most parts of the 'modern sector', the colonies lacked an autonomous indigenous bourgeoisie capable of acting as entrepreneurs and accumulators of capital. Indeed, almost all the modern sector was in foreign hands. This in turn meant that most of the surplus generated by the economy flowed overseas as profits, leaving the colony unable to generate essential savings for investment and dependent on overseas loans and grants. In every way, therefore, the new post-colonial states found themselves deprived of their inherent potential for development; they were 'underdeveloped' in the sense that their eventual condition left them less free to move in desired directions than they might have been before they were linked with the metropolitan and international economies.

The opposite 'conservative' way of looking at the colonial inheritance emphasizes the positive achievements of colonialism and the foundations it provided for future growth. The key to this approach is the proposition that there was never any possibility of rapid or easy economic development in tropical Africa. Although recent research has emphasized that many of these societies possessed far more sophisticated commercial and industrial structures than was suggested by the old stereotypes of 'backward' or 'pre-capitalist',[1] most revisionist writers agree that the scope for sustained development of even the most complex economies (as in West Africa) was limited by the size of local markets, by technological lag and by political and social factors which checked the growth of capitalist modes of production. Thus their innate capacity for development was inhibited by adverse circumstances: in common with most other countries, they needed to be linked more effectively with wider markets and sources of technological development than was possible so long as these links depended mainly on, for example, a tenuous trans-Saharan camel trade. That is, their development was contingent on incorporation into the more dynamic world economy.

This incorporation did not necessarily depend on their becoming colonies; but it can be argued that, given the circumstances of the nineteenth and early twentieth centuries, this was the best way in which it could have been done. The main contribution of colonial rule was that, in their own interests, the European rulers 'opened up' the interior of Africa and linked virtually every part of the continent with the outside world. By imposing their own absolute rule over areas far larger than any singly indigenous state, they removed political obstacles to the movement of men, goods and ideas. By building railways and improving rivers, they made it possible for areas far distant from the ports to initiate or expand commercial production of cash crops and to consume imported goods. Given the political structures of pre-colonial Africa, it seems very unlikely that comparable results could have been achieved in any foreseeable period without the imposition of colonial rule.

Yet, even if this is conceded, the question remains whether the best or even good use was made by the imperial powers of the sixty or seventy odd years during which they ruled Black Africa. The case for the prosecution is that far too little was achieved because the imperial powers were only interested in promoting a limited level of development, stopping short once Africa produced a sufficiency of commodities at minimum cost to the imperialists. The case for the defence is commonly stated as follows. Since almost all these colonies were deficient (so far as was known) in exploitable minerals (the Gold Coast, Northern Rhodesia and the Belgian Congo being the main exceptions), and since none of them initially possessed manufacturing industries capable of competing with those of the West, their main potential for growth lay in exploiting their three main assets – land, labour and climate – which gave them a comparative advantage in production of commodities which could not profitably be produced in industrial countries. The function of colonialism was to maximize the exploitation of these advantages; and their success in doing this is shown in the very dramatic increase in the volume and value of the export trades from the later nineteenth century to at least 1914. So long as the commodity market operated in the interests of the producers (as shown by favourable trends in the terms of trade), this strategy provided clear benefits for Africans, who were usually quick to respond to new market opportunities: the cocoa farmers of the Gold Coast, who built up their own industry with minimal official help or stimulus, are the classic success story, though producers of cash crops in many different places also did well. In principle, at least, the relative affluence of these producers should have enabled them to save, to invest in expanded production, to diversify, even to invest in non-agricultural enterprises. Moreover, the taxation made possible by increased economic activity and trade could be used by the colonial state to provide improved public services, including communications and other infrastructural essentials, education and medicine. Thus, the main defence of the colonial economic system was that it enabled Africans to do the only things that they could do well at that stage of their development.

Clearly, however, the actual benefits Africans had received by the mid-1940s fell far short of what had been predicted earlier in the century. More serious, there seemed no evidence of sustained growth or structural development. On the contrary, during the 1920s and 1930s the real return to most producers actually fell, few new crops were established, the state did not expand its services and there was very little diversification into industry. Colonialism had apparently lost its early momentum. The defenders of colonial rule, however, had their explanation and justification for this. The main blame was laid, first, on the disruptive effects of the First World War, which (apart from the period of commodity shortage from 1919 to 1921) seriously reduced world demand for tropical products; then, on the effects of the slump from 1929, which lifted only about 1937; and, finally, on the Second World War, which again disrupted the commodity trades. Given these two and a half decades of generally adverse world economic circumstances, it was not surprising that African countries, whether or not colonies, should have shared the experience of virtually every other part of the world. These adverse trends were, in any case, reversed after about 1945, when booming commodity markets, together with large loans and grants from metropolitan treasuries, stimulated an unprecedented expansion of African economies which was still under way when the colonies received their independence. Thus the last years of the colonial period demonstrated that the inter-war period was the exception not the rule and that in the end the African economies, far from being 'underdeveloped', were well equipped for sustained development, provided that they maintained the sensible policies previously imposed on them by the colonial authorities.

These two approaches to the colonial impact on Black Africa have one common feature: both assume that colonial rule had a decisive effect, the one generally adverse, the other potentially good. But these are clearly polarities, Aristotelian extremes. Modern research suggests that there is a third, median, position which accords more closely with historical realities. Marxist and dependency theories assert that colonialism involved the transformation of all existing relations of production into capitalist relations, so that Africans lost control of the means of production and capital accumulation. In its most acute form this would imply transforming peasants into a rural or urban proletariat; more probably it implied reducing the autonomy of the peasant household to the point at which its male members were compelled to take wage labour on capitalist farms or factories. Yet such conditions were in fact very rare: outside South Africa very few Africans became proletarians in the sense that, like the working classes of industrial Europe, they had no alternative means of subsistence. What, then, becomes of the 'international division of labour' which is central to dependency theory?

Similar doubts arise from closer examination of the colonial impact as described by the right. Africa does not seem to have been incorporated fully into a more dynamic international economy, and colonial rule did not in most places result in the evolution of a progressive African capitalism which reproduced the dynamics of European industrial or agricultural development. This is why there seems to be room for a third general approach to the colonial inheritance which stands somewhere between these two extremes and attempts to measure the actual colonial impact more precisely.

John Lonsdale has used the term 'syncretic articulation' to describe the muted effects of colonial rule and foreign capital on indigenous African economies and societies; Frederick Cooper has written of Africans 'straddling' the two systems.[2] The essence of their arguments, if they can be conflated, seems to be roughly as follows.

The most important feature and consequence of colonial rule was precisely that neither political nor economic forces proved sufficiently strong to change the essential character of African societies, except possibly in parts of South Africa. Very few Africans become capitalists in a European sense of depending exclusively on their ownership of the means of production to extract surplus value from others. Capitalism did not become the dominant mode of production. Nor did most Africans become proletarians entirely dependent on selling their labour. Most remained in some sense peasants with the option of moving out of wage labour into rural self-sufficiency. But equally peasant production did not remain unaffected by the pressures and attractions created by the colonial state and links with international capitalism. What happened was that foreign capitalism, together with the fiscal demands and economic planning of the colonial state, compelled or persuaded the majority of Africans to become linked with the international economy. They did so variously, as producers of cash crops, as small businessmen, as middleman traders or as paid employees of other Africans, of Europeans or of the government. On the other hand, very few indeed adopted any one of these roles exclusively, so breaking their links with their indigenous social and economic background. Cocoa and coffee producers could grow food crops if commodity prices slumped. Owners of trucks or shops and middleman traders kept their footholds in village and family economies. Paid workers on plantations or in the towns might also be smallholders, using wages to supplement agricultural incomes and remaining free to revert to their peasant role if necessary. In short, colonial rule had a limited impact on African society and economy, sufficient to enable Western capitalism to deepen its operations, insufficient to carry through a complete transformation or to make Africa entirely dependent on international capitalism. This is the meaning of 'syncretic articulation'.

Why the colonial impact was, in this interpretation, so limited is beyond the purpose of the present analysis. Broadly, explanations are likely to fall into two general categories: the weakness or uncertainty of exogenous economic or political forces making for change, or the strength of African resistance to these forces. Under close examination it is clear that colonial states were very ambivalent about allowing economic forces free rein; they were certainly not mere tools of capitalists. Capitalism commonly found it more rewarding to maintain indigenous structures and to articulate them with itself than to attempt to destroy them. For their part African peasants demonstrated their ability to straddle both worlds and keep their options open by retaining access to land. They remained, in Hyden's term, 'uncaptured', with results that will be examined in more detail in Chapter 4.

But whatever the reasons, this argument suggests that the impact of colonialism was very much less than either its critics or its defenders have claimed. If this is correct, there is an interesting corollary. If neither the colonial state nor the batteries of capitalism were strong enough to transform African economies over a period of sixty years or more, it would not be surprising if the impact of successor states in the course of some two decades after 1960 was also limited. It is important to bear this in mind when considering the 'policy' approach to post-independence development in later chapters.

Right or wrong, these alternative interpretations of the general significance of colonialism for Black Africa at least provide a rough conceptual framework for analysing the inheritance left by the imperial powers to the new African states in the mid-twentieth century.

The Late-Colonial Economies, *c*.1945–*c*.1960

In most respects the statistics suggest an unprecedented developmental achievement in colonial Black Africa after 1945 which was still gathering momentum at the time of colonial independence. Between 1947 and 1960 the value of exports (at current prices) from British Africa, excluding South Africa, increased from £120.1m. to £591m.; between 1948 and 1953 that of the exports from French sub-Saharan Africa from $291m. to $484m.[3] The average per capita growth rate of GDP (measured in current US dollars) for all Africa (excluding South Africa) between 1950 and 1960 was 2.4 per cent, as compared with 2.2 per cent for 1960–70. While there were wide differences between countries and although there are gaps in the available data, a number of French and British colonies did well in this decade. For example, the average per capita growth rate of Cameroon was 1.5 per cent, of Ghana 1.9 per cent, of Kenya (despite the Mau Mau crisis) 1.0 per cent, of Nyasaland 1.6 per cent, of Mali 1.2 per cent, of Nigeria 2.1 per cent, of Senegal 4.4 per cent, of Sierra Leone 2.5 per cent and of

Tanganyika 3.7 per cent.[4] Of these only Cameroon, Kenya and Nyasaland (Malawi) did better in the 1960s.

These general statistics conceal wide variations in actual performance in this late-colonial period. The decade before 1960 was in general relatively good for agricultural production. The index of volume (1952/3 = 100) for all Africa rose from 88 in 1948/9 to 120 in 1958/9; for food products from 88 to 118, for non-food products from 87 to 133 and for livestock from 92 to 114. Per capita production also rose slightly, despite accelerating population growth: from 97 to 103 for all agricultural products, from 97 to 101 for food and from 95 to 114 for non-food products.[5] In manufacturing also there had been quite substantial growth, particularly in consumer goods. By 1960 the share of manufacturing in total GDP of 'developing Africa' had risen to 10.5 per cent.[6] By a broader definition, by 1960 'industry' accounted for a weighted average of 16 per cent of the domestic product of all sub-Saharan countries, though this varied between 6.3 per cent in Zambia (mostly mining) to about 10 per cent in a number of places.[7] Moreover, in absolute terms, a very large proportion of total value added by manufacturing in 1960 came from a very few countries. Egypt with 31.2 per cent had the largest single share in Africa as a whole, while Zaire (8.9 per cent) and Nigeria (6.3 per cent) had the largest shares in sub-Saharan Africa; the next largest – Kenya and Ghana, each with 2.2 per cent of the total, Ivory Coast with 1.7 per cent, and Zambia with 1.1 per cent – were the only other countries with a significant share of the total.[8] These were for the most part predominantly light consumer industries, such as food, beverages, tobacco, textiles and clothing, with only the beginning of chemical and petrochemical industries in a few places.

There had, therefore, been significant growth in late-colonial Africa, helped immensely by the long postwar boom. Nevertheless, there were many aspects of the colonial economy which called its benefits into question. First, peasant agriculture still had relatively low yields, wherever these can be compared with comparable production elsewhere. In terms of kilograms per hectare (world = 100), in 1961–3 sub-Saharan cocoa was 94, coffee 83, tea 90, maize 42, rice 62, wheat 67, groundnuts in shell 95, pulses 71, roots and tubers 60, seed cotton 46 and tobacco 69. Only in millet at 107 and sugar cane on 100 did sub-Saharan Africa match or rise above the world average.[9] Colonial Africa's level of industrialization was self-evidently very low. In social terms, life expectancy at birth averaged 39 in 1960, as compared with 70 in industrialized countries; the average population per physician was 50,096 as compared with 830 and enrolment in primary schools 36 per cent of the age group as against 114.[10] The average GNP of all Africa in 1950 was only $150 as compared with $2,378 in all OECD countries; and between 1950 and 1960 the absolute gap between these widened from $2,208 to $3,006.[11]

Another main and often emphasized limitation in the character of the modern sector in African colonial economies was that much of it was foreign owned or controlled. This was true of almost all modern manufacturing, banking, the import–export trade, shipping, mining and a number of plantations, timber enterprises and so on. Conversely, there were very few African entrepreneurs or even men holding senior managerial posts in foreign-owned firms. Thus almost all the commanding heights of the colonial economy were occupied by expatriates, leaving the colonial peoples to fill the role of peasant producers or urban proletariat.

Clearly, then, there had been growth in the late-colonial period, though its absolute achievements by about 1960 were limited. The more important question is whether the successor states inherited dynamic economies with the capacity for rapid and sustained growth, or whether the colonial inheritance included structural obstacles which expansion since about 1945 had not destroyed. To attempt an answer to this question it is proposed to examine six main areas, all of which are important measures of development potential: human resources, infrastructure, agricultural productivity, levels of saving and capital formation, manufacturing development and potential, and the level of public indebtedness.

Human Resources

Probably the least promising aspect of the situation in about 1960 was the supply of educated and skilled people. Colonial states had been able to spend little on public education, relying heavily on mission schools; moreover the common assumption was that it was unnecessary and probably dangerous to produce large numbers of people with advanced Western-style qualifications in societies which could not employ them adequately. The bald statistics indicate the general lack of school provision. Thus, while the average for all sub-Saharan Africa was 36 per cent of the age group in primary schools, this varied from under 10 per cent in very poor countries such as Niger, Mauritania and Upper Volta (as also, significantly, in independent Ethiopia) to 96 per cent in Southern Rhodesia, with over 50 per cent in a number of places. In Africa as a whole only some 16 per cent of adults were literate in 1960. A still greater weakness, however, lay in secondary and tertiary education. In 1960 the average enrolment in secondary schools was only 3 per cent of the age-group, no continental colony having more than 6 per cent (Southern Rhodesia) and only three (Gold Coast, Swaziland and Gabon) 5 per cent.[12] Tertiary education was so rare that it produced few recorded statistics. There were very few colonial universities or university colleges and these dated only from the later 1940s or early 1950s. By 1960 there were still no universities in French territories, just two in Zaire, and a handful of university colleges in the main British colonies (Sierra Leone, Gold Coast, Nigeria, Southern Rhodesia, Uganda and Kenya). Probably the majority of Africans with university training had received it abroad: in 1960, for example, there were 396 Kenyans at Makerere University College in Uganda but 1,655 at university abroad.[13] Perhaps more important, there were very few technical schools or colleges to provide training in industrial and managerial skills. The general results were that most African societies were predominantly illiterate and innumerate; that there was no stock of men trained in the skills of Western business; and that the tiny elites with university degrees stood out as distinctively as did expatriates, anxious to fill the more lucrative and prestigious positions in government or education but rarely equipped or motivated to engage in productive enterprises.

Infrastructure

By contrast with education, provision of infrastructure was taken seriously by the colonial state as its main contribution to economic development; and in most of British and French Africa (apart from British Central Africa) most utilities were publicly owned and operated. The first and most important of these were the railways. Built to serve a mixture of economic and strategic functions, most of them ran from ports to inland areas of production and the greater part of the mileage had been constructed before 1914. By international standards sub-Saharan Africa was poorly provided. Total track in British Africa (excluding South Africa) was only 13,638 km in 1946. In French West and Equatorial Africa there were some 4,389 km. Much of this was narrow gauge with limited capacity and high freight charges which seriously affected the international competitiveness of inland producers. Moreover, there were few branch or lateral lines and almost no railways ran from one colonial territory to a foreign colony, the main exceptions being the Benguela railway from Katanga through Angola and the various rail links from Nyasaland, the Rhodesias and South Africa to Beira and Lourenço Marques. Hence there were no rail links, for example, between the multiple adjacent colonies of West Africa.

These limitations made roads even more essential; but here the colonial state, partly because of its stake in rail freights, was slow to act. Africa had a large nominal road network – an estimated 946,291 km in 1963 excluding Mozambique and Angola; but only about 10 per cent was sealed and many roads were only passable in good weather. Nevertheless, roads and the petol-driven truck, coming in during the 1920s, were critical factors in economic development, opening up new areas to production for the market and incidentally providing one of the main opportunities for Africans to become capitalists and entrepreneurs.

By Western standards other forms of infrastructure barely existed. In 1960 energy consumption per capita (measured in kilograms of coal equivalent) was only 76 in Black Africa compared with 356 for all low-income countries and 4,486 for industrialized countries.[14] The late-colonial period saw the start of some large-scale hydroelectric schemes, notably the Volta scheme in the Gold Coast (although this did not come into operation until the mid-1960s) and the Kariba scheme in the Rhodesias, begun in 1955; and between 1948 and 1961 total electricity production in Black Africa increased from 4,141m. kWh to 18,544m. kWh.[15] But by international standards this was still very low indeed and most areas outside the main towns were not provided with electricity. Much the same was true of other types of public utility: later colonial Africa was severely handicapped by lack of a modern infrastructure, and this was to compel the successor states to devote a very large part of their development expenditure to providing essential amenities, particularly in the rapidly growing towns that were also the main focus of industrial expansion.

Agricultural Productivity

But almost certainly the most important weakness in the late-colonial economy was agriculture. There is, of course, a paradox here. On the one hand there are the classic success stories of African response to international demand for cash crops, resulting in quite spectacular growth during the colonial period. The five-yearly average of cocoa exports from the Gold Coast increased from 106,000 tons in 1916–20 to 263,000 tons in 1936–40. Exports of Nigerian palm kernels rose from 85,624 tons in 1900 to their peak of 464,111 tons in 1954 and of palm oil from 45,508 tons to 208,482 tons in the same years. French West African groundnut exports rose from 242,000 tons in 1913 to 382,889 tons in 1954.[16] These were among the main show-cases of colonial agriculture. But there are less impressive aspects of the record. As has been seen above, in most major crops, except for millet, sugar cane and groundnuts, Black African yields per hectare were well below the world average, even where the main competition came from other peasant societies. Yields of most locally consumed food crops, which do not appear in most statistics because very little information on them is available, were probably as low or even lower: African rice production, for example, averaged 1,249 kg/ha in 1961–3 as compared with a world average of 2,026. Already, by the early 1960s, Black Africa was having to import substantial quantities of basic foods: 464,000 tons of rice, 394,000 tons of wheat, 197,000 tons of maize, with a total cereal importation of 1,177,000 tons in 1961–3.[17] Some commentators, including Samir Amin, have attributed this growing dependence on imported food, which was most acute in Senegal with its huge concentration on groundnut production, to compulsory over-specialization and have argued that, given adverse trends in the terms of trade for commodities, the effect was to reduce the consumption of many Africans; that is, the principle, of comparative advantage did not work satisfactorily in relation to African agriculture.[18]

That is debatable. The certain fact is that the great increase in agricultural production of all types was almost entirely the result of extension of land under cultivation and the use of more labour; it owed very little to improvements in agricultural techniques or the application of more animal or mechanical power. There may have been good economic reasons for this. So long as ample new land and additional labour were available, it was rational for peasants to use these cheap means of increasing production rather than invest in relatively expensive technology and inputs which might not be justified by the marginal increase in profits. The situation only became serious when no more good new land was available or when labour became scarce or relatively expensive, or when these methods of production no longer provided goods that were competitive in price and quality on the world market. Although they recognized that agriculture was critical for both economy and public revenues, none of the colonial powers put significant resources into agricultural research or extension programmes until the early 1940s. Thereafter considerable effort was put into research on tropical crops and their special problems and into the dissemination of new methods through the expanded agricultural departments of the colonies. Some quite substantial improvements resulted, but at the same time most attempts to persuade or compel Africans to make major changes in their methods of production and attitudes to livestock, tree diseases, soil erosion, etc., met with great resistance in many areas, as they were to do after independence. At the end of colonial rule the African peasant remained, in Hyden's term, largely 'uncaptured': that is, while prepared to produce for the market so long as he deemed it profitable to do so, he had effectively retained his freedom of action and his preference for risk avoidance and generally refused to adopt new systems of production which were incompatible with his existing life-style.[19]

Saving and Capital Formation

One of the major unknown elements in the late-colonial economy is the level of domestic saving and capital formation. Investment funds came from five main sources: foreign (mainly imperial) governments; colonial government borrowing abroad; foreign private investors, both direct and portfolio; colonial government taxation; and private savings in the colonies. The first, second and fourth of these are reasonably accessible through the public accounts; but foreign private investment is to some extent conjectural and private investment by Africans except in government stock and company shares is unknowable. Yet properly to assess the dynamics and potential of colonial economies at the time of independence one ought to be able to assess their capacity to provide their own investment funds and to service external borrowing. The standard statistical sources are of little use here: there are no figures for colonial domestic savings in the British *Statistical Abstract*, the French *Annuaire statistique* or the UN *Statistical Yearbook* for that period; the very measurement of this and other indicators of growth seems to begin only in the 1960s for most African countries. The UN *Statistical Yearbook* provides information on fixed capital formation as a percentage of GNP for a very few colonies from the mid-1950s, though these probably include overseas capital flows. The available data are summarized in Table 2.1. But for the majority of the African states the earliest data on the percentage of GDP devoted to domestic savings is in the Berg Report and relates to 1960; this is summarized for the countries dealt with individually in this study and a few other major African countries in Table 2.2.

The significance of these figures is strictly limited: they are of dubious accuracy and uniformity, and the importance of a percentage is relative to the national income or domestic product – for a very poor country the absolute investment implied by even a relatively large percentage of GDP may be very small. Nevertheless, and even allowing for the fact that most of the countries included in Table 2.1 are relatively big and not among the poorest African colonies, the size of fixed capital formation is in most cases surprisingly large; significantly it was highest in the mineral-extracting countries in the period before 1958, but substantial also in Ghana and Tanganyika. Only Togo, very underdeveloped at the time, had a very low level of fixed capital formation. Table 2.2 generally supports this impression. All but the poorest colonies (Nigeria in the 1950s before the expansion of oil extraction was still one of the poorest in per capita terms) had a gross domestic saving rate of more than 10 per cent and it is significant that foreign capital inflows (reflected here by a negative resource balance) enabled the gross domestic investment rate to be above 10 per cent. How long these levels of savings and investment ratios had existed is impossible to say, since earlier data are not available; but it is clear that at least at the end of the colonial period capital formation, helped in most cases by overseas aid, had risen to quite respectable levels.

This does not, of course, mean that any of these societies had an adequate stock of capital, whether in the form of public utilities or private productive enterprises. It is quite impossible to calculate the capital invested in or by these colonies, partly because so much of it was in the 'traditional' sector and had never been monetized: the huge African investment in sylvan and other forms of agricultural

Table 2.1 *Fixed Capital Formation as a Percentage of GNP (at market prices) for Selected African Countries, 1950–1964*

Country	1950	1954	1955	1958	1959	1960	1963	1964
Zaire	22	—	—	24	18	—	—	—
Ghana	—	—	15	14	—	21	—	17
Malawi	—	10	—	17	—	16	14	—
S. Rhodesia	—	28	—	33	—	23	—	14
Tanganyika	—	18	—	16	—	12	—	12
Togo	—	—	—	—	—	—	8	—
Zambia	—	32	—	33	—	20	—	18

Source:
UN *Statistical Yearbook 1965* (New York, 1966), table 181.

production is one obvious example. The only figures available, many of them highly speculative, relate exclusively to the modern sector and consist mainly of colonial government borrowing on capital account, metropolitan grants and the share issues of the larger foreign enterprises. Unfortunately the best recent estimates for French territories, by Marseille, are not broken down by territory or region of the French empire; and most other calculations relate to the pre-1940 period. S. H. Frankel's estimate of combined public and private listed overseas capital in sub-Saharan Africa in about 1936 suggests that, except for the mining colonies – the Rhodesias and the Belgian Congo – the average per capita investment was under £10 a head and was much less in many places; £4.8 in British West Africa as a whole, £2.1 in French West Africa, £8.1 in British East Africa (including Tanganyika and Nyasaland).[20] Other estimates vary widely but there can be no doubt that the modern sectors of all these territories were very poorly capitalized before the Second World War.

Far more public and private investment occurred after 1945 and some estimates of French investment were given in Chapter 1. Some speculative calculations of my own suggest that between 1947 and 1955 French public investment in Black Africa (excluding Madagascar) may have been about 245b. francs, plus about 63.5b. francs of new private investment, making a total of some 308b., equivalent to about £314m. With a total estimated population of the area in 1960 (the earliest date for which such calculations of total population seem available) of some 35.5m., the total post-1945 foreign investment was around £8.8 a head, four times the 1936 figure, but not substantially larger after inflation is allowed for.[21] A comparable rough calculation for British tropical Africa is even more difficult and probably misleading. From 1946 to

Table 2.2   *Gross Domestic Investment (GDI), Gross Domestic Saving (GDS) and Resource Balance (RB) as a Percentage of Gross Domestic Product in Selected African Territories, 1960*

Territory	GDI	GDS	RB
Mali	14	9	−5
Malawi	10	−4	−14
Tanganyika	14	19	+5
Zaire	12	21	+9
Uganda	11	16	+5
Togo	11	4	−7
Kenya	20	17	−3
Senegal	16	15	−1
S. Rhodesia	23	22	−1
Zambia	25	41	+16
Ivory Coast	15	17	+2
Congo	45	−21	−66
Nigeria	13	7	−6
Gabon	50	50	+1
Weighted average for:			
Sub-Saharan Africa	15	13	−3
All low-income countries	18	16	−2
All middle-income countries	21	19	−2
Industrialized countries	21	22	+1

Source:
World Bank, *Accelerated Development in Sub-Saharan Africa* (Washington DC, 1981), Appendix 5.

1955 new official loans and grants may have amounted to around £90m. In 1962 the Board of Trade put total cumulative British direct investment in Black Africa at £373.4m.; and of that £125.6m. was in Central Africa, most of it in mining.[22] Disregarding pre-war investments, British public and private post-1945 investment in Black Africa by the later 1950s may thus have been of the order of £500m., allowing for continuing public loans and grants from 1955 to 1960. The total population of about 80 million gives a per capita figure of post-war British investment of around £6.25. Excluding the Rhodesias, total investment might have been about £350m., and population around 73 million[23], giving a per capita investment of *c.*£4.8.

These, it must be emphasized, are hardly more than guesses, but they probably indicate the rough order of magnitude of foreign investment in the late-colonial period. The only point that is certain is that, by Western standards, capital investment in the modern sector was very small indeed, and most of it in public utilities and commerce; fixed industrial investment was minute. Even so, the level of public provision of quite elementary amenities, as has been seen, was extremely low. Clearly, despite the relatively high level of domestic saving and investment in many colonies by the 1950s, the backlog was huge. This, of course, was one of the main 'structural' problems as perceived by development economists of the 1950s and 1960s, whose arguments in support of massive Western grants and loans to back up much greater levels of domestic saving in Africa as the only way to break through the low-level equilibrium trap are discussed below in Chapter 3. It is also obviously one main factor likely to have limited growth in most post-colonial societies: so much investment was required to lay the foundations of a modern economy capable of sustained expansion that relatively little might be available for directly productive purposes.

Why colonial Africa was so generally lacking in capital investment is beyond the scope of this study; but, in so far as there may have been continuity between the colonial and post-colonial periods, some tentative hypotheses may be put forward. First, the cliché that poverty breeds poverty holds good. The domestic product per capita of all these African countries both before and after independence – averaging only $106 in 1960 for all Africa excluding South Africa[24] – allowed for very limited public consumption, however high the proportion transferred from private use. Secondly, African private capital showed little interest in investing in the modern sector, particularly in production. For this there are many possible explanations: the superior attraction of alternative forms of investment, particularly urban property; the difficulty of raising medium- to long-term credit; the absence of colonial stock exchanges or indeed available shares in local enterprises; the existence of foreign firms with superior technology and know-how in most parts of the modern economy; the absence of any indigenous tradition of investment in corporate, as contrasted with family, enterprises; lack, under colonial conditions, of evidently promising investment opportunities, particularly in industry. Thirdly, foreign investors found little to attract them, except in mining and trade and, in a few places such as Central Africa, public utilities. The reasons for this limited attraction have been much canvassed and need not be rehearsed here; but among the most important in discouraging investment in manufacturing were limited markets, lack of protection against metropolitan or international competition, the common lack of local inputs better or cheaper than could be obtained in their home countries, and the fact that colonial governments made little or no attempt to provide favourable conditions. Other types of potential foreign investment, such as plantations, were positively discouraged by British and French administrators where these were thought incompatible with established social and political norms, as in much of West Africa.

It has often been suggested that a main cause of limited investment and therefore development in colonial Africa was early imperial selfishness and the inability of colonial governments to conceive of or plan conditions attractive to greater capital investment. How important such factors were cannot be examined here; what is certain is that the turning-point came at least a decade before the formal transfer of power in most territories. A drive for maximum saving and public and private investment was intrinsic to the post-1945 development plans prepared by all the imperial powers. It was, of course, too late to make good the backlog of under-investment; but it is important that the main lines of post-independence capital raising (for example, through the marketing boards of British West Africa, government to government loans and grants, parastatal organizations such as the British Colonial (later Commonwealth) Development Corporation) were established long before the transfer of power. So also was the drawing up of medium-term plans and the use of large state or parastatal enterprises in the colonies to spend the funds made available. What the new independent governments added was readiness to borrow far beyond what colonial governments had regarded as prudent, to extract a greater proportion of the domestic product for public spending than had seemed politically safe before and to provide attractions to potential foreign and indigenous investors in industry which derived from nationalist rather than economic calculations. In short, they ignored even the much higher speed limits set by the colonial governments during the last expansionist phase. The result was a very considerable increase in levels of capital accumulation and investment, but also a far greater exposure to risk. The consequences of this new departure are basic to the main themes of later chapters.

Manufacturing Development and Potential

This is particularly true of manufacturing, which was obviously one of the weakest sectors of colonial economies. Table 2.3, taken from Kilby's very useful short survey of the extent and character of manufacturing in Black Africa, summarizes the essential points.[25]

Perhaps three main features stand out. First, in only two countries – the Belgian Congo and Southern Rhodesia – did manufacturing (which here excludes construction and utilities) exceed 10 per cent of the GDP, though in Senegal and Kenya it was 9.5 per cent. In six of these countries it was under 5 per cent. The two places with relatively high manufacturing components had also large mining enterprises

Table 2.3 *Population, Income and Manufacturing Output in Selected African Countries, 1960*

	Population (m.)	GDP Gross domestic product ($ m.)	Per capita income ($)	Manufacturing production ($ m.)	Share of manufacturing in GDP (%)
Nigeria	40.0	3,500	88	157.5	4.5
Ethiopia	20.7	1,021	49	61.3	6.0
Congo	14.1	910	58	127.4	14.0
Sudan	11.8	909	77	43.6	4.8
Tanganyika	9.6	671	67	20.1	3.0
Kenya	8.1	641	79	60.9	9.5
Gold Coast	6.8	1,503	222	94.7	6.3
Uganda	6.7	583	87	37.9	6.5
Angola	4.8	726	151	31.2	4.3
Cameroon	4.7	511	109	30.6	6.0
S. Rhodesia	3.6	751	206	120.2	16.0
N. Rhodesia	3.2	511	155	28.1	5.5
Ivory Coast	3.2	584	181	31.0	5.3
Senegal	3.1	678	218	64.4	9.5
Dahomey (1965)	2.4	175	74	4.6	2.6
Sierra Leone (1965)	2.3	316	133	19.9	6.3
Togo (1965)	1.6	150	92	6.2	4.1
Gabon	0.4	131	294	8.0	6.1

Note:
Manufacturing excludes utilities and construction. All values expressed in US 1964 dollars. Population data from OECD, Development Centre, *Population of Less Developed Countries* (Paris, 1967). For Nigeria, income data from Nigeria, Federal Office of Statistics, *Gross Domestic Product of Nigeria, 1958–1966* (Lagos, 1968). For the Gold Coast, columns 4 and 5 from Peter Robson and D. A. Lury, *The Economies of Africa* (Evanston, Northwestern University Press, 1969), p. 112. All other data from World Bank, Economics Department, *World Tables* (Washington DC 1968).

Source:
P. Kilby, 'Manufacturing in Colonial Africa', in P. Duignan and L. H. Gann (eds), *Colonialism in Africa*, Vol. 4, *The Economics of Colonialism* (Cambridge, 1975), p. 472.

(though it did not necessarily work the other way round: Zambia, with a very large copper mining industry, got only 5.5 per cent of GDP from manufacture). The four colonies with the largest proportion of GDP from manufacturing had sizeable European populations. Secondly, there was clearly some correlation between size of population and that of the manufacturing sector. Thus, although manufacturing in Nigeria was very small in relation to GDP, it was absolutely the largest in Black

Africa. Finally, there was some correlation between per capita incomes and levels of industrial production, though this was not very strong and in the case particularly of the Portuguese colonies did not exist at all. How does one account for these variations and characteristics? Was limited industrialization intrinsic to colonialism or was it likely to continue to be characteristic of post-colonial Africa?

A main point is that different answers are necessary for different places and regions. The Belgian Congo was a special case. Although 99 per cent of the population in the later 1950s were indigenous, 95 per cent of total assets, 82 per cent of the largest units of production and 88 per cent of private savings belonged to foreigners. Moreover, in 1958 the 1 per cent of foreigners received 12.9b. francs in salaries, 7.0b. francs from property and business enterprises, 5.9b. from amortization and 1.3b. from corporate savings. Total foreign consumption was 12.1b. francs; that of Africans 19.0b.[26] Here, then, was a society in which about 110,000 whites (by the 1958 census) and a few very large overseas firms controlled almost the entire modern economy, possessed very considerable purchasing power and constituted a relatively large market for local manufactures as well as imports.

This alone does not, however, explain the rapid growth and relatively large size of manufacturing in the late-colonial Congo, especially between 1950 and 1958, when the value of industrial output jumped from 12 to over 19 per cent of the total value of industrial exports and local consumer goods production rose from 30 to 44 per cent of total available imported and locally produced manufactured consumer goods.[27] How does one explain the early establishment of a consumer goods industry and its rapid eventual expansion?

For the period before the later 1940s the most important single reason was the relatively high transport cost of imports, particularly of bulk goods. Although transport costs declined substantially as a proportion of the import price over time, the absolute cost of carriage from the coast, including unavoidable transfers between river and rail, remained high. Thus, in periods of prosperity in the mining sector, rising demand, particularly in the European sector, encouraged the large investing corporations to diversify into consumer production and construction. After 1945 new factors were at work. With rising productivity in the mines and agriculture and a state policy of increasing public investment and welfare provision, African wages rose both relatively and absolutely. Real incomes rose: between 1950 and 1958 the price of a piece of cloth declined from 61 to 41 per cent of average monthly wages in rural areas, in Leopoldville from 26 to 13 per cent, in Elizabethville from 40 to 15 per cent. In the same period average African wages in the transport sector rose from 2 to 4 per cent of European salaries and African wage-earners' incomes increased from 5.1b. to 14.1b. francs.[28] Here was a booming domestic market fuelled by increased public expenditure which provided the necessary stimulus for investment in industry. While most of the new industrial investment was by big foreign corporations, the greater part of private consumption was now by Africans.

The Congo was a special case, particularly in its golden 1950s. So favourable a conjunction of circumstances for manufacturing was very rare. Yet in different degrees many of the factors that made possible the Congo's manufacturing development may be found elsewhere and help to explain differences between one colony and another.

Though both Southern Rhodesia and Kenya had substantial European populations and relatively high manufacturing components, patterns of development were different. In Rhodesia small-scale manufacturing began in the late nineteenth century, stimulated by the high cost of carriage from the coast. Until 1938, however, most firms were small and the labour force then only 2,798 Europeans and 14,756 Africans. The Second World War provided a great stimulus. Between 1938 and 1953 net industrial output rose from £2.3m. to £26m. (about £16.2m. in 1938 prices) and the scale of industry rose through concentration and the greater role of large foreign firms. By 1957 68 per cent of total gross output was provided by 9 per cent of firms.[29] This expansion was helped by the huge influx of white settlers after 1945, by the expansion of agricultural and mineral exports, by the enlarged market created by the Central African Federation after 1953, which resulted in a flow of resources from Northern to Southern Rhodesia, by the availability of local iron ore and coal at competitive prices and by the activity of the state as entrepreneur. Conversely, protective tariffs and controls played no important role; duties were generally low and for revenue purposes. The most important single factor was a growing market which stimulated foreign importers to protect established markets by setting up local manufacturing subsidiaries.

Kenya also had a relatively high manufacturing component of GDP in 1960, but this was associated with the needs and activities of the minority of Europeans and again the impulse provided by the Second World War rather than mining. Before 1939 settlers established small consumer goods factories and also plants for processing agricultural products such as sisal, pyrethrum and coffee and some British firms moved in to produce soda ash and cement and to process tea and wattle extract. The war provided a great stimulus and the state, partly to provide for British military needs in the Middle East zone, established a number of industrial enterprises run by the Industrial Development Corporation. By 1957 there were 1,038 manufacturing establishments employing 53,800 with a gross product of £56.6m. and net output of £17.1m.[30] This expansion was helped by other factors. The East African Common Market, which included Uganda and Tanganyika, increased the market of 7m. Kenyans to about 25m. Tariff policy favoured local manufactures. Import duties provided 66.6 per cent protection on some luxury goods and 33.3 per cent on a range of consumer goods, with a general tariff of 25 per cent. There were drawbacks of duties on imported raw materials and intermediates. Perhaps most important was the increase in African incomes. Earlier figures do not seem to be available, but from 1954 to 1961 average earnings of Africans in employment rose by 70 per cent in industry and commerce, by 55 per cent in agriculture and by 90 per cent in public service, though these figures must be offset by inflation of above 15–20 per cent between 1954 to 1961.[31] Thus Kenya provides an example of considerable growth in manufacturing during the colonial period, though its further extension was conditioned by low African incomes which only began to rise significantly in the 1950s.

The contrast between these territories and the bulk of colonial Africa is so great that it is tempting to ascribe it to one or more simple factors: the absence of large mineral deposits (but Zambia had these) and the lack of many European settlers. The more salient facts are that in these other colonies almost all production (except for a few European-owned plantations) was in the hands of African peasants and that their marketed product was mainly cash crops for export. None of these places had manufacturing sectors which provided more than 6.5 per cent of GDP by 1960 except Senegal, which had a special position as capital of French West Africa with a large number of expatriates. In most other colonies there were very few industries indeed and most of these were set up in the 1950s. One has therefore to explain two things: the almost total lack of manufacturing before about 1950 and its quite substantial growth by 1960.

For the earlier period several obvious general explanations of limited industrialization are available, most of which have little to do with the colonial situation. Markets were open to world or (in the French and Portuguese case) metropolitan imports, which could undersell all but the cheapest indigenous products and discouraged expatriate investment. Markets were small because there were few affluent Europeans and African cash incomes were very low. The cost of transport to most coastal colonies was too low to provide natural protection for any but the most bulky goods and even where local raw materials – cotton, vegetable oils, timber, etc., – provided a potential advantage to local production, this was usually too small to offset higher unit costs. There were few Africans with entrepreneurial ability, know-how and access to capital. The main impact of the colonial state was negative. It was not hostile to local manufacture in principle but it did not positively encourage it except in wartime. By refusing protective duties, providing no incentives or special aids (state credit, etc.) and, in West Africa, by discouraging the immigration of Europeans and Lebanese (broadly for fear of their effects on Africans) the state did nothing to offset the inherent obstacles to manufacturing development.

Much of this, however, would apply also to the Congo. One main difference was the role played by large-scale foreign enterprise which in the Congo did, but in most other places did not, invest in local manufacturing. Kilby has summarized what is now a general consensus view in arguing that it was the role of large-scale capital which, more than anything else, prevented the early establishment of manufacturing for local consumption in 'peasant Africa' but, by changing its attitudes and activities, was mainly responsible for such industrial growth as took place during the last decade of colonialism. His argument, briefly, is as follows.

Until the later 1940s, and particularly in West Africa, colonial economies were dominated by a handful of foreign import–export firms whose profits depended on maximizing the volume of their trade in each direction. With markets for consumer goods limited by low African incomes, there was no room for additional firms of any size and oligopoly ensured a satisfactory rate of return for those in the ring. These firms had, therefore, no incentive to engage in local manufactures or, indeed, any other form of fixed investment. After 1946, however, conditions changed substantially. Booming prices for agricultural exports greatly increased demand for consumer goods and simultaneously colonial governments expanded public expenditure and investment. The expanding market in turn created space for the entry of competitors in the trading system: in West Africa for Levantines, Greeks, Indians and African entrepreneurs (whose share of Nigerian imports rose from c.5 to c.20 per cent from 1949 to 1963) and also foreign manufacturers, who began to set up their own distributive networks. In the face of this new competition the older trading firms found it no longer profitable to maintain their huge networks of retail outlets and were in danger of being undersold or bypassed by others. Moreover, with the increasing probability by the early 1950s of a transfer of political power to African politicians, it became likely that nationalist economic policies would be adopted which would benefit firms within the country and threaten outsiders. In British colonies the role of the marketing boards as sole purchasers of commodities further reduced the traditional activities of traders. The result was that the big trading firms, led by UAC, completely transformed their activities. They virtually moved out of trade and into manufacturing, commonly acting as partners of European industrial firms for whom they provided local know-how and part of the equity. In this way foreign capital was primarily responsible for the establishment of large-scale manufacturing in West Africa and some other areas and their lead was to some extent followed by indigenous and foreign entrepreneurs.

In this argument the key fact is the expansion of the market due to expansion of the marketed agricultural product after 1945. This had little or nothing to do with the character of colonialism and was a by-product of the postwar commodity boom. But the late-colonial state did play an important part. An increasing flow of metropolitan money, mainly in salaries to expatriates and grants and loans, helped to lubricate the economy. Colonial governments were now unprecedentedly active. In Nigeria, for example, they provided accelerated depreciation allowances, tax holidays and import duty relief for new businesses. The first steps were taken towards moderate tariff protection. Governments provided more credit and established some (ultimately unsuccessful) industrial estates. Large infrastructural projects were begun. Many aspects of the first post-independence development plans were merely a continuation of these policies.

What, then, was the industrial inheritance from the colonial states? Clearly by the standards of the West and many Latin American countries, though not of South Asia, manufacturing still provided a relatively small part of the domestic product by 1960. To the extent that the colonial powers had done little before 1945 to encourage industrial growth in Africa and in a few cases (for example, limitation of the proportion of Senegalese groundnuts that could be processed before export to France) actively discouraged it, they were at least partly responsible. After 1945 more positive measures were taken but even so, industrialization was less rapid than it was to be in most countries after independence. Yet the basic constraint was not alien rule but the intrinsic difficulty of established viable manufactures in poor countries with small markets in a world system which could, except in war, provide an unlimited supply of manufactures at prices with which few less developed countries could compete. The important difference between colonial and post-colonial development was that in the first case industries existed because they had natural advantages and could make a positive contribution to the national income, whereas in the second a large proportion existed because they were given some artificial stimulus. It is significant that most of those industries which were efficient by international standards during the two decades after 1960 were established before independence and would have existed without the stimulants provided by the new states. Thus the colonial inheritance was the principle of viability which, in most African circumstances, also meant limited industrialization.

Public Indebtedness

Finally there is the position of the African colonies as debtors or creditors at the time of independence. This not only reflects the economic consequences of colonial rule but also provides a point of comparison with the effects of two decades of independence. A preliminary technical comment is necessary. Information on colonial debts and credits is limited. Since no British or French colony in Africa was an autonomous monetary unit, colonies did not hold foreign exchange: all assets were in the metropolitan currency, so that it would be meaningless to ask what their dollar holdings were. In the case, moreover, of France, individual colonies did not hold measurable currency reserves even in francs. From the early 1950s each colony was given a current account with the metropolitan treasury into which it paid all foreign earnings and from which it drew whatever currency it required. By and large, colonies were expected to break even on current account, though in practice, as has been seen in Chapter 1, the French Government used funds allocated through FIDES to balance these accounts. As a result the French official records do not provide credit or debit figures for the colonies: the only relevant data on public transactions relates to pre-1939 colonial borrowing; and private indebtedness is notoriously difficult to calculate. Moreover, the French colonies, by contrast with the British, did not have to maintain cover for their currencies in Paris. Thus the figures for public foreign liquidity shown in Table 2.4 reflect only the position of the current acccounts of the Francophone states that remained within the franc zone at that time, rather than accumulated reserves. They are not strictly comparable with those of British colonies, which held substantial reserves in London to cover both their trade and currency, both of which were available for use by newly independent governments.

Let us consider first the liquidity position of the colonies at or around the time of independence and then their long-term public debt in relation to the GNP or GDP and to foreign exchange earnings. Table 2.4 shows the liquidity position of selected colonies about 1960 compared with that in 1982 and also with that of three other countries of very different types. Despite wide variations, the first essential point is that the overseas currency holdings of the main West African colonies at the time of independence ranged from very strong to sound. Ghana in 1955 held $532m., or $83.1 a head. This was the combined result of booming cocoa prices and compulsory limitation of imports before the mid-1950s, which resulted in large blocked sterling balances. By 1962 these reserves had been significantly depleted but were still substantial. Nigeria also had substantial reserves. Outside the sterling area the main commodity-exporting colonies − Belgian Congo, Gabon, Senegal and Ivory Coast − were all in strong positions. The rest had smaller per capita overseas assets, but all were proportionately larger than those of India and were not much below those of Peru. The 1982 figures do not allow for inflation; but even so the obvious fact is that by then only the oil-exporting countries and Togo were significantly better off in reserves than they had been in c.1960, and many were much worse, notably Zaire, Ghana, Ivory Coast and Senegal. Moreover,

Table 2.4 International Liquidity of Selected African Colonies at or about the Time of Independence, Compared with their Position in 1982 (US$.; population m.)

Country	Date	External assets ($ m.)	Population	External assets per cap. ($)	Date	External assets ($ m.)	Population	External assets per cap. ($)
Cameroon	1960	19.2	4.7	4.1	1982	81	9.3	8.7
Chad	1960	12.2	2.9	4.2	1982	18	4.6	3.9
Congo	1960	5.1	0.7	7.2	1982	42	1.7	24.7
Zaire ⎰	1956	338	14.1	23.9	1982	312	30.7	10.2
Zaire ⎱	1960	63	14.1	4.5				
Benin	1962	8.9	2.3	3.8	1982	10	3.7	2.7
East Africa[a]	1962	144.6	22	6.5	1981/2	286	51.4	5.5
Gabon	1960	9.5	0.45	21.1	1982	318	0.7	454.3
Ghana ⎰	1955	532	6.4	83.1	1982	318	12.2	26.0
Ghana ⎱	1962	196	6.4	30.6				
Ivory Coast	1962	34	3.4	10.0	1982	23	8.9	2.5
Mali	1962	11	4.0	2.7	1982	25	7.1	3.5
Nigeria ⎰	1959	498	42.9	11.6	1970	223	66.2	3.4
Nigeria ⎱					1982	1927	90.6	21.3
Senegal	1962	76	3.1	24.5	1982	25	6.0	4.2
Togo	1962	7.3	1.5	4.8	1982	173	2.8	61.7
Australia	1960	915	10.5	87.1				
India	1960	670	435.5	1.5				
Peru	1960	76	9.9	7.7				

Sources: External assets c. 1960: UN, Statistical Yearbook 1965, table 187.
Population c. 1960: UN, Survey of Economic Conditions in Africa, 1973 (New York, 1974), p. 203.
Nigerian data for 1970: World Bank, World Tables (2nd edn., Washington DC, 1980).
1982 data: World Bank, Toward Sustained Development in Sub-Saharan Africa (Washington DC, 1984).
Note: a. East Africa = Kenya, Uganda and Tanganyika, which were grouped together in contemporary British accounts.

in 1960 or so, the ratio of international reserves to import of goods and services of those colonies for which information is available ranged from satisfactory to excellent.

Turning to long-term indebtedness and its burdens, it is difficult to find reliable figures for the end of the colonial period which are directly comparable with those available for later periods. Tables 2.5 to 2.7 summarize some of the available evidence. It is weak on the period for which it is most needed here, that is the 1950s, but enables a reasonably reliable answer to be given to the vital questions: how heavily burdened were the colonies by debt at or soon after independence, and consequentially, how much capacity had they to undertake new borrowing for development purposes?

Consider first the total burden of public indebtedness in relation to government revenue and GNP (Tables 2.5 and 2.6, which are taken from different sources). Both absolutely and in relation to public revenues and to GNP, public debt and debt interest were low or moderate in all the colonies for which the relevant information is available. In 1957 Ghana, hitherto the most prosperous West African colony, had £22.1m. public debts, which represented 42.5 per cent of public revenues and 5.1 per cent of GNP. In 1960 interest on the debt was only 1.2 per cent of public revenues and 0.2 per cent of GNP. Indeed, Ghana's liquid assets in 1955 were more than seven times its long-term debts. Nigeria had public debts of £49.2m. in 1960, which represented 55 per cent of public revenues and 4.1 per cent of GNP. Interest on the debt represented 4.1 per cent of public revenues and 0.15 per cent of GNP. Malawi, Tanganyika and Zambia were in much the same position as Nigeria as regards debts and revenues, but less well placed when measured by debt as a percentage of GNP. Togo, which had undertaken very little borrowing or development, was more lightly burdened than any but Ghana. It is interesting that the two colonies with substantial white settler populations, Kenya and Southern Rhodesia, had far higher levels of public indebtedness in relation to both revenues and GNP than any of these.

In many ways the better test of the indebtedness of these countries is the ratio between the cost of servicing the overseas debt and the value of their exports of goods and services. This is shown in Table 2.7, though the earliest date for which standard figures seem available is 1965, which is too late to reflect accurately the position of some colonies at the time of independence, particularly of Ghana.

The main significance of this data is that, except for Ghana and Mali (whose position seems to have improved so markedly later that the statistics must be in doubt), there was little change between 1965 and 1970 − almost the last moment before the economic crisis sparked off by the Organization of Oil-Exporting Countries (OPEC) oil price increase. The great deterioration came later, leaving most countries in a very serious position by 1982 as a result of deteriorating terms of

Table 2.5   *The Public Debt of Selected British Colonies*
at or about the Date of Independence, Showing its Relationship
to Public Revenue and GNP (£m.)

Country	Date[a]	A Public debt[b]	B Public revenue[c]	C GNP	A/B (%)	A/C (%)
Ghana ⎫	1957	22.1	52.0	n/a	42.5	—
Ghana ⎭	1960	82.3	71.6	430[d]	114.9	19.1
Nigeria ⎫	1959	34.1	77.3	n/a	44.0	—
Nigeria ⎭	1960	49.2	88.8	1,199.5	55	4.1
N. Rhodesia[e]	1964	100.6	31.8	216	316.3	46.5
N. Rhodesia	1964	33.1	31.8	216	104.0	15.3
S. Rhodesia	1962	70.9	25.2	307.5	281.3	23.0
Nyasaland	1963	4.2	8.5	7.4	49.4	5.6
Tanganyika	1962	24.5	21.2	344.9	115.5	7.1

Notes:
a. The month of the year at which the accounting year ended varied from one colony to another. The date shown is the year in which the accounting year ended.
b. 'Public debt' includes both domestic and external debts.
c. 'Public revenue' is current revenue and excludes 'Development Funds'.
d. 1961.
e. The Public Debt of Northern Rhodesia in 1964 reflected the very large sums allocated to the colony on the breaking up of the Central African Federation in 1963. The lower figures show the debt of N. Rhodesia without the addition of this Federal debt to make it comparable with the figures for Southern Rhodesia and Nyasaland.

Sources:
Columns A and B are taken from British official statistics in the annual Audit Department reports of the colony concerned. These sometimes differ from the figures in UN and World Bank publications, which may be based on different assumptions.
Column C: World Bank, *World Tables* (Washington DC, 1976).

trade, the effects of declining export volumes, greatly increased borrowing and higher interest rates. For most countries, therefore, the external debt service situation was far better in the early years of independence than at any later time. Only those which had relied mainly on grants rather than borrowing (for example, Chad and Mali) and had very modest development programmes, were better off than at the start of their independent careers.

It is very difficult to generalize usefully about the economic inheritance of Black African states at the end of the colonial period, but the evidence and arguments used here suggest one modest general proposition. At the time of independence none of these places could be regarded as a dynamic economy clearly moving along the traditional

Table 2.6 *Public Debt as a Percentage of Public Revenue and GNP of Selected Colonies and Other Countries at or about the Time of Independence (US$m.)*

Country	Date	A Interest[a]	B Revenue	C GNP	A/B (%)	A/C (%)
Ghana	1960	2.52	196.5	1,203	1.2	0.2
Kenya	1960	6.5	104.7	762.9	6.2	0.8
Malawi	1960	0.75	18.9	177.5	3.9	0.4
Nigeria	1960	5.2	125.6	3,358.6	4.1	0.15
S. Rhodesia	1961	9.8	87.1	847	11.2	1.1
Tanganyika	1961	3.1	65.9	690	4.7	0.4
Togo	1960	0.14	9.7	118.2	1.4	0.1
Zambia	1960	3.08	70.0	526.5	4.4	0.6
Australia	1960	57.1	2,735.0	14,896	2.0	0.4
India	1961	383.4	2,579.4	36,675	14.8	1.0
Peru	1960	18.5	329.2	2,055.0	5.6	9.0

Notes:

The data for Columns A and B are taken from a different source from Column C, so the figures may not be directly comparable. But as the same sources were used for all these countries, the same relationship AC should apply to them all.

a. Interest excludes repayment, sinking funds, etc., and so is not equivalent to debt service, for which adequate information was not available for all these colonies.

Sources:
Columns A and B: UN, *Statistical Yearbook 1965*, table 192.
Column C: World Bank, *World Tables* (Washington DC, 1976).

Western road to affluence. All were predominantly agricultural, with very low levels of productivity. Some had highly developed commercial export crops which provided relatively large per capita incomes (Ghana, Senegal, Ivory Coast) but even there agriculture was technically almost static. Industry contributed a small proportion of GNP and a large part of 'manufacturing' consisted in processing export commodities. Provision of infrastructure was limited by low public revenues, which in turn reflected both low income levels and inadequate systems of taxation. Savings and investment levels looked respectable in relation to the national income but were small absolutely for the same reason, resulting in heavy reliance on external loans and grants for development. Most domestic capital formation was on public account through taxation: very few Africans used their savings for productive investment except in extending agricultural production.

These were hallmarks of limited development and a low-level equilibrium poverty trap. But then were also some signs of dynamism and development potential. The 1950s were a period of expansion,

Table 2.7 *External Public Debt Service Ratio of Selected African Countries, 1965, 1970 and 1982*

Country	A 1965	B 1970	C 1981/2
Benin	3	2.2	n/a
Chad	3.2	3.9	0.4
Congo	6.5	n/a	22.6
Ghana	19.0	5.0	6.8
Ivory Coast	4.5	6.8	36.9
Kenya	5.9	5.4	20.3
Malawi	6.4	7.1	22.8
Mali	8.4	1.2	3.5
Nigeria	3.2	4.2	9.5
Tanzania	4.5	4.9	5.1
Togo	2.2	2.9	n/a
India	15.0	28.0	
Peru	6.8	13.7	

Note:
Payments on external public debt or publicly guaranteed debt as a percentage of the value of the exports of goods and non-factor services.
Sources:
Column A (and Column B for India and Peru): World Bank, *World Tables* (Washington DC, 1976), table 11.
Columns B and C: World Bank, *Toward Sustained Development*, Appendix 13.

with production and investment at unprecedented levels. The metropolitan states were now for the first time making substantial transfers and providing essential technical advice and services. Increasing public investment stimulated many forms of local production, including manufacturing. Above all, perhaps, all these new states had relatively low levels of public and private indebtedness and many had substantial foreign assets. Their capacity to borrow for development was therefore excellent, helped by the unprecedented availability of grants, loans on soft terms, and IMF and commercial credit. If they were still undeveloped, they did not lack the resources for further development: their powder was, so to speak, still dry.

How well they performed would be influenced by many factors: trends in the world economy, the pattern of external relationships which replaced the imperial systems and, perhaps most important, the character and ability of their post-colonial governments. Most of these and other influences will be considered in later chapters; but it is necessary first, under the heading of the colonial inheritance, to consider briefly the colonial background to later systems of government and the special economic relationship between ex-colonies and one-time metropolises which succeeded the imperial economies.

The Nature of the Late-Colonial State

The formal transfer of the symbols of sovereignty to African rulers at independence perhaps came nearer to creating genuinely new political organisms than ever happens in societies with more continuous histories. But in fact both the nature of the post-colonial state and many of the problems it experienced during its first two decades were heavily affected by its colonial inheritance and especially by the changes that took place in the last decade of empire.[32]

The essential feature of the colonial state in Africa was that it was in many respects alien; it did not grow from the soil but was built on the surface of indigenous society, hence the concept of the 'specificity of the colonial state'. This state system, as it was created after effective occupation and completed during the first decade of the twentieth century, was absolutist and bureaucratic. Power descended from the imperial metropolises to be exercised by administrators responsible to them. In degrees and styles which varied from one colony and imperial state to another, all colonial rulers used and relied on indigenous collaborators – chiefs, emirs, tribal elders, etc. – but this cannot be regarded as genuine power-sharing; these were agents, not independent actors. Nor, as a rule, did Europeans in Africa adopt the traditionalist position of inheriting the authority or style of African predecessors, as the British did in India. None, not even Britain with its tradition of gradual concession of 'self-government' to appropriate colonies, seriously started to construct an alternative basis for legitimacy in elective democracy before the later 1940s. Their claim to rule was based on power and justified by the claim to constructive 'trusteeship'.

The exogenous character of the colonial state had one other characteristic that was to be very important after independence. Most sub-Saharan territories had been defined quite arbitrarily as part of European diplomacy, their boundaries often cutting across historic political, economic or ethnic lines. During the colonial period this had little significance. Because it was external, the state could and did maintain a more or less impartial supervision over the disparate elements over which it ruled. In its own interests it stopped traditional warfare and settled territorial and other disputes, often arbitrarily and in ignorance of legitimate rights and claims. It did not expect its subjects to feel any emotional attachment to the territory as a whole, rather emphasizing common loyalty to the metropolis. The effect for Africans was the security and equality of a Hobbesian state. As in the Austro-Hungarian and Ottoman empires before 1914, most African groups, however disparate, could live and move confidently under the umbrella of the colonial power.

The later significance of this is obvious. When the external sovereign power was removed, people who had never had to come to terms with each other because their relationships were defined for them had to face standard questions. What claim had the new 'national state' to the obedience that had once belonged to smaller groups? What right had those groups which had been dominant by reason of colonial favour to retain their position? The character and success of post-decolonization African states depended largely on how successfully these major problems could be resolved.

It is important that very little had been done before the transfer of power to prepare for this transition. The main need was to build domestic political structures which could provide the same stability as the colonial state but without depending on external compulsion. In practice, given that all but Portugal of the imperial powers were democracies, this would mean evolving democratic systems in the colonies through which individuals and groups could associate freely and accept a national sovereign authority based on a common will. In no Black African country had this process had time to mature before independence. The colonial powers began to establish democratic institutions very late, starting with British West Africa in the later 1940s. No colony had a decade of rule by democratically elected Africans before the transfer of power, some had only a couple of years, the Belgian Congo not even that. There was, therefore, no time for the proto-nation state to establish its legitimate claim to universal obedience or for a realistic shakedown of competing groups within a new political framework.

To say this is not to criticize the imperial powers for not providing a longer period of preparation, nor the nationalist leaders for demanding full sovereignty before their colonies had been transformed into self-conscious nations. Under the circumstances of the two decades after 1945, when decolonization in South Asia had set the dominoes falling, it was inevitable that African intellectuals should demand independence at once. Equally, once a colonial power had committed itself in principle to abdicating, it had admitted that it had no right to rule and became a caretaker government. There was, therefore, no possibility of a phased devolution of power of the sort some Colonial Office officials were talking of privately in 1947.[33] The result was that only a very partial metamorphosis of the colonial state and society had taken place before decolonization; the new nation state inherited a tradition of autocracy barely tempered by democracy and a society united only by the now irrelevant call to eject the imperialists.

Yet in the transitional period from *c*.1945 to *c*.1960 the colonial powers did, in fact, add one new dimension to earlier concepts of the state in Africa which was to influence the character of and create problems for successor states. This was the prospect of economic and social improvement with the state as main provider and controller. In the colonial context this may to some extent be seen as a means of buying time and providing a new legitimacy for continuing imperial rule. In the longer perspective, welfare policies added new dimensions to the state Africans were to inherit. The development ideal justified much greater central government power and intervention. It was expressed in planning, higher taxation, tight economic regulation, state monopoly of commodity pricing and purchase, pressures on peasants to improve production methods and a larger bureaucracy. Nationalists took over development as a vital political tool, claiming that they could provide it faster than the imperialists. After independence it was used to legitimize any policy governments chose to adopt.

The political inheritance of colonialism in Black Africa can, therefore, be summed up in over-simplified form as a tradition of bureaucratic autocracy, scarcely yet affected by democracy and bolstered by the development imperative, and social pluralism only transiently overlaid by the nationalist myth. These were political structures in transition which could either move forwards to true democracy or backwards to centralized authoritarianism. The prospects were in fact bleak, despite the immense euphoria of the moment of inheritance. The colonial state, given its inherent limitations, had been efficient, impartial as between groups, relatively cheap and uncorrupt. It was viable so long as Africans did not seriously dispute its legitimacy and claim the right of participation at the highest levels. In its last decade it became increasingly vulnerable because it was incapable of providing the development it promised at sufficient speed. The successor states had only one advantage over their predecessors: they could claim legitimacy based on nationality. For the rest they could not claim the impartiality of an alien administrator. They were encumbered with layers of claimants to power and wealth whom they could not satisfy. They were saddled with promises of rapid economic and social development which were unrealizable. The common result was fundamental political instability usually concealed under monopolistic or oligopolistic authoritarian regimes.

The economic consequences of these political structures are evident throughout the rest of this book; two of the major reasons for limited or even arrested development in Black Africa were the character of governments and their methods of retaining power. To a considerable extent their deficiencies and problems can be seen as consequences of the nature of the colonial state and the way in which it transferred its power to Africans; though that is not to suggest that, given the character of colonialism and the circumstances of the period after 1945, any better solution could have been found.

Post-Colonial Economic Relations between African States and One-Time Metropolises

It has been suggested (though not demonstrated) above that in the last few years of colonial rule the Western imperial powers made it a prime objective in preparing to hand over political power to lay foundations for continued close relationships with their one-time colonies. Their motives for this were mixed. Many who had believed that empire was essential to national greatness and wealth were content to accept decolonization on the assumption that the new states would remain within a looser but still significant collectivity – the British Commonwealth or French Community – or at least maintain close special relationships. There were cultural ambitions, particularly in France, and economic hopes. Colonies had been very important markets and sources of imports. British Africa (excluding South Africa) took 12.87 per cent of total British exports in 1956 and sent 42.5 per cent of its exports to the United Kingdom; French colonies took 28.2 per cent of French exports and provided 20.3 per cent of French imports in 1959.[34] The colonies were important for particular metropolitan industries and interest groups, notably the big trading, mining, banking and investment corporations. In the recent past, colonial foreign currency earnings had provided vital support for metropolitan currencies. Finally, there were less specific but important concerns about world power relationships. Although Black Africa had little or no strategic significance, there was fear that the new states might drift into the communist camp and affect the general world balance, particularly of some strategic resources. For all these and less specific reasons the metropolitan states were clearly anxious to prepare an institutional framework within which African states might retain close links with their former masters.

The results may be outlined very briefly for Britain and France; Belgium maintained no special formal links with Zaire, though she retained a very considerable stake there through her big investment corporations. To consider Britain first, the irony is that, although it already possessed the unique instrument of the Commonwealth to which all African states were admitted if they chose, British links with its ex-colonies rapidly became weak and had little institutional basis. There were intermittent meetings of heads of state; from 1965 a Commonwealth Secretariat in London provided information and organized meetings on specialized topics; there were many residual private networks and much educational exchange. Until the 1970s Commonwealth citizens had free entry to Britain. Britain, moreover, continued to send most of its aid to its own ex-colonies, maintaining the pattern of disbursement established under the CD&W Acts. Thus, in 1964, out of total bilateral aid of £175m., £108m. went to independent Commonwealth countries and £46m. to still-dependent British territories, leaving only £21m. to other countries. Moreover, British direct overseas investment continued to move towards Commonwealth countries more than to the rest of the world: in 1964 British firms invested £160m. in the overseas sterling area as against £102m. in the rest of the world, though the majority of new 'portfolio and other' investment (including oil) was in non-sterling areas (£107m. as against £29m. in the sterling area in 1964).[35]

Yet in two major respects – currency and trade – the Commonwealth did not constitute a formal institutional framework to replace empire. Briefly, although the sterling area continued into the mid-1980s and although many one-time colonies (along with other states) continued to use the pound sterling as their medium of international exchange for a long time (though decreasingly from the 1970s), their link with sterling was in fact weak. Until decolonization all British Black African countries had currencies tied to the pound sterling by the colonial sterling exchange standard system, which in effect meant that their currency was fully convertible into British pounds at par but that they kept 100 per cent cover for their fiduciary issues of notes and coins in London. This was thought during the 1950s to be excessively restrictive, with the result that at or shortly after independence all sterling countries took responsibility for supporting their own currencies, using central banks and varying forms of domestic cover to maintain its value. Initially most tied their exchange values to the pound sterling (typically at two local units for one pound) but in course of time and the decline of sterling this relationship slipped and many countries related their currencies to the US dollar. Ghana, for example, devalued its currency in relation to the pound in 1967. Nigeria revalued its currency to maintain the existing dollar exchange rate when Britain devalued in 1967, as did most other Anglophone African states. In short, since Britain did not provide backing for the currencies of these countries, their monetary relationship was the same as with any other foreign country and the sterling area ceased to be a linking force.

Nor did tariff preference long remain a significant bond. Many of the colonies had never given or received preferential rates, notably Ghana, Nigeria and Tanganyika. Some others could and did give Britain preferences under the 1932 Ottawa agreements; but in practice Britain could give none of these commodity-exporting countries useful preferences at home because there were no import duties on these goods. Under the 1948 GATT agreements imperial preferences were in any case being run down and were quite unimportant by the 1960s. The effect was that after independence there were no special stimuli to intra-Commonwealth trade except residual institutional connections; and the share of Britain in Black African markets and vice versa declined quite rapidly.

The French case was substantially different.[36] Although the Community established by de Gaulle in 1958 was dissolved in 1961, its institutions designed to maximize economic and political relations between the African states and France survived. From the start France signed with each new state (except for renegade Guinea) *accords de coopération* which covered a wide range of subjects and essentially ensured that France would continue to provide most of the services it had provided before independence. The continuity was remarkable. Within France many research and other institutions set up to serve the colonies continued almost unchanged; within the ex-colonies many former colonial officials remained as employees of the new governments and were frequently responsible for the early development plans; it was not until the 1970s that nationalist feeling began seriously to affect this position. In 1972 there were still more than 11,000 French citizens in the Francophone territories under the co-operation agreements, plus some 2,000 teachers in universities and agronomic institutions and many working for private firms and international organizations. More important economically, were the two main institutional links between France and these countries: commercial relations and the monetary system.

French colonies had, of course, been more closely linked with France than most British colonies with Britain: by institutional factors, by preferential tariffs in each direction, by quotas and, on exports of certain tropical commodities to France, by the *surprix* system, which ensured that colonial producers received prices above those on world markets to compensate them for paying inflated prices for French imports. Initially these arrangements survived decolonization; but by then France had joined the EEC and the Treaty of Rome provided for the progressive sharing of French colonial benefits and burdens with other members. This meant that the Francophone states were from the start associate members of EEC, that their markets would gradually be open to all EEC countries on equal terms, that their exports would eventually enter all EEC markets on the same preferential terms, and that Europe as a whole would contribute to the cost of economic and social development. These initial arrangements were eventually extended and modified by the Yaoundé Agreements of 1963 and 1969 and later by the Lomé Conventions of 1975, 1980 and 1985.

The effects were that in the early 1960s, and culminating in 1967, the Francophone territories lost the subsidies on commodity exports to Europe, thereafter having to sell at market prices, but retained absolute freedom of entry there. Europe as a whole gradually replaced France as their largest trading partner. Imports from France declined from 70 per cent in 1959 to 32 per cent in 1978 as other EEC members increased their share, though the proportion of African exports to France declined only from 50 to 40.6 per cent in the same period.[37] In addition the new states received aid from EEC on a scale France alone could not have provided. EEC thus offered the ex-French colonies an indefinite continuation of the protected economic environment once provided by France. They chose to remain there because it gave advantages they could not obtain elsewhere and in due course they were joined as associate members by virtually every other independent state in Black Africa. This, of course, encouraged the continuation of long-established patterns of production and exchange, a point of criticism by those who disapprove of such patterns.

Perhaps equally significant was continuing African membership of the franc zone, which was more rigorous in its effects than membership of the sterling area for Anglophone states. All the French colonies (except for Guinea and Mali between 1962 and 1967) continued to use the CFA franc which was originally twice the value of the old French franc and retained its relationship at 50 CFA francs = 1 franc when the metropolitan franc was called down by 100. Independence made almost no difference. The Bank of West Africa became the Central Bank of West African States; the Bank of Equatorial Africa became the Central Bank for the States of Equatorial Africa and Cameroon and the metropolitan Caisse de la France d'Outre-Mer became the Comité Monétaire de la Zone Franc. These central African banks, preserving one essential feature of the dead federations, continued to keep their foreign currency reserves in French francs in deposit accounts at the French Treasury. The Bank of France guaranteed their currencies without requiring fixed cover, though they had to remain in credit, and provided unlimited foreign exchange in return for francs. To ensure that sound monetary policies were maintained, the French government had a number of representatives on the boards of the African central banks.

The system provided these small and often financially unstable states with a currency as stable and fully convertible as that of France, which was a major advantage in attracting foreign investment and in commercial relations. Assuming that the French franc was correctly priced in relation to other currencies, this ensured that Francophone African exchange rates were realistic and removed the temptation to overvalue their currencies, as was done in a number of other African countries, with serious distortion of productive and trading patterns. As against this the system denied these states the possibility of using exchange rates and money supply as tools of economic management and implied a degree of dependence on a foreign state which would have been obnoxious to nationalist feeling in most other states of post-colonial Africa.

To assess the colonial inheritance of Black Africa as a factor influencing its later economic development is clearly very difficult. The danger is that, by emphasizing pre-independence structures and the element of continuity (as has been done in this chapter), one may imply that what happened after independence was predestined, that it was all a consequence of the colonial past and the continuing influence of neo-colonial relationships. Thus, if post-colonial Black African states experienced economic stagnation or disaster in the following two decades, these could be attributed directly to their damned inheritance.

This, of course, would be an entirely false conclusion because it underestimates the vital force of national sovereignty. The new regimes of the early 1960s and beyond were in many ways constrained by what they inherited; yet they had also very considerable freedom of future action in rapidly changing conditions. If they were all relatively poor, all had experienced considerable development in the 1950s and could reasonably expect to sustain at least the same rate of growth. If they inherited patterns of production that were excessively skewed towards commodity exports, they had the ability gradually to modify them, as many, for better or worse, were to do in the next two decades. If institutional factors linked them with their former metropolitan states, these links could be broken, as they were by Guinea, or adjusted. International developments facilitated reorientation. EEC offered a wider European partnership. Development funds were available from multilateral agencies. The UNO provided a political forum. They could play the Western powers against Soviet Russia and China for political and economic support. The world, that is, was not standing still and the colonial inheritance was not immutable.

Certainly the mood of the 1950s and early 1960s was not pessimistic; if anything it was over-optimistic about the possibilities offered by the post-colonial future, as will be suggested in Chapter 3 below. We can now see that much of that optimism was misplaced, but that should not lead to an equally misplaced determinism. The evidence surveyed in this chapter suggested a more moderate summary of what the new states inherited from their past. They were in most cases poorly endowed in human skills, in modern technology, in infrastructure and in some aspects of natural endowment. Their politicians and indigenous civil servants had little experience in running a modern state. They lacked ethnic or historical unity. They were accustomed to close dependence on foreigners for many services. On the other hand, almost all had been on an upward curve for at least a dozen years. Most had vast unused resources of land and labour. They had well-established commodity production. Many began with substantial foreign assets, low public debts and considerable capacity to borrow for development from a developed Western world then anxious to provide whatever resources these countries needed. At the start the new governments could draw on huge and unrenewable reserves of proto-nationalist support for whatever they chose to do.

All this points to the cautious conclusion that, while there was little ground for the wilder hopes that these intrinsically poor and underdeveloped countries could reach levels of affluence comparable with those in the West within any foreseeable period, equally there was little reason to fear that they would remain as poor as they then were, still less that some would slide into endemic economic crisis and become pauperized dependants on external philanthropy. It is a main aim of this book to discover why, by the early 1980s, most of the promise of the moment of decolonization had evaporated, leaving most Black African states in a condition that can only be called checked development or worse.

Notes

1 See, for example, A. G. Hopkins, *An Economic History of West Africa* (London, 1973); J. Iliffe, *The Emergence of African Capitalism* (London, 1983).
2 J. Lonsdale, 'States and Social Processes in Africa: an Historiographical Survey'; F. Cooper, 'Africa and the World Economy'; both in *The African Studies Review*, Vol. 24, nos 2/3 (1981). The following argument is based mainly on these two very perceptive articles, which were originally commissioned for the twenty-fourth meeting of the African Studies Association in Bloomington, Indiana, in October 1981.
3 Central Statistical Office, *Statistical Abstract for the British Commonwealth*, 71, 81; OEEC, *Foreign Trade Statistical Bulletin*, Series 1 (Paris, 1954).
4 D. Morawetz, *Twenty-Five Years of Economic Development, 1950–1975* (Washington DC, 1977), Statistical Appendix table A1, p. 77.
5 M. Crowder (ed.), *The Cambridge History of Africa*, Vol. 8 (Cambridge, 1984), p. 212.
6 ibid., p. 216.
7 World Bank, *Accelerated Development in Sub-Saharan Africa* (Washington DC, 1981), Appendix table 3 (hereafter *AD* App. 3).
8 *Cambridge History of Africa*, Vol. 8, p. 219.
9 *AD* App. 27.
10 *AD* App. 34, 37, 38.
11 Morawetz, *Twenty-Five Years*, tables A.1, A.8.
12 *AD* App. 38.
13 *Cambridge History of Africa*, Vol. 8, p. 446.
14 *AD* App. 6.
15 P. Duignan and L. H. Gann (eds), *Colonialism in Africa*, Vol. 4, *The Economics of Colonialism* (Cambridge, 1975), p. 407.
16 ibid., pp. 146, 446, 455.
17 *AD* App. 27, 29.
18 S. Amin, *Neo-Colonialism in West Africa* (New York and London, 1973), *passim*, especially ch. 1.
19 G. Hyden, *Beyond Ujamaa in Tanzania* (London, 1980), *passim*.
20 S. H. Frankel, *Capital Investment in Africa* (London, 1938), p. 170.

21 These rough estimates are based on my essay, 'The Economic Exploitation of Africa', in P. Gifford and W. R. Louis (eds), *France and Britain in Africa* (New Haven, 1971), pp. 627–31. Population figures are taken from UN, *Survey of Economic Conditions in Africa, 1973* (New York, 1974), p. 203. For the French empire as a whole, J. Marseille, *Empire colonial et capitalisme français. Histoire d'un divorce* (Paris, 1984), p. 105, suggests that, in constant 1914 francs, total French investment from 1940–1958 at 11.9b. francs was nearly as much as total pre-1914 investment at 13.7b. francs. His proportion of postwar private/public investment is about 20 per cent, whereas my calculations suggested about 11 per cent; but his figures include North Africa.

22 Fieldhouse, 'The Economic Exploitation', p. 632; *Board of Trade Journal*, vol. 187 (1964), p. 293, vol. 189 (1965), p. 230.

23 Based on UN *Survey of Economic Conditions in Africa, 1973*, p. 203; World Bank, *World Tables 1976*.

24 UN *A Survey of Economic Conditions in Africa, 1960–1964* (New York, 1968), p. 20.

25 Probably the most balanced short overview of the subject is Peter Kilby's 'Manufacturing in Colonial Africa', in Duignan and Gann (eds), *Colonialism in Africa*, Vol. 4, ch. 12, on which the argument of this section leans heavily.

26 J.-P. Peemans, 'Capital Accumulation in the Congo under Colonialism: the Role of the State', in Duignan and Gann (eds), Vol. 4, pp. 181, 197.

27 Calculated from ibid., table 37, pp. 186 and 193.

28 ibid., pp. 194, 195, 197.

29 Kilby, pp. 480, 481.

30 World Bank, *The Economic Development of Kenya* (Baltimore, 1963), p. 152.

31 ibid., p. 219.

32 My ideas on this issue have been sharpened by a draft paper, 'The Colonial State and its Connection to Current Political Crises in Africa' given by Professor Crawford Young to the conference on 'African Independence', University of Zimbabwe, Harare, January 1985, which will be published in revised form as part of the proceedings of the conference by the Yale University Press.

33 There is, of course, a large literature on Colonial Office plans around 1947. See, in particular, R. D. Pearce, *The Turning Point in Africa* (London, 1982); R. E. Robinson, 'Andrew Cohen and the Transfer of Power in Tropical Africa', in W. H. Morris-Jones and G. Fischer (eds), *Decolonization and After: the British and French Experience* (London, 1978); J. W. Cell, 'On the Eve of Decolonization', *Journal of Imperial and Commonwealth History*, vol. 7 (1980); D. K. Fieldhouse, 'The Labour Governments and the Empire–Commonwealth, 1945–51', in R. Ovendale (ed.), *The Foreign Policy of the British Labour Governments, 1945–1951* (Leicester, 1984).

34 *Statistical Abstract for the British Commonwealth*, 81; *Annuaire statistique de la France* (Paris, 1966).

35 Central Statistical Office, *United Kingdom Balance of Payments, 1965* (London, 1965), p. 14.

36 The section on French policy leans on a draft paper by Professor Catherine Coquery-Vidrovitch, 'Economic Decolonization in French Africa', given at

the conference on 'African Independence', University of Zimbabwe, Harare, January 1985.
37 ibid., table p. 24.

PART TWO

Economic Performance and Explanations, 1960–1980

3

Performance, Expectations and the 'Policy' Approach

Historians must always be aware of the dangers of a *post hoc ergo propter hoc* argument. To describe the dominant patterns of economic development in Black Africa from about 1960 in terms of 'the economic consequences of decolonization' is not to suggest that what happened was necessarily the direct consequence of the transfer of political power. There were both continuities and decontinuities and it is in most cases impossible to draw a hard line between them. On the one hand, successor states and development economists may point to dramatic increases in national incomes or to rapid industrialization, and claim that these were only possible because of the beneficent forces liberated by decolonization. On the other hand, critics of Third World regimes may suggest that in fact the best years for Africa were just before independence, perhaps in the booming 1950s, and that the almost universal economic disasters of the 1970s and 1980s demonstrate the unwisdom of adopting the types of economic management common in most post-colonial African states. There is no way of adjudicating between these standpoints. The basic question is rather whether it is possible to pinpoint specific factors which were characteristic of the economic development of these states after they became independent and which may, at least partially, explain their fluctuating fortunes since about 1960.

Surveying the literature, two distinct general approaches can be seen. First there is what can broadly be described as a 'policy' interpretation: whether things went well or badly, they must be seen as primarily the outcome of policies adopted by the successor states of Africa. Success may be attributed to their greater devotion to economic development and the wisdom of the means they employed, failure to their incompetence or misguided strategies. Secondly, there is what can equally loosely be described as a 'non-policy' approach, which reduces or even eliminates the responsibility of African governments, particularly for disasters. One strand of this approach has already been described in Chapter 2, where it was suggested that the colonial inheritance circumscribed but did not dictate the options open to the new states. Other explanations include the influence of the international environment (terms of trade, changing interest rates, etc.) and adverse endogenous factors, such as geology, climate and African attitudes to development. All such explanations of what happened after independence have their supporters; all, in some degree, are clearly relevant. It is the aim of this chapter and Chapter 4 to survey the range of such arguments. Evidence for a number of African countries will then be presented in Part Three of the book and an attempt will be made to assess their relative significance in the concluding chapter.

There is, however, an underlying assumption which must be made explicit. This is that economic performance is most likely to be influenced by one or both of two major factors. The first is strictly economic and will largely be determined in any one country by the interaction of domestic and international movements in supply and demand, reflected in prices, terms of trade and ultimately an increase or decrease in real incomes. The second is broadly political – the actions of governments which attempt to regulate domestic economic activity in pursuit of whatever objectives they may adopt. In terms of decolonization, the economic effects of the transfer of power are potentially minimal; the act of pulling down the imperial flag changes neither the facts of the domestic economy nor its relations with the international economy. If the successor regime made no changes in its approach to production, exchange, taxation or investment, the economic development of the ex-colony would barely be affected. Conversely, an interventionist government can radically affect the character of the domestic economy, even if it cannot significantly control the impact on it of external forces.

It is precisely because most post-colonial governments have attempted, or at least claimed to attempt, to develop the domestic economy in ways different from those of the imperialists that one can usefully consider the economic implications of decolonization. Putting it bluntly, have these political interventions made much difference? If there has been growth (taken here to imply an increase in the real national income) and development (the restructuring of the economy to increase the rate of growth and to enable it to be sustained indefinitely), was this because governments were active and successful? Or was it because, in the decades after the mid-1950s, international conditions became generally very favourable to these African economies? Conversely, if growth and development were less than one might reasonably have expected, or if they lost momentum at some point, given international comparisons, was this because governments adopted ill-advised (even if well-intentioned) policies, or because expectations had been pitched too high, or because there were factors beyond governmental control obstructing further progress? These are the fundamental problems to be considered, even if the available evidence is too limited and the statistics too unreliable to provide final answers.

General Trends in Black Africa, 1960–1980: an Overview

Of one thing at least there can be no doubt: as the summary Tables 3.1–3.6, for the whole of Black Africa, make clear, the quarter century after 1950 was a period of growth in Africa which may (though, since no comparable statistics are available for earlier periods, this is largely speculative) have no precedent. In those years the overall per capita growth rate for the whole continent averaged 2.4 per cent compared with 1.7 per cent for South Asia and 2.6 per cent for Latin America. So impressive a performance cannot, however, be attributed simply to the transfer of power. For many countries there are no GNP or GDP figures before 1960; but in those for which these are available, the 1950s with a per capita growth rate of 2.4 per cent were marginally better than the 1960s, at 2.2 per cent and nearly as good as the period 1970–5 at 2.8 per cent. Moreover, in some countries the 1960s were markedly less satisfactory than the 1950s: in Ghana the growth rate on a per capita basis slowed from 1.9 to 0.7 per cent; in Senegal from 4.4 to 1.6 per cent; and in Zambia from 2.7 to 0.5 per cent.[1]

These were, nevertheless, excellent years for most parts of Africa. The latter 1970s and early 1980s saw a serious slowing down of the rate of growth. According to the World Bank, the rate of growth of GDP for the whole of sub-Saharan Africa slowed from 3.9 per cent in the 1960s to 2.9 per cent in the 1970s (excluding Nigeria from 4.1 to 1.6 per cent); while per capita income growth overall slowed from 1.3 to 0.8 per cent. If Nigeria is excluded, the low- and middle-income countries actually had a negative per capita growth rate in the 1970s.[2] Thus the basic question with which all students of recent African history must be concerned is why the apparent promise of these earlier decades appears to have evaporated.

Within this generalized picture, however, there are marked contrasts between different sectors of African economies. In most countries industry grew fast, with a growth rate of 3.3 per cent in the 1970s, rising from 16 to 31 per cent of GDP in sub-Saharan Africa between 1960 and 1979.[3] General infrastructure and welfare indicators also suggest a quite impressive performance. For example, energy consumption per capita rose from 76 to 128 kgs coal equivalent; life expectancy rose from an average of 39 at birth in 1960 to 47 in 1979; and between 1960 and 1978 the proportion of the appropriate

Table 3.1 Black Africa, 1960-1982: Basic Indicators

	Population (millions) mid-1982	Area (thousands of square kilometres)	GNP per capita Dollars 1982	GNP per capita Average annual growth rate (per cent) 1960-82[a]	Average annual rate of inflation (per cent) 1960-70	Average annual rate of inflation (per cent) 1970-82[b]	Life expectancy at birth (years) 1982	Index of food production per capita (1969-71=100) average for 1980-82
Low-income economies	**213.5 t**	**12,992 t**	**249 w**	**0.7 w**	**2.6 m**	**10.8 m**	**49 w**	**86 w**
Low-income semiarid	**29.3 t**	**4,714 t**	**218 w**	**-0.1 w**	**3.4 m**	**9.8 m**	**44 w**	**85 w**
1 Chad	4.6	1,284	80	-2.8	4.6	7.8	44	95
2 Mali	7.1	1,240	180	1.6	5.0	9.8	45	83
3 Burkina Faso	6.5	274	210	1.1	1.3	9.7	44	95
4 Somalia	4.5	638	290	-0.1	4.5	12.6	39	60
5 Niger	5.9	1,267	310	-1.5	2.1	12.1	45	88
6 Gambia, The	0.7	11	360	2.5	2.2	9.7	36	74
Low-income other	**184.2 t**	**8,278 t**	**254 w**	**0.9 w**	**2.6 m**	**11.7 m**	**49 w**	**86 w**
7 Ethiopia	32.9	1,222	140	1.4	2.1	4.0	47	82
8 Guinea-Bissau	0.8	36	170	-1.7	.	7.1	38	88
9 Zaire	30.7	2,345	190	-0.3	29.9	35.3	50	87
10 Malawi	6.5	118	210	2.6	2.4	9.5	44	99
11 Uganda	13.5	236	230	-1.1	3.2	47.4	47	86
12 Rwanda	5.5	26	260	1.7	13.1	13.4	46	105
13 Burundi	4.3	28	280	2.5	2.8	12.5	47	96
14 Tanzania	19.8	945	280	1.9	1.8	11.9	52	88
15 Benin	3.7	113	310	0.6	1.9	9.6	48	100
16 Central African Rep.	2.4	623	310	0.6	4.1	12.6	48	104
17 Guinea	5.7	246	310	1.5	1.5	3.3	38	89
18 Madagascar	9.2	587	320	-0.5	3.2	11.5	48	94
19 Togo	2.8	57	340	2.3	1.3	8.8	47	89
20 Ghana	12.2	239	360	-1.3	7.5	39.5	55	72
21 Kenya	18.1	583	390	2.8	1.6	10.1	57	88

22 Sierra Leone	3.2	72	390	*0.9*	..	12.2	38	81
23 *Mozambique*	12.9	802	..	..	..	..	51	68
Middle-income oil importers	**56.1** t	**5,959** t	**634** w	**0.9** w	**2.4** m	**11.4** m	**49** w	**91** w
24 Sudan	20.2	2,506	440	−0.4	3.9	15.2	47	87
25 Mauritania	1.6	1,031	470	1.4	2.1	8.7	45	73
26 Liberia	2.0	111	490	0.9	1.9	8.5	54	88
27 Senegal	6.0	196	490	(.)	1.8	7.9	44	93
28 Lesotho	1.4	30	510	6.5	2.7	11.4	53	84
29 Zambia	6.0	753	640	−0.1	7.6	8.7	51	87
30 Zimbabwe	7.5	391	850	1.5	1.1	8.4	56	87
31 Botswana	0.9	600	900	6.8	2.4	11.5	60	73
32 Swaziland	0.7	17	940	4.2	2.4	12.8	54	107
33 Ivory Coast	8.9	322	950	2.1	2.8	12.4	47	107
34 Mauritius	0.9	2	1,240	2.1	2.2	15.0	66	110
Middle-income oil exporters	**110.3** t	**3,256** t	**889** w	**3.2** w	**4.5** m	**12.6** m	**50** w	**92** w
35 Nigeria	90.6	924	860	3.3	4.0	14.4	50	92
36 Cameroon	9.3	475	890	2.6	4.2	10.7	53	102
37 Congo, People's Rep.	1.7	342	1,180	2.7	4.7	10.8	60	81
38 Gabon	0.7	268	4,000	4.4	5.4	19.5	49	93
39 *Angola*	8.0	1,247	..	..	..	..	43	77
Sub-Saharan Africa	**380.0** t	**22,207** t	**491** w	**1.5** w	**2.7** m	**11.4** m	**49** w	**88** w
All low-income countries	**2,266.5** t	**29,097** t	**280** t	**3.0** w	**3.2** m	**11.5** m	**59** w	**110** w
All lower middle-income countries	**669.6** t	**20,952** t	**840** w	**3.2** w	**2.9** m	**11.7** m	**56** w	**108** w
All upper middle-income countries	**488.7** t	**22,079** t	**2,490** w	**4.1** w	**3.0** m	**16.4** m	**65** w	**115** w
Industrial market economies	**722.9** t	**30,935** t	**11,070** w	**3.3** w	**4.3** m	**9.9** m	**75** w	**114** w

Notes:

t = total; w = weighted average; m = median.

a. Because data for the early 1960s are not always available, figures in italics are for periods other than that specified.

b. Figures in italics are for 1970–81, not 1970–82.

Source: World Bank, *Toward Sustained Development in Sub-Saharan Africa* (Washington DC, 1984), Appendix Table 1.

Table 3.2 Black Africa, 1960–1982: Growth of Production

	GDP		Agriculture		Industry		Manufacturing[a]		Services	
	1960–70[b]	*1970–82[c]*	*1960–70[b]*	*1970–82[c]*	*1960–70[b]*	*1970–82[c]*	*1960–70[b]*	*1970–82[c]*	*1960–70[b]*	*1970–82[c]*
Low-income economies	4.0 w	1.8 w	..	1.6 m	..	2.3 m	..	0.5 m	..	4.3 m
Low-income semiarid	2.4 w	2.6 w	..	1.4 m	..	2.9 m	..	0.1 m	..	5.4 m
1 Chad	0.5	−2.6	..	−1.0	..	−2.0	..	−3.2	..	−5.5
2 Mali	3.3	4.3	..	3.8	..	2.1	..	..	..	5.4
1 Burkina Faso	3.0	3.4	..	1.4	..	2.9	..	3.4	..	5.4
4 Somalia	1.0	3.8	3.4	−2.4	4.0	..	4.0	..	4.2	..
5 Niger	2.9	3.4	13.9	3.2	..	10.8	..	..	(.)	6.9
6 Gambia, The	6.2	4.5	6.1	..	..	7.4	..	..	6.2	4.6
Low-income other	4.2 w	1.7 w	..	1.7 m	..	2.0 m	..	0.5 m	..	4.0 m
7 Ethiopia	4.4	2.2	..	0.9	7.4	2.0	8.0	2.9	7.8	4.1
8 Guinea-Bissau	..	3.1	..	0.5	..	2.4	..	..	..	8.4
9 Zaire	3.4	−0.2	..	1.5	..	−0.9	..	−2.3	..	−0.4
10 Malawi	4.9	5.1	..	4.1	..	5.4	..	5.4	..	6.0
11 Uganda	5.6	−1.5	..	−0.6	..	−8.7	..	−8.9	..	1.3
12 Rwanda	2.7	5.3	..	..	..	..	..	..	..	..
13 Burundi	4.4	3.5	..	2.3	..	8.6	..	6.4	..	4.0
14 Tanzania	6.0	4.0	..	2.8	..	1.5	..	0.5	..	5.8
15 Benin	2.6	3.3	..	..	..	..	..	..	..	..
16 Central African Rep.	1.9	1.4	5.4	2.3	5.4	4.0	..	−4.3	1.8	0.3
17 Guinea	3.5	3.8	..	..	..	..	..	..	..	..
18 Madagascar	2.9	0.2	..	0.3	..	−0.7	..	..	..	0.4
19 Togo	8.8	3.0	..	1.7	..	5.5	..	−10.0	..	2.9
20 Ghana	2.2	−0.5	..	−0.2	..	−2.4	..	−1.5	..	−7.5
21 Kenya	5.9	5.5	..	4.1	..	8.1	..	9.0	..	5.6

Average annual growth rate (per cent)

22 Sierra Leone	4.3	2.0	..	2.5	..	-3.1	..	3.9	..	4.5
23 *Mozambique*	..	..	..	..	..	..	..	..	..	..
Middle-income oil importers	4.2 w	3.7 w	..	3.4 m	..	5.8 m	..	4.8 m	..	5.2 m
24 Sudan	0.7	6.3	..	4.1	..	5.8	..	6.0	..	8.5
25 Mauritania	6.7	2.0	1.4	3.4	14.1	-3.5	9.2	5.2	7.4	5.2
26 Liberia	5.1	0.9	..	3.5	..	-0.7	..	4.5	..	1.0
27 Senegal	2.5	2.9	2.9	2.3	4.1	3.8	6.2	0.8	1.8	2.8
28 *Lesotho*	5.2	6.6	..	*0.3*	..	*21.1*	..	*13.4*	..	*5.5*
29 Zambia	5.0	0.9	..	1.9	..	0.4	..	1.4	..	1.3
30 Zimbabwe	4.5	2.2	..	1.8	..	-1.9	..	-4.1	..	2.9
31 Botswana	5.7	*12.6*	1.6	3.7	12.6	*16.0*	..	..	7.6	*15.2*
32 Swaziland	7.7	4.4	6.3	11.4	10.8	15.7	..	..	5.9	-0.5
33 Ivory Coast	8.0	5.7	4.2	4.5	11.5	8.6	11.6	5.4	9.7	5.4
34 Mauritius	1.7	5.8	..	-2.6	..	8.1	..	..	..	9.7
Middle-income oil exporters	3.5 w	4.1 w	..	1.9 m	..	12.0 m	..	8.4 m	..	6.7 m
35 Nigeria	3.1	3.8	-0.4	-0.6	14.7	4.8	9.1	12.0	2.3	6.7
36 Cameroon	3.7	7.0	..	3.4	..	12.2	..	8.4	..	7.2
37 Congo, People's Rep.	3.5	6.8	1.8	1.9	7.4	12.0	..	3.3	2.8	5.1
38 Gabon	4.4	2.0	..	..	..	..	..	..	..	..
39 *Angola*	..	..	..	..	..	..	..	..	..	..
Sub-Saharan Africa	**3.8 w**	**3.0 w**	..	**2.1 m**	..	**3.9 m**	..	**3.4 m**	..	**4.9 m**
All low-income countries	**4.5 w**	**4.5 w**	**2.2 m**	**2.3 m**	**6.6 m**	**4.2 m**	**5.5 m**	**3.4 m**	**4.2 m**	**4.5 m**
All lower middle-income countries	**4.9 w**	**5.3 w**	**3.0 m**	**3.1 m**	**6.2 m**	**5.8 m**	**6.5 m**	**5.5 m**	**5.2 m**	**5.4 m**
All upper middle-income countries	**6.4 w**	**5.4 w**	**4.0 m**	**2.6 m**	**9.1 m**	**5.7 m**	**8.4 m**	**5.8 m**	**7.2 m**	**6.3 m**
Industrial market economies	**5.1 w**	**2.8 w**	**1.4 m**	**1.8 m**	**5.9 m**	**2.3 m**	**5.9 m**	**2.4 m**	**4.5 m**	**3.2 m**

Notes:

a. Manufacturing is part of the industrial sector, but its share of GDP is shown separately because it typically is the most dynamic part of the industrial sector.

b. Figures in italics are for 1961–70, not 1960–70.

c. Figures in italics are for 1970–81, not 1970–82.

Source: World Bank, *Toward Sustained Development,* App. 2.

Table 3.3 Black Africa, 1960–1982: Structure of Production

	GDP (US$ millions)		Agriculture		Industry		Manufacturing[a]		Services	
	1960	1982[b]	1960	1982[b]	1960	1982[b]	1960	1982[b]	1960	1982[b]
Low-income economies			51 w	50 w	12 w	13 w	6 w	6 w	37 w	37 w
Low-income semiarid			60 w	39 w	11 w	19 w	5 w	8 w	29 w	42 w
1 Chad	180	*400*	52	*64*	11	*7*	4	*4*	37	*29*
2 Mali	270	*1,030*	55	*43*	10	*10*	5	*5*	35	*47*
3 Burkina Faso	200	*1,000*	55	*41*	16	*16*	9	*12*	31	*43*
4 Somalia	160		71	*..*	8	*..*	3	*..*	21	*..*
5 Niger	250	*1,560*	69	*31*	9	*30*	4	*8*	22	*39*
6 Gambia, The	27	*213*	39	*26*	11	*..*	..	*..*	50	*..*
Low-income other			49 w	50 w	12 w	12 w	6 w	6 w	39 w.	38 w
7 Ethiopia	900	4,010	65	49	12	16	6	11	23	36
8 Guinea-Bissau	..	*132*	..	*..*	..	*..*	..	*..*	..	*..*
9 Zaire	130	*5,380*	30	*32*	27	*24*	13	*3*	43	*44*
10 Malawi	160	1,320	50	..	10	..	5	..	40	..
11 Uganda	540	8,630	52	82	12	4	9	4	36	14
12 Rwanda	120	*1,260*	80	*46*	6	*22*	1	*16*	14	*32*
13 Burundi	190	1,110	..	56	11	17	..	10	..	27
14 Tanzania	550	4,530	57	52	11	15	5	9	32	33
15 Benin	160	830	55	44	8	13	3	7	37	43
16 Central African Rep.	110	660	51	35	11	19	3	8	38	46
17 Guinea	400	1,750	..	41	..	23	..	2	..	36
18 Madagascar	540	*2,900*	37	*41*	10	*15*	4	*..*	53	*44*
19 Togo	120	800	55	23	15	29	8	6	30	48
20 Ghana	1,220	31,220	41	51	10	8	..	5	49	41
21 Kenya	730	5,340	38	33	18	22	9	13	44	45

22 Sierra Leone	..	1,130	..	32	..	20	..	5	..	48
23 *Mozambique*	..	..	..	..	..	..	..	..	..	..
Middle-income oil importers			**24 w**	**25 w**	**32 w**	**25 w**	**10 w**	**14 w**	**44 w**	**50 w**
24 Sudan	1,160	9,290	..	36	..	14	..	7	..	50
25 Mauritania	90	640	44	29	21	25	3	8	35	46
26 Liberia	220	950	..	36	..	28	..	7	..	36
27 Senegal	610	2,510	24	22	17	25	12	15	59	53
28 Lesotho	30	300	..	23	..	22	..	6	..	55
29 Zambia	680	3,830	11	14	63	36	4	19	26	50
30 Zimbabwe	780	5,900	18	15	35	35	17	25	47	50
31 Botswana	35	*949*	54	..	11	..	..	..	35	..
32 Swaziland	34	*522*	32	..	24	..	..	..	44	..
33 Ivory Coast	570	7,560	43	26	14	23	7	12	43	51
34 Mauritius	134	929	15	15	24	25	..	..	61	60
Middle-income oil exporters			**60 w**	**21 w**	**12 w**	**40 w**	**5 w**	**6 w**	**28 w**	**39 w**
35 Nigeria	3,150	71,720	63	62	11	39	5	6	26	39
36 Cameroon	550	7,370	..	27	..	31	..	11	..	42
37 Congo, People's Rep.	130	2,170	23	6	17	52	10	5	60	42
Gabon	140	3,254	32	7	34	62	..	..	34	31
39 *Angola*	..	..	..	..	..	..	..	..	..	..
Sub-Saharan Africa			**47 w**	**33 w**	**17 w**	**27 w**	**7 w**	**8 w**	**36 w**	**40 w**
All low-income countries			**49 w**	**37 w**	**26 w**	**32 w**	**13 w**	**14 w**	**25 w**	**31 w**
All lower middle-income countries			**37 w**	**23 w**	**22 w**	**35 w**	**15 w**	**17 w**	**41 w**	**42 w**
All upper middle-income countries			**18 w**	**11 w**	**33 w**	**41 w**	**25 w**	**22 w**	**49 w**	**48 w**
Industrial market economies			**6 w**	**3 w**	**40 w**	**36 w**	**30 w**	**24 w**	**54 w**	**61 w**

Notes:

a. Manufacturing is part of the industrial sector, but its share of GDP is shown separately because it typically is the most dynamic part of the industrial sector.

b. Figures in italics are for 1981, not 1982.

Source: World Bank, *Toward Sustained Development*, App. 3.

Table 3.4 Black Africa, 1960-1982: Growth of Consumption and Investment

| | Average annual growth rate (per cent) | | | | | |
| | Public consumption | | Private consumption | | Gross domestic investment | |
	1960-70	1970-82[a]	1960-70	1970-82[a]	1960-70[b]	1970-82[a]
Low-income economies	**4.8 m**	**5.0 m**	**3.6 m**	**3.0 m**	**5.2 m**	**2.6 m**
Low-income semiarid	**4.4 m**	**6.5 m**	**2.8 m**	**2.8 m**	**4.3 m**	**3.2 m**
1 Chad	4.4	-3.8	-0.7	-1.8	2.3	-5.4
2 Mali	6.2	6.5	2.8	4.4	4.9	3.1
3 Burkina Faso	..	8.7	..	2.8	..	3.2
4 Somalia	3.7	..	0.4	..	4.3	..
5 Niger	2.0	2.4	3.9	3.4	3.0	6.6
6 Gambia, The	4.9	7.5	5.5	2.5	6.2	26.9
Low-income other	**6.7 m**	**4.2 m**	**3.7 m**	**3.1 m**	**5.7 m**	**2.0 m**
7 Ethiopia	8.1	7.7	4.3	2.7	5.7	0.7
8 Guinea-Bissau	..	1.4	..	-1.5	..	-2.1
9 Zaire	8.5	1.0	3.5	-3.3	9.6	5.7
10 Malawi	4.6	8.0	3.7	4.1	15.4	2.0
11 Uganda	—[c]	—[c]	5.6	-4.0	7.5	-8.0
12 Rwanda	1.1	11.8	4.3	3.2	3.5	14.9
13 Burundi	19.2	4.2	3.2	3.3	4.3	15.0
14 Tanzania	—[c]	—[c]	6.6	4.4	9.8	3.4
15 Benin	1.7	2.6	4.9	3.1	4.2	12.2
16 Central African Rep.	2.2	-2.9	3.0	2.7	1.3	-7.5
17 Guinea	..	..	..	..	..	..
18 Madagascar	3.0	2.0	1.9	-0.5	5.4	-1.4
19 Togo	6.7	9.4	7.6	4.0	11.1	6.3
20 Ghana	7.2	5.7	1.7	-0.4	-3.1	-5.1
21 Kenya	10.0	8.4	2.9	5.9	10.3	2.1

22 Sierra Leone	..	-2.2	..	3.5	..	-1.1
23 *Mozambique*	..	..	..	..	..	..
Middle-income oil importers	**6.5 m**	**8.1 m**	**4.9 m**	**5.3 m**	**4.7 m**	**6.6 m**
24 Sudan	12.1	2.3	-2.5	7.8	3.2	9.0
25 Mauritania	(.)	8.1	2.6	3.1	-2.0	6.6
26 Liberia	5.6	2.5	0.7	3.1	-3.9	2.1
27 Senegal	-0.2	6.4	3.3	3.3	1.1	1.8
28 Lesotho	(.)	*15.5*	6.5	*8.0*	20.7	*19.6*
29 Zambia	11.0	1.0	6.8	3.0	10.6	-10.5
30 Zimbabwe	..	9.9	..	2.9	..	2.5
31 Botswana	10.8	*14.2*	6.9	*10.3*	25.3	7.4
32 Swaziland[d]	7.4	5.6	14.9	5.6	6.1	10.8
33 Ivory Coast	11.8	9.8	8.0	5.3	12.7	10.1
34 Mauritius	2.1	8.1	2.4	7.5	-6.7	5.7
Middle-income oil exporters	**7.3 m**	**6.6 m**	**2.3 m**	**5.9 m**	**4.3 m**	**9.1 m**
35 Nigeria	10.0	11.7	0.6	5.6	7.4	8.8
36 Cameroon	6.1	4.7	2.7	6.1	9.3	9.4
37 Congo, People's Rep.	5.4	6.3	1.9	0.3	1.1	12.2
38 Gabon	8.5	6.9	8.8	7.3	-2.1	8.0
39 *Angola*	..	..	..	..	..	..
Sub-Saharan Africa	**5.9 m**	**6.4 m**	**3.4 m**	**3.3 m**	**5.2 m**	**5.7 m**
All low-income countries	**4.5 m**	**5.0 m**	**3.2 m**	**3.3 m**	**4.9 m**	**3.3 m**
All lower middle-income countries	**5.9 m**	**6.4 m**	**4.8 m**	**4.8 m**	**7.6 m**	**6.6 m**
All upper middle-income countries	**7.0 m**	**6.3 m**	**5.5 m**	**6.1 m**	**7.6 m**	**7.3 m**
Industrial market economies	**4.2 m**	**3.2 m**	**4.3 m**	**2.7 m**	**5.8 m**	**0.6 m**

Notes: For data comparability and coverage see the technical notes.
a. Figures in italics are for 1970–81, not 1970–82.
b. Figures in italics are for 1961–70, not 1960–70.
c. Separate figures are not available for public consumption, which is therefore included in private consumption.
d. Swaziland data are for 1970–80, not 1970–82.
Source: World Bank, *Toward Sustained Development,* App. 4.

Table 3.5 Black Africa, 1960–1982: Structure of Demand

Distribution of gross domestic product (per cent)

	Public consumption 1960	Public consumption 1982[a]	Private consumption 1960	Private consumption 1982[a]	Gross domestic investment 1960	Gross domestic investment 1982[a]	Gross domestic saving 1960	Gross domestic saving 1982[a]	Exports of goods and nonfactor services 1960	Exports of goods and nonfactor services 1982[a]	Resource balance 1960	Resource balance 1982[a]
Low-income economies	**11 w**	**12 w**	**77 w**	**86 w**	**15 w**	**10 w**	**12 w**	**5 w**	**21 w**	**11 w**	**-3 w**	**-5 w**
Low-income semiarid	**11 w**	**17 w**	**83 w**	**84 w**	**11 w**	**19 w**	**6 w**	**-1 w**	**14 w**	**20 w**	**-5 w**	**-20 w**
1 Chad	13	23	82	102	11	9	5	-25	23	35	-6	-34
2 Mali	12	25	79	79	14	15	9	-4	12	19	-5	-19
3 Burkina Faso	10	20	94	89	9	15	-4	-9	9	14	-13	-24
4 Somalia	8	..	86	..	10	..	6	..	13	..	-4	..
5 Niger	9	9	79	79	12	26	12	12	9	21	(.)	-14
6 Gambia, The	15	..	79	..	7	..	6	..	45	..	-1	..
Low-income other	**11 w**	**12 w**	**76 w**	**86 w**	**16 w**	**9 w**	**13 w**	**5 w**	**22 w**	**10 w**	**-3 w**	**-4 w**
7 Ethiopia	8	16	81	81	12	11	11	3	9	12	-1	-8
8 Guinea-Bissau	..	—[b]	..	..	..	..	..	..	..	..	..	..
9 Zaire	*18*	*17*	*61*	*90*	*12*	*16*	*21*	*10*	*55*	*29*	*9*	*-6*
10 Malawi	17	16	87	71	10	20	-4	13	18	21	-14	-7
11 Uganda	9	b	75	95	11	8	16	5	26	5	5	-3
12 Rwanda	*10*	*17*	*82*	*75*	*6*	*22*	*8*	*8*	*12*	*12*	*2*	*-14*
13 Burundi	3	13	92	86	6	14	5	1	13	9	-1	-13
14 Tanzania	9	22	72	70	14	20	19	8	30	11	5	-12
15 Benin	16	13	75	87	15	37	9	(.)	12	30	-6	-37
16 Central African Rep.	19	12	72	97	20	9	9	-9	23	18	-11	-18
17 Guinea	..	*17*	..	*66*	..	*13*	..	*17*	..	*28*	..	*4*
18 Madagascar	20	15	75	81	11	14	5	4	12	13	-6	-10
19 Togo	8	17	88	78	11	26	4	5	19	28	-7	-21
20 Ghana	10	7	73	92	24	1	17	1	28	2	-7	(.)
21 Kenya	11	19	72	64	20	22	17	17	31	25	-3	-5

22 Sierra Leone	..	9	..	92	..	12	..	-1	..	14	..	-13
23 *Mozambique*	..	..	..	..	..	..	..	..	..	..	..	..
Middle-income oil importers	11 w	19 w	69 w	71 w	18 w	21 w	20 w	10 w	33 w	26 w	2 w	-11 w
24 Sudan	8	13	81	89	9	16	11	-2	15	9	2	-18
25 Mauritania	25	31	71	64	38	41	4	5	15	43	-34	-36
26 Liberia	7	23	58	57	28	22	35	20	39	46	7	-2
27 Senegal	17	20	68	74	16	20	15	6	40	31	-1	-14
28 Lesotho	17	31	108	146	2	29	-25	-77	12	14	-27	-106
29 Zambia	11	30	48	65	25	17	41	5	56	27	16	-12
30 Zimbabwe	11	20	67	59	23	27	22	21	..	..	-1	-6
31 Botswana	15	..	88	..	8	..	-3	..	23	..	-11	..
32 Swaziland	21	..	49	..	17	..	30	..	44	..	13	..
33 Ivory Coast	10	18	73	58	15	24	17	24	37	39	2	(.)
34 Mauritius	13	13	82	69	26	21	6	18	27	46	-20	-3
Middle-income oil exporters	7 w	13 w	86 w	68 w	16 w	26 w	8 w	18 w	15 w	21 w	-8 w	-8 w
35 Nigeria	6	13	87	71	13	25	7	16	14	19	-6	-9
36 Cameroon	..	8	..	65	..	25	..	27	..	31	..	2
37 Congo, People's Rep.	15	15	97	37	53	56	-12	48	21	55	-65	-8
38 Gabon	10	14	40	30	..	50	50	..	32	..	..	..
39 *Angola*	..	..	..	..	..	..	..	..	..	..	..	..
Sub-Saharan Africa	10 w	14 w	77 w	75 w	16 w	19 w	13 w	12 w	23 w	17 w	-3 w	-7 w
All low-income countries	8 w	11 w	78 w	73 w	19 w	24 w	18 w	21 w	7 w	9 w	-1 w	-3 w
All lower middle-income countries	10 w	13 w	76 w	70 w	15 w	23 w	14 w	17 w	15 w	20 w	-1 w	-6 w
All upper middle-income countries	12 w	15 w	67 w	67 w	22 w	24 w	21 w	23 w	18 w	24 w	-1 w	-1 w
Industrial market economies	15 w	18 w	63 w	62 w	21 w	20 w	22 w	20 w	12 w	19 w	1 w	(.) w

Notes:
a. Figures in italics are for 1981, not 1982.
b. Separate figures are not available for public consumption, which is therefore included in private consumption.
Source: World Bank, *Toward Sustained Development,* App. 5.

Table 3.6 Black Africa, 1960–1982: Growth of Merchandise Trade

	Merchandise trade (US$ millions)		Average annual growth rate in real terms (per cent)			
			Exports		Imports	
	Exports 1982[a]	Imports 1982[a]	1960–70	1970–82	1960–70	1970–82
Low-income economies	**6,736 t**	**11,045 t**	**6.0 m**	**–2.5 m**	**6.2 m**	**0.0 m**
Low-income semiarid	**997 t**	**1,727 t**	**6.0 m**	**7.9 m**	**5.6 m**	**6.5 m**
1 Chad	101	132	6.0	–8.6	5.1	–3.6
2 Mali	146	332	2.9	6.6	–0.4	6.6
3 Burkina Faso	56	346	14.5	9.1	8.1	6.7
4 Somalia	317	378	2.5	9.1	2.7	3.8
5 Niger	333	442	5.9	20.8	12.1	11.0
6 Gambia, The	44	97	6.4	–1.7	6.1	6.4
Low-income other	**5,739 t**	**9,318 t**	**5.7 m**	**–4.0 m**	**6.2 m**	**–2.1 m**
7 Ethiopia	404	787	3.7	1.3	6.2	0.2
8 Guinea-Bissau	12	50	..	..	..	..
9 Zaire	569	480	–1.7	–5.6	5.4	–12.4
10 Malawi	262	314	11.7	5.1	7.6	1.2
11 Uganda	371	339	6.9	–9.2	6.2	–7.9
12 Rwanda	90	286	16.0	2.4	8.2	11.5
13 Burundi	88	214	..	..	..	..
14 Tanzania	480	1,046	3.8	–5.8	6.0	–1.5
15 Benin	34	889	5.2	–4.4	7.5	5.2
16 Central African Rep.	106	91	9.6	2.6	4.5	–0.2
17 Guinea	411	296	..	..	..	..
18 Madagascar	433	522	5.4	–3.6	4.1	–3.4
19 Togo	213	526	10.5	0.3	8.6	8.6
20 Ghana	873	705	0.1	–4.7	–1.5	–4.8
21 Kenya	979	1,683	7.5	–3.3	6.5	–2.7

22 Sierra Leone	111	298	2.5	−6.6	1.9	−2.6
23 *Mozambique*	303	792	6.0	−13.3	7.9	−14.5
Middle-income oil importers	**6,058 t**	**7,097 t**	**4.1 m**	**−0.1 m**	**2.9 m**	**3.0 m**
24 Sudan	499	1,285	2.1	−5.1	0.5	3.5
25 Mauritania	232	273	53.8	−0.1	4.6	3.0
26 *Liberia*	531	477	18.5	0.5	2.9	−2.4
27 Senegal	477	974	1.4	−1.8	2.3	1.3
28 Lesotho						
29 Zambia	1,059	831	2.3	−0.5	9.7	−6.8
30 Zimbabwe	663	704				
31 Botswana						
32 Swaziland						
33 Ivory Coast	2,235	2,090	8.9	2.6	10.0	4.6
34 Mauritius	362	463	4.1	5.2	−0.2	5.5
Middle-income oil exporters	**25,296 t**	**24,721 t**	**7.1 m**	**−1.1 m**	**7.9 m**	**9.7 m**
35 *Nigeria*	19,484	20,821	6.6	−1.6	1.5	17.2
36 Cameroon	998	1205	7.1	4.0	9.2	5.2
37 Congo, People's Rep.	923	970	6.4	1.4	−1.0	9.1
38 Gabon	2,161	724	11.1	−1.1	7.9	10.2
39 *Angola*	1,730	1,001	9.7	−15.8	11.5	0.0
Sub-Saharan Africa	**38,090 t**	**42,863 t**	**6.2 m**	**−0.8 m**	**6.0 m**	**3.0 m**
All low-income countries	**42,619 t**	**56,205 t**	**5.4 m**	**0.3 m**	**5.4 m**	**1.2 m**
All lower middle-income countries	**97,855 t**	**119,668 t**	**5.3 m**	**1.6 m**	**6.8 m**	**3.3 m**
All upper middle-income countries	**231,703 t**	**260,541 t**	**5.4 m**	**7.1 m**	**5.5 m**	**7.4 m**
Industrial market economies	**1,148,808 t**	**1,212,975 t**	**8.5 m**	**5.6 m**	**9.5 m**	**4.3 m**

Note:
a. Figures in italics are for 1981, not 1982.
Source: World Bank, *Toward Sustained Development*, App. 7.

age-groups in education rose from 36 to 63 per cent in primary schools and from 3 to 13 per cent in secondary education.[4]

Other aspects of economic development were, however, much less promising. Most serious was the trend of agriculture. The overall growth rate (volume) was only 1.3 per cent in the decade 1969/71–1977/79, or −1.4 per cent in per capita terms.[5] Since most African exports are agricultural, it is not surprising that agricultural decline resulted in lower exports. The average annual growth in exports during the 1960s was 5.9 per cent, but this dropped to −0.8 per cent in 1970–9.[6] Breaking this down into percentage shares of total exports, fuels (almost all Nigerian petroleum) rose from 3 to 49 per cent between 1962 and 1978; minerals rose from 7 to 10 per cent; but 'food and beverages' declined from 62 to 31 per cent and 'other primary products' from 21 to 9 per cent. Manufactured products also declined from 7 to 4 per cent.[7] Between 1960 and 1978 Africa's share of world non-fuel exports declined from 3.1 to 1.2 per cent.[8]

Declining exports (except from Nigeria) and increasing dependence on imported food in many countries, coupled with large imports of goods and extensive borrowing abroad, inevitably resulted in an increasingly adverse balance of payments and thus in external indebtedness. Between 1970 and 1979 the debt service of sub-Saharan Africa rose from 1.4 to 2.0 per cent of total GNP and from 5 to 6.9 per cent of the value of exported goods and services. On average these figures were not high; but for individual countries they could be overwhelming. Thus the debt service ratio as a percentage of the value of exported goods and services in 1979 was 59 per cent in Guinea-Bissau, 33 per cent in Sudan, 24.4 per cent in Togo and 19.7 per cent in Zambia, to take a few of the worst examples. In fact, the weighted average for Black Africa as a whole was greatly improved by Nigeria, with a debt service ratio of only 1.5 per cent.[9] For many African states this meant virtual bankruptcy, postponed by foreign aid and further borrowing, which in turn implied greater dependence.

Thus the general picture, ignoring the vast differences between countries which are obscured by these aggregate statistics, is of very considerable growth since the 1950s which was slowing up by the mid-1970s and appeared to be seriously at risk in the early 1980s. Within this, however, there were marked sectoral contrasts. Industry and the provision of infrastructural and welfare services grew very fast; but this was offset by a serious lag in the growth of agriculture. Food production was not keeping up with population growth and many of the staple commodity exports were in decline. The result was increasing dependence on imported food and international aid, coupled with balance of payments deficits, heavy overseas borrowing and deteriorating debt service ratios. By the early 1980s most parts of Black Africa were in varying degrees of crisis. The golden dreams of the independence era were in ruins: it was no longer possible to hope that Black Africa would be able to sustain rates of growth and patterns of development which might enable her to close the gap on the affluent West.

It is this disappointment that has resulted in the use of such terms as 'arrested' (in the meaning used by dependency theorists to indicate structural blockage), checked, limited or decelerating development during the two decades after 1960. Equally it has become a main preoccupation of those concerned not only with African history but with Third World development as a whole to find an explanation. The purpose of the rest of this chapter and of Chapter 4 is to survey the range of explanations currently on offer.

False Expectations and their Origins

Disappointment may result from unreasonable expectations. It is, therefore, prudent to begin by considering on what grounds it was widely supposed around 1960 that political freedom would lead to rapid and sustained economic and social growth and development.[10]

In retrospect it is one of the most astonishing features of post-1950 African history that there should have been so general an expectation that independence would lead to very rapid economic growth and affluence. There was, after all, no historical precedent. The wealth of Western Europe and North America had been accumulated over a long period: even if we accept the hypothesis that income levels in Europe were no higher than those in Africa and Asia in the earlier eighteenth century,[11] it took a century or more of relatively slow growth before these countries achieved comparative affluence; and it was at least possible that this achievement was special, a unique product of congruent conditions not present elsewhere. Moreover, the record of those non-European states which had never been colonies, or (apart from the United States) which had been liberated by the early nineteenth century, did not suggest that political freedom by itself was guaranteed to result in rapid and sustained growth: indeed, Latin America provided a depressing case study in post-colonial poverty. Why, then, the almost universal optimism that accompanied decolonization in Africa?

The main reason appears to be that decolonization coincided with the birth and, as it turned out, short life-span, of a brand of applied economics which claimed to have solved the problem of the origins and nature of poverty and to be able to provide formulas which could ensure its eradication. The fundamental idea was that poverty, rather than affluence, was the abnormal human condition; so that, if one could isolate its causes, affluence should follow naturally. In the 1950s a broad consensus emerged, based on the new economic analysis of the nature of growth that emerged in the 1930s. Poverty resulted from a pathological condition from which any economy could suffer and whose main cause or symptom was an inadequate rate of capital accumulation.

For this various causes were assigned. Ragnor Nurkse attributed it either to limitation of the division of labour, resulting from the extent of the market, which in turn inhibited capital accumulation by preventing a rise in national income; or, adopting a Keynesian consumption function, to low productivity and incomes keeping per capita incomes low and thus creating a vicious circle of poverty.[12] Leibenstein further defined this 'low level equilibrium trap', in which low initial levels of income growth stimulated population increases which would overtake the growth of national income and force down per capita incomes. Thus only a substantial increase in per capita incomes could break the circle.[13] Many others also emphasized the inhibiting effects of low initial incomes in less developed countries; for example, Gunnar Myrdal,[14] W. W. Rostow[15] and S. Kuznets.[16] Clearly the only way out of the poverty trap was in some way to raise national and per capita incomes to the point at which savings and capital accumulation were possible on a sufficient scale; and, in analysing how this might be achieved, all these theorists assumed that the social value of an act of investment exceeded its private value because it expanded the size of the market and so tended to attract further investments. Tibor Scitovsky in particular emphasized the importance of externalities resulting from initial acts of investment, particularly in 'import-competing' industries for domestic consumption rather than for export, since in these a larger proportion of the profit was retained locally instead of being shared with the exporting firms and the country to which exports were sent.[17]

Growth, then, depended on investment levels which were above the capacity of most unimproved less developed countries. What was the way out of this dead end? It is important that most economists of the 1950s and 1960s rejected the two standard remedies of previous thought: export-led growth and foreign direct investment. Exports and, by extension, concentration on export commodities on the principle of comparative advantage, could no longer perform the functions defined by classical economics – that is, by widening the market and providing a surplus for investment. Nurkse explained this primarily in terms of declining demand for tropical raw materials as the wealthy countries evolved synthetic substitutes and of markets in more developed countries blocked by protectionism.[18] H. W. Singer, a pioneer of the structuralist school of development economics, using United Nations statistics, held that there had been an adverse trend in the terms of trade of less developed countries since the 1870s (thus providing an argument that was widely used by the left during the next decades),[19] so that exporting commodities provided declining returns. Moreover, the economies of less developed countries were too inflexible for them to be able to respond to market signals of this type. Such arguments, heavily reinforced by evidence drawn from the depressed 1930s, were widely accepted and expanded into a broad denunciation of 'lop-sided' or 'skewed' economies that were over-dependent on a limited range of commodities. Clearly comparative advantage was no longer theoretically respectable.

Nor was foreign direct investment the panacea of colonial development schemes. Although the main attack on multinationals did not develop until the later 1960s, dependency theory was evolving in the early 1950s and with it criticism of foreign direct investment, based mainly on Latin American experience. The central argument, initiated by Singer and Paul Prebisch[20] and taken up by a wide range of theorists who included the Latin American dependency school, Myrdal, Hla Myint and others,[21] was that foreign direct investment was normally concentrated in 'enclaves', insulated from the rest of the host economy. These foreign firms paid low wages to indigenous workers, employed few local managers or technicians (so contributing little to the local stock of skills), bought little from the host economy, exported most of their products (so providing few downstream stimuli) and, above all, transferred their profits rather than reinvesting them locally. Foreign enterprises did not, therefore, contribute significantly to the process of domestic capital accumulation or the creation of local skills and know-how: if anything, they caused a drain of real resources. Clearly, such investment could not help less developed countries to break out of the poverty trap.

If these two well-established escape routes were now blocked, other gradualist solutions based on conventional capitalist assumptions were also discarded. Small markets in the new states led to scale problems, monopoly, imperfect factor markets and dualistic economies; all of which, coupled with poor information flows, resulted in low elasticities of supply. Entrepreneurs also seemed to be in very short supply. In primitive economies the price mechanism had little value. In short, if left to the operation of conventional market forces within a capitalist environment, these countries would almost certainly continue to stagnate. Organic evolution was blocked by structural problems.

This pessimism was the starting-point of the new approach to economic development of the 1950s. The broad consensus was now that a special prescription was necessary for the less developed countries of the modern world: hence the concept of development economics as a specific branch of applied economics. Killick has defined five basic assumptions common to all, or most, of those who pioneered this field.[22]

(1) Economic development in the tropics was a discontinuous process, involving structural transformation; it was not a natural growth.

(2) This transformation consisted primarily of increasing the level of capital accumulation; once a critical threshold had been reached, the process should be self-sustaining.

(3) An initial 'big push' was needed to break the mould of poverty and to make this possible.

(4) This push involved a massive increase in the capital investment/national income ratio. It was assumed that the rate of growth of the economy would be roughly in line with the increase of the invested share of the GDP; and it seemed generally agreed (though without any evidential base) that a minimum level of 10 per cent was essential for what Rostow emotively called 'the take-off'.

(5) Finally, industrialization was essential to growth and development; and the arguments for this are important. Industry was more likely to be 'modernizing' than agriculture. Productivity should be higher. Industry would provide a market for increased agricultural production and its products would provide an incentive for farmers to earn the money to buy consumer goods. Import-substituting industry was best, because this would provide both backward and forward linkages into the economy and capture all the benefits.[23] Some, notably (Sir) Arthur Lewis, did not accept this last point entirely, but most swallowed the import-substitution argument whole.

This, then, became the grand strategy of the 1950s and early 1960s. There remained the question of tactics: how best to get the 'big push' going. One almost universal assumption was that colonialism must end before anything serious could be done. Despite their deathbed repentance and the extensive projects carried out by the metropolitan states after about 1950, it was regarded as axiomatic that a colonial state could not wish to carry out the structural changes that were necessary because these would be inconsistent with its own economic interests. Moreover, the colonial state lacked the legitimacy, and therefore the self-confidence, to undertake fundamental social engineering. The onus, therefore, must be on the first successor states just beginning to be visible in Africa, with Ghana moving towards independence and the rest assumed to be following not far behind. On these states and their character the economists – like the eighteenth-century *philosophes*, with whom they had much in common, before them – placed great faith. Their rulers were assumed to be both enlightened and efficient, and so fit to be the main instruments of change and development. The reason was that the economists put great emphasis on economic management and planning as the alternative to the market. The main case for this preference, as expounded as Scitovsky in 1954, was that the price mechanism could not give true signals about the future, especially where factor and product markets were as imperfect and entrepreneurs and resources as scarce as they were deemed to be in less developed countries. Moreover, new econometric techniques made indicative planning possible for the first time, and also, of course, exciting for economists. Development, therefore, must be planned and executed by the post-colonial state.

In expounding this doctrine of planning the economists showed several biases that were to have significant consequences. They preferred to deal in national aggregates (saving and investment ratios) and showed little interest in the detail of micro-economic implementation. They postulated closed rather than open economies. They adopted long time-horizons, which implied state rather than private provision of capital. This the state would do through taxation (on the assumption that the state's propensity to consume was lower than that of private individuals), by the creation of new credit institutions and probably by deficit financing. Inflation was not regarded as a serious problem. W. A. Lewis, for example, thought that it would be self-correcting. The main area of disagreement was over whether the state should take a direct role in economic life, as owner of factories, farms, banks, etc., in addition to providing infrastructure and social services. But this was only on the margins of the new consensus. Those who disagreed in principle were few and, for the time being, regarded as old-fashioned and obscurantist; they included S. H. Frankel, who stuck to gradualist or organic micro-economic solutions,[24] P. T. Bauer, always a convinced free-trader[25] and J. Viner.[26]

Why, then, was the battle won so easily? One answer is that, since conventional prescriptions for economic development appeared to have failed in the past – with the disastrous 1930s still taken as the most relevant example rather than what proved to be the booming 1950s – there was a general desire for new courses. Intellectually the new economics found ready allies on the left, where Marxist economists such as Maurice Dobb[27] and Paul Baran[28] were able to fit them readily into the Marxist–Leninist schemata and, indeed, added influential ideas concerning the possibility of extracting savings from the indigenous wealthy and from foreign enterprises. But by far the most important fact was that these arguments for 'economic independence' and state control of the economy were extremely attractive to the leaders of nationalist movements in the colonies, the future rulers of the new states. In the so-called struggle for independence, the assertion that colonialism and its associated collection of economic practices and institutions were a bar to progress provided excellent propaganda, both in Africa and Europe. Nkrumah, for example, as early as 1949, made the famous prophecy that 'If we get self-government, we'll transform the Gold Coast into a paradise in ten years'.[29]

Once independence was achieved the economists' prescription had even more to offer. Their emphasis on state power was a useful rhetorical weapon against liberals and political opponents. Economic nationalism was a multi-purpose tool which could be used against all foreign interests and justified a wide range of potentially unpopular devices, such as control over imports, credit, productive capacity and prices. The primary role allotted to industry could be used to justify penal taxation of primary producers whose surplus was urgently needed to support the new state apparatus. The need for huge quantities of investment capital, accepted by the West, made it possible to borrow very extensively. The near-promise that, if the 'push' was big enough, the structural obstacles to growth would be removed suggested that the new states could achieve affluence and self-sufficiency in accumulation in a very short time-span. But, above all, it was probably the nationalist element – the rejection of internationalism and dependence on overseas markets and investors – that was the most attractive feature of the new development economics for the African countries. In short, one way or another, the new development economics was almost universally accepted, with gratitude, by the new states and their leaders. It would have been amazing had it been otherwise.

Thirty years later most of this optimism seems to have been misplaced. No Black African state has 'taken off'. Despite considerable growth of real incomes in some states and often impressive performance in the provision of welfare and infrastructural services and in the relative importance of industry, there has been very limited development in the structural sense. Clearly there were many false expectations. But were the strategies themselves misguided or were they incorrectly executed? The argument of this book is that both factors must be held responsible for relative failure – relative because in fact there were very substantial real achievements in most new states. On the one hand, few of the theorists had any deep understanding of the realities of African life and the problems of overcoming obstacles to growth. On the other, none of the new states proved capable of carrying out the complex requirements of the new development codes. These failures will become apparent when we consider the actions of African governments in pursuit of affluence.

Weakness at the Centre: African Governments as a Prime Cause of Limited Development

There is one proposition common to all who see the roots of limited development within rather than outside modern African states: that governments as at present constituted are unable, unwilling, or both, to carry out satisfactorily the functions prescribed for them by the development economists, and indeed by their own plans. Why this should be so varies with ideological standpoint. The left tends to explain it in terms of self-seeking bourgeois or petty bourgeois regimes, representing small elites, who use political power to extract the surplus from the masses and so accumulate private capital, freely collaborating with international capital as their main ally and source of finance.[30]

Class analysis is thus the appropriate framework for understanding the paralysis and incompetence of the post-colonial African state. The alternative 'conservative' assessment, typified by publications of multilateral agencies such as the World Bank, accepts the basic premiss of governmental lack of wisdom, but discounts the political emphasis of the radical approach on the grounds that it does not in fact make much difference what political label or style African rulers adopt. Rather the main block to more effective development lies in the peculiar basket of assumptions and policies adopted by the great majority of African states, as indeed by many Third World countries elsewhere.[31] Expositions of this new 'conservative consensus', and explanations of what may appear to be perverse policies, can be found in a wide range of published work, but one of the clearest and most recent statements is in Douglas Rimmer's *The Economies of West Africa*; and, although his evidential base is mostly in West Africa, his argument can be used to relate to any part of Black Africa.

The basis of the argument is that the main policy assumption of African governments is that development depends on central government control of all aspects of the economy and society, and that wise central direction can produce infinite improvement. The main instruments of control can be divided into external and internal. External controls include manipulation of exchange rates (commonly with over-valued domestic currencies); imposition of trade controls (licensing imports and sometimes exports, import and export tariffs); a monopoly of foreign borrowing; and membership of external organizations, such as IMF, Lomé and regional unions. Internal policy instruments aim to gear all available resources to official objectives. Taxation transfers a maximum share of the national product to public rather than private consumption, including quasi-taxation through marketing boards for commodities and commercialized food. Price fixing is used to offset over-valued currencies. New productive enterprises require governmental licence. Deficit financing is common, linked to government-controlled central banks and credit institutions. Development planning is almost invariable to allocate scarce resources. Governments aim at high levels of investment, relying mainly on tax revenues and foreign loans.

All these are justified by their authors as necessary means to the end of economic development, which in turn has five main objectives: provision of welfare − schools, amenities and public health; a sectoral shift of resources to industry, on the assumption that this alone can provide higher productivity and create urban employment;[32] high levels of investment, on the assumption that all investment is good investment; 'autonomy', in the sense of making a break with the external constraints imposed by the international economy; and urbanization, as essential to industrialization and modernization.

Rimmer considers that, both in concept and execution, these policy aims are largely responsible for Africa's limited economic success. Such aims and instruments of policy, as prescribed by the development economists, were based on highly theoretical assumptions, above all on what Rimmer calls the 'investment fetish' – belief that massive investment was essential to higher productivity and would necessarily create it – though this assumption had no basis in the history of Western development and was even more irrelevant to tropical Africa. The unprecedented availability of foreign loans, etc., made it all too easy for African states to adopt this prescription; and the use of indicative planning for long gave the impression that these resources were being efficiently used and would produce the growth rates projected in the plans. Much growth did, in fact, take place; but there was also great waste, major distortion of economies unable to adapt at sufficient speed, increasing indebtedness not balanced by increased production or productivity and heavy dependence on overseas sources of credit and goods. Above all, perhaps, the underlying aim of 'autonomy' was dangerous. It implied expansion of industry and food production on a scale not compatible with the principle of comparative advantage (which many development economists and African rulers specifically rejected); and, since most new African states were too small in resources and population to constitute viable autonomous units, the result was bound to be the creation of inefficient new enterprises and the discouragement of established export industries, notably in agriculture.

From that position the conservative consensus moves on to two consequential issues: first, what African states should have done and should now do in the future to retrieve the situation; secondly, why most African regimes adopted such unrewarding policies and stuck to them even after two decades had shown that many of them were unsatisfactory or even disastrous.

On the first of these there is considerable agreement, though with difference in detail. African states must accept the discipline of economic management. Exchange rates must be made realistic in order to help exports, discourage imports and eliminate the huge 'black' sectors of their economies. Protectionism must be modified so that only potentially viable domestic industries survive. State enterprises should be overhauled to eliminate inefficiency, overmanning, etc., and, if improvement is impossible, dismantled. Conversely, a larger role should be given to private enterprise, both foreign and indigenous. The government itself must be made more efficient; in particular, its size and costs must be reduced. The growth rate of public consumption since 1960 has been far greater than that of the domestic product in most African states: for African states as a whole 6.0 per cent in the 1960s, 5.8 per cent in the 1970s, compared with an average annual growth rate of GDP of 3.9 per cent and 2.9 per cent respectively.[33]

Above all, however, agriculture must be made more productive. Its growth rate has been poor: an average of 2.3 per cent in the 1960s, 1.3 per cent in the 1970s, compared with a rate of population increase of 2.7 per cent.[34] Export production rose in the 1960s but fell in the 1970s, so that the volume was no greater at the end than twenty years earlier.[35] Food production also showed a declining trend in productivity, leading to a rapid increase in the import of basic foods by many states.[36] To reverse such trends the World Bank (together with most conservative commentators) proposes a broad strategy for stimulating producers by paying more realistic prices for export crops and food supplies, providing more extension services, fertilizers, etc., to increase productivity and conducting more research into improved seeds, etc. This strategy is based on the peasant (or 'smallholder' in World Bank terminology), who is assumed to be a conventional economic man who can and will respond to market forces if these are favourable. He can be stimulated by the example of larger, more productive modern farms, but these cannot replace him. That is, disenchanted with the inefficiency of almost all large-scale agricultural enterprises in Africa, from the Groundnut Scheme to the large new farms of northern Ghana and Nigeria, the multilateral experts have rediscovered the peasant as being the only person involved in African agriculture who knows what he is doing and can be relied upon to work hard if he is given sufficient incentive to do so. Not everyone agrees with this, as will be seen below; but it appears to be a necessary assumption for any conservative formula to improve African agricultural production in the near future.

The now standard conventional neo-classical explanation of limited African development is, therefore, that market forces have been fundamentally disrupted by the imposition of ill-calculated or badly managed plans for modernization. 'Policy', that is, has been counter-productive, and development has been limited or arrested mainly because governments have adopted the wrong strategies and tactics. This, however, leads to the second question: why did so many African states not only adopt such policies initially but cling to them long after it was clear that they were not conducive to sustained development?

On the answer to this question also there is now a broad consensus with considerable variations in detail, much of which is accepted by radicals as well as conservatives. Perhaps the bluntest argument is

provided by Rimmer.[37] African governments have never, despite their
protestations, been primarily concerned with economic growth but
rather with maintenance of political power and the distribution of
wealth to themselves and their supporters. The reason lies not in their
special greed or malevolence but rather in the fact that rulers of new
states cannot afford the luxury of disinterested public service because
their position as rulers is fundamentally unstable. As was suggested in
Chapter 2 above, the states they inherited were artefacts, lacking
natural cohesion. The 'national' parties the first nationalist leaders
cobbled together with great skill to put pressure on their rulers to
abdicate had no ethnic, class or ideological cement. The fact that they
became the first free governments was partly an accident of history:
they happened to be in a dominant position at the moment of
decolonization. The danger, which became a reality in many states,
was, therefore, that these parties would disintegrate into competing
factions, with consequences that were politically fatal for their original
leaders and possibly disastrous for the integrity of the new states. On
both private and public grounds they, therefore, had to create support
for their continuing rule.

They found it in the promise of planned development. As an ideal
it might hold the nation together, a substitute for the goal of independence. In practical political terms it would provide the resources,
foreign and domestic, for buying political support for the dominant
party. Investment funds would provide money and economic
management the excuse for ministerial power, both of which could be
converted into the political currency of patronage.

But to be effective such patronage had to be specific: only those
whose support mattered and who gave it must receive a share of
the strictly limited stock of benefits. This largely explains why, in the
words of Rimmer, 'the administration of West African economic life
. . . shows a marked predisposition in favour of particular rather than
general inducements'.[38] Licensing of all kinds is desirable because
licences can be used either as rewards or as threats. Price controls to
balance over-valued currencies are preferable to rational monetary
policies because they can be used selectively. It is better to offer
selective benefits (fertilizer subsidies, use of tractors, etc.) to small
groups of larger farmers rather than to help all farmers by paying
higher prices for their produce. Such practices have become endemic
and the expectations and institutions they generate have ossified, even
though they may be recognized as dangerous economically. Parastatals
are denounced by most reformist regimes, but never dismantled,
bureaucracies admitted to be too large but never pruned. Thus, except
in the area of public welfare and infrastructure, which provide many
social as well as political returns, state intervention in the economy has
probably been counter-productive, mainly because the motivation

behind policies has been political, not economic. Only if the political interests of the ruling class fortuitously coincide with the needs of the main productive sectors of the economy (as, allegedly, in Ivory Coast and Kenya) have the effects not been disastrous.

A slightly different version of this argument is adopted by Tony Killick in his detailed study of Ghana in the 1960s and 1970s.[39] He argues that there the roots of the managed economy, with all the biases described by Rimmer, derived more from Nkrumah's preferences, which coincided with those of the development economists, than from consciously political motives; but he admits that the major policy shift undertaken in 1961 owed something to the urgent political need to satisfy party supporters, offset urban unemployment and speed up industrialization as the only way to increase the national income quickly. The results, however, were as disastrous as in any other account, and for the same basic reasons as are defined by Rimmer; and successive regimes after 1966, all of which stated their intention of removing the corruption and inefficiency endemic in the Nkrumah system, failed to make any radical changes. Killick's basic explanation of such failures lies in the inapplicability of these development models to Ghana at that time, compounded by the inability of both the bureaucracy and those who administered state enterprises to do so efficiently.[40] Unfortunately, once a certain level of maldistribution of resources and inefficiency had been established, a number of factors made it almost impossible to change direction. Each element in Nkrumah's system had created vested interests – civil servants, managers in parastatals, recipients of licences to import or manufacture, urban consumers of artificially cheapened agricultural products, industrial beneficiaries of protection, and so on. Such a system could only be dismantled gradually, but the aim must be to get back to something like a market economy in which the state would still play a major role but individual Ghanaians would have greater scope for making full use of their undoubted skills, enterprise and assets.

This theme, of the determining influence of interest groups on government policy, has been taken further by R. H. Bates[41] and others. Setting out to explain the apparent irrationality of agricultural and industrializing policies in all parts of tropical Africa, despite their evident failure to increase the national income, Bates arrives at what, in Gladstone's words, might be described as a classes against masses explanation. The process began with the new states' 'revenue imperative': they needed money urgently to support their proposed modern sectors and saw agriculture, initially the reserves of the marketing boards, as the only immediately available resource. These funds, and later policies designed to keep down agricultural prices and to raise industrial prices, were used to help and therefore gain the support of a wide range of interest groups who nevertheless constituted a small proportion of the population: industrialists, who got protected markets; a few wealthy farmers who got cheap inputs; those who ran state farms, managers of parastatals and the bureaucracy, all of whom got well-paid jobs; and the urban workers, who got increased employment and low food prices. Once this pattern had been created, its beneficiaries joined in an informal federation of interest groups with a common interest against change, particularly change which implied payment of higher prices for agricultural produce, fewer jobs or reduced markets for protected high-price industrial production.

This alliance was successful partly because the state had sufficient coercive power to suppress rural resistance, partly because it could buy selective support where it really mattered; but above all because the beneficiaries of these policies could form effective organized groups with access to the highest levels of government or, in the case of the urban proletariat, posed a real threat to political stability. By contrast, the mass of rural producers had little chance of forming cohesive pressure groups and were denied electoral power by one-party state systems and the suspension or manipulation of elections. Bates points out that the beneficiaries of these inefficient systems of national economy also suffered from high prices for industrial products and the general inefficiency of the supply system. Why do they not rebel? His answer is that the urban classes, especially the proletariat, spend some 60 per cent of their incomes on food and are therefore prepared to accept the defects of the pricing structure for other goods as a necessary price to pay for maintaining the system from which most of their advantages derive.

Bjorn Beckman, concentrating on Ghana and from a different angle, has provided a simplified version of the same hypothesis.[42] The post-colonial Ghanaian state, with its strong bias towards urbanization and modernization through industry, founded these superstructures on the basis of peasant earnings from cocoa; it extracted an increasing proportion of the surplus through the marketing board. The main agents and beneficiaries of this process of sectoral transfer were the politicians, bureaucrats and general public service, whose salaries were essentially a first charge on cocoa earnings. Their plans assumed that world cocoa prices would remain as high as in the 1950s and early 1960s and that production would not decline in response to the low prices paid to producers. They were wrong on both counts. Apart from the temporary rise between 1973 and 1977, the trend of cocoa prices was downward from the mid-1960s; and production declined by between a half and a third between the early 1960s and later 1970s. The result was that the peasant base proved inadequate to sustain the weight of the complex modern state and urban economy built upon it: hence the endemic economic and fiscal problems of Ghana from the mid-1960s. Significantly, however, even when major reforms were attempted after 1966, those who had constructed this unstable system – the state administrative class and a variety of entrenched vested interests (larger farmers, industrialists, etc.) – were able to avoid any significant reduction in the scale of their benefits.

The conservative consensus is not, therefore, uniform; but its common propositions can be summarized as follows. The main cause of limited African economic development after 1960 lay in the deplorable inefficiency of most parts of the modern sector of the economy, especially industry, and in the relative decline of agriculture. These failures are attributable to public policies which aimed to develop the modern sector at almost any cost, and in particular at the cost of rural producers, who (apart from a favoured minority of larger farmers) were bled by means of low prices and artificially high exchange rates. Rural production and exports therefore failed to expand as fast as population growth and the needs of the modern sector required. To resolve these problems involved a progressive dismantling of the instruments of economic mismanagement and a return to a market economy. Once this was achieved, all genuinely productive sections of society would respond, especially the peasant agriculturalists, resulting in larger exports, more food production and a genuine increase of the domestic market for the products of the modern industrial sector.

There are, perhaps, three main tests one can apply to the conservative explanation of limited economic development in particular countries. First, whether the state has tended to engulf the economy, is basically inefficient and has adverse effects on economic growth. Secondly, whether the import-substitution policy adopted by most states was successful in inaugurating progressive industrialization and capital accumulation, in particular whether it assisted in the growth of indigenous capitalism. Finally, whether the limited success of agriculture in most places can be put down to poor state management, and, in particular, whether the evidence suggests that payment of higher prices or a free market would stimulate peasants to greater production.

Conversely, in terms of the radical analysis, the main question to be asked is whether these same policies and their weakness flow from the class interest of the dominant socio-economic groups. This can be tested by examining the class structure of regimes, the distribution of rewards and the extent of class differentiation. In practice the same evidence is relevant to both the radical and the conservative approach. These two sets of questions, although not rigorously adhered to, will, therefore, be the frame of reference for examining in greater detail the experience of Ghana, Nigeria, Kenya, Tanzania, Ivory Coast and Senegal in Part Three of this book.

Notes

1 D. Morawetz, *Twenty-Five Years of Economic Development, 1950–1975* (Washington DC, 1977), Statistical Appendix, table A1, p. 77.

2 World Bank, *Accelerated Development in Sub-Saharan Africa (AD)* (Washington DC, 1981), Appendix table 2 and table 1.1.

3 *AD* App. 3, 4.

4 *AD* App. 6.

5 *AD* App. 25. It must, however, be said that these pessimistic assumptions are based on very inadequate data and may be misleading. World Bank information relies on reports by individual countries; and of many African states, notably large states such as Nigeria, Zaire, Ethiopia and the Sudan, which greatly influence overall statistics, it has been commented (by Michael Lipton in a confidential paper) that 'crop data, except for commercial export crops with minimal smuggling, are little better than random numbers at national level'. Of Nigeria, E. Rice, in a World Bank report, remarked that there is 'a discrepancy between orthodox trend lines showing mounting food deficits, and what we now believe to be reasonably stable per capita supplies of subsistence crops, implying increased production – at a rate above the rate of growth of farm population [despite] unfavourable price incentives'. Such doubts must be borne in mind when reading my account of the conseqences of government policies, particularly the effects of artificially low state-fixed prices. The fact is that we just do not know for certain how much food is produced and how serious the food situation is.

6 *AD* App. 7.

7 *AD* App. 7, 8.

8 *AD* table 3.4, p. 19.

9 *AD* App. 40, 17.

10 The following section is based mainly on the following: I. M. D. Little, *Economic Development. Theory, Policy and International Relations* (New York, 1982); T. Killick, *Development Economics in Action* (London, 1978) and 'Trends in Development Economics and their Relevance to Africa', *Journal of Modern African Studies (JMAS)*, Vol. 18, no. 3 (1980); R. H. Bates, *Markets and States in Tropical Africa* (Berkeley and Los Angeles, 1981) and *Essays on the Political Economy of Rural Africa* (Cambridge, 1983); D. Rimmer, *The Economies of West Africa* (London, 1984); A. M. Kamarck, *The Economics of African Development* (New York, 1971) and *The Tropics and Economic Development* (Washington DC, 1976); Anne Phillips, 'The Concept of Development', *Review of African Political Economy (RAPE)*, Vol. 8 (1977).

11 For a statement of this see P. Bairoch, 'The Main Trends in National Economic Disparities since the Industrial Revolution', in P. Bairoch and M. Levy-Leboyer (eds), *Disparities in Economic Development since the Industrial Revolution* (London, 1981).

12 R. Nurkse, *Problems of Capital Formation in Underdeveloped Countries* (Oxford, 1953), ch. 1.

13 H. Leibenstein, *Economic Backwardness and Economic Growth* (New York, 1957).

14 *Economic Theory and Under-Developed Regions* (London, 1957).

15 *Stages of Economic Growth* (Cambridge, 1960).

16 *Post-War Economic Growth* (Cambridge, Mass., 1964).

17 T. Scitovsky, 'Two Concepts of External Economies', *Journal of Political Economy* (April 1954).

18 R. Nurkse, *Patterns of Trade and Development* (Stockholm, 1959).

19 See, for example, A. Emmanuel, *Unequal Exchange* (London, 1971); S. Amin, *Unequal Development* (Hassocks, Sussex, 1976).

20 H. W. Singer, 'The Distribution of Gains between Investing and Borrowing Countries', *American Economic Review Papers and Proceedings* (May 1950); R. Prebisch, *The Economic Development of Latin America and its Principal Problems* (New York, 1950).

21 G. Myrdal, *An International Economy* (New York, 1957); *Economic Theory and Under-Developed Regions*; H. Myint, 'An Interpretation of Economic Backwardness', *Oxford Economic Papers* (June 1954).

22 Killick, *Development Economics*, p. 17f.

23 See A. O. Hirschman, *The Strategy of Economic Development* (New Haven, 1958), which followed Prebisch's argument; and Scitovsky, 'Two Concepts'.

24 See, for example, his essay in *The Economic Impact on Under-Developed Societies* (Oxford, 1953).

25 At this time expressed mainly in his *West African Trade* (Cambridge, 1954) and, with B. S. Yamey, *The Economics of Under-Developed Countries* (Cambridge, 1957). Bauer later summed up his views in *Dissent on Development* (Cambridge, Mass., 1973).

26 *Studies in the Theory of International Trade* (New York, 1937).

27 For example, *Economic Growth and Underdeveloped Countries* (London, 1963).

28 'On the Political Economy of Backwardness', *Manchester School of Economic and Social Studies* (January 1952); *The Political Economy of Growth* (New York, 1957).

29 Quoted by Killick, *Development Economics*, p. 34.

30 For a typical and clear statement of this approach, see S. W. Langdon, *Multinational Corporations in the Political Economy of Kenya* (London, 1980).

31 Well summarized in *AD*.

32 The original argument was set out by Hirschman, *Strategy of Economic Development* who followed Prebisch's *The Economic Development of Latin America*. Recent restatements include those by A. Singh, 'Industrialization in Africa: a Structuralist View' and F. Nixson, 'Import-Substituting Industrialization', both in M. Fransman (ed.), *Industry and Accumulation in Africa* (London, 1982).

33 *AD* App. 2, 4; table 4.1; p. 42.

34 *AD* App. 25.

35 *AD* table 5.1.

36 *AD* table 5.3.

37 'The Crisis of the Ghanaian Economy', *JMAS*, Vol. 4 (1966); 'The Abstraction from Politics', *Journal of Development Studies* (April 1969); *The Economies of West Africa*, ch. 7.

38 Rimmer, *The Economies of West Africa*, p. 262.
39 Killick, *Development Economics*.
40 ibid., pp. 228–62.
41 *Markets and States; Essays on the Political Economy of Rural Africa* (Cambridge, 1983), especially ch. 5, 'The Nature and Origins of Agricultural Policies in Africa'.
42 *Organizing the Farmers: Cocoa Politics and National Development in Ghana* (Upsala, 1976); 'Ghana 1951–78', in J. Heyer, P. Roberts and G. Williams (eds), *Rural Development in Tropical Africa* (London, 1981).

4

'Non-Policy' Explanations of Limited Development

There are two main ways of looking at African economic development after independence which do not turn on the effects of African governmental policies and their execution. The first is to see African states in the context of an international economic system which largely decided how well or badly they could perform. The other is to look at factors within African societies which were likely to condition that performance, whatever the international economy was doing and to a great extent irrespective of the actions of African governments. These two approaches will be examined in turn in this chapter. One might, of course, include under this heading the continuing effects of the colonial inheritance; but some of the main features of that inheritance have been summarized above in Chapter 2 and here it will be assumed that all African states started with and had to take account of certain inherited advantages and handicaps. Their later performance must be assessed in relation to where they began.

Africa and the International Economy

The significance of the international economy for Africa can again be approached from two contrasting though overlapping standpoints. The first is that of the 'political economy' or 'dependency' school, the second that of neo-classical economics. It is not proposed to recapitulate 'dependency' arguments in detail: these have been set out by many writers from different standpoints and are too complex to summarize, but a very short résumé of some of their central and relevant assumptions is necessary because they have set the terms on which the current debate is conducted.[1]

Dependency theory essentially states that the development opportunities open to African countries after political independence were constricted by the limited scope allotted to them as 'peripheral' units within the capitalist world system. That system was constructed by western Europe as it expanded its economic and political power from the sixteenth century onwards, culminating in the late-nineteenth- and early twentieth-century colonial occupation of Black Africa. In this system Africa was cast in the role of consumer of Western manufactured exports and supplier of a variety of unmanufactured commodities. Europe's initial advantage lay in superior mobility, technology, capital and political power. To a large extent the new economic relationship was established by 'informal' means, but from the partition of Africa 'formal' colonial rule (colonialism) was used to break down obstacles to total capitalist penetration of the continent. The results, as they stood by the 1950s, were that European firms dominated the import–export trade, European capital controlled large-scale enterprises such as mining, plantations, banking and communications, and only those regions and products that were of value to Europe were developed. For their part Africans were allotted the role of peasant producers of export commodities, for which they received inequitably low monopsonic prices from the trading companies. In the colonial situation there was no place for large-scale indigenous enterprise: expatriates controlled all the heights of the economy.

The outcome was that most colonial economies had common adverse features. They were 'dual economies', in which the modernized 'enclaves' (mines, plantations, a few factories, banking) had few links backward or forward into the indigenous economy. There was very little industry because tariff policies kept doors wide open for imports. Most of the surplus generated locally, which might otherwise have been available for development, was syphoned overseas as profits accruing to foreign capital. As a result, African societies were very ill-equipped to undertake modernization after independence. Levels of education and health were low and life expectancy was short. Communications and public utilities were quite inadequate. Moreover, even within the parameters of commodity export economies, the long-term trend in the terms of trade between primary-producing and industrial countries were adverse from about 1870. W. A. Lewis's calculations (on a world basis, 1913 = 100) show a decline from 111.3 in 1870 to around 95 from 1884 to 1912. Then, after a drop to under 80 during the slump of 1921–2, they hovered around 90 until 1930, dropping to a low point of 65.1 in 1932 and remained in the 70s for most of the rest of the 1930s. In 1950 the ratio was 102.[2]

Many of these things could be ascribed to the effects of colonialism; but dependency theory asserts that, while the transfer of power changed many things, it did not alter the essential dependence of Black Africa (along with most other parts of the Third World) because most internal as well as external constraints remained. Internal factors were critical because these ensured that dependence would remain. Most new states continued to be dominated by feudal or capitalist elites who determined public policy in their own interests rather than those of the masses; and this involved maintaining close ties with the capitalist West. Policies represented their class interest. Unable, given the limitations of their inherited economic and social structures, to accumulate capital sufficiently fast for essential development, the new states borrowed abroad, thus putting themselves at the mercy of international agencies such as the World Bank and IMF. To industrialize quickly they invited or permitted foreign multinationals to establish subsidiaries, which led to foreign ownership and control of much of the expanding modern sector, to intensification of the existing dualism of the economy, and to transfer overseas of much of the profits (the available 'surplus' in Baran's term). Although a new race of African entrepreneurs evolved, helped by new state agencies, few of these were genuine capitalists; rather they were 'auxiliary' capitalists who depended heavily on foreign companies for credit, technology and know-how. Although industry often developed fast, for the most part this was merely substituting for previously imported consumer goods. The capital equipment, most of the intermediate goods and even raw materials were imported, so that there was often negative value added; it would have been cheaper at international prices to import the finished products. Meantime the dominant political groups developed as a new bourgeoisie, accumulating capital on the basis of high salaries, access to patronage and corrupt relations with foreign capital.

Most new African states, therefore, contributed heavily to their own economic problems; but unfavourable external factors made these far worse. Trends in the terms of trade, particularly after the OPEC price increases for petroleum of 1973 and 1979, became generally adverse as a result of a relatively declining demand in the West for tropical raw materials and protectionist obstacles to manufactured exports to industrialized countries. Even the Lomé Conventions, which purported to help African states associated with EEC, in fact merely consolidated the old economic relationship. As a general consequence, and after a short-lived bonanza period, the new states found themselves as dependent as ever on the international system and international capital, becalmed in a sea of debts at low levels of income and growth. From all this the standard deduction is that further development must depend on these states breaking free from international capitalism, adopting socialist solutions and struggling for true 'autonomy'.

The accuracy of this fundamentally pessimistic appraisal is much debated within the 'dependency' school; some who previously accepted it as generally valid are now making substantial reservations.[3] It is not proposed to offer any assessment at this point. It is necessary, however, to look briefly at the implications of the international economy for African states from a conventional, neo-classical standpoint and to ask whether exogenous factors do, in fact, appear to have acted as a serious constraint after independence. Four main points need examination: the terms of trade; availability of overseas markets; the provision of investment, loans and aid by the West; and changing rates of interest and terms of debt repayment.

Terms of Trade

Generally speaking there appears to be no strong case for explaining African economic problems as the result of adverse trends in the terms of trade after 1960, though exceptions have to be made for particular countries and commodities.[4] For sub-Saharan Africa as a whole the net barter terms of trade (1975 = 100) were 108 in 1960, 117 in 1970 and 100 in 1979. The income terms of trade in the same years (taking account of the volume of exports) were 57,114 and 105. Obviously the 1960s were a favourable period, whereas the 1970s, mainly because of the petroleum price increases and the resultant world recession, were bad for all but the oil exporters. Even so, there was no dramatic overall trend in the barter terms of trade and the income terms improved sharply. But if we break down these figures into three types of African economy – oil exporters, mineral exporters and the remaining commodity exporters – strikingly different patterns emerge.

For the oil exporters (Angola, Congo, Nigeria and Gabon) the barter terms of trade between 1960 and 1979 (1975 = 100) improved from 54 to 109 and the income terms of trade from 18 to 183, while for Nigeria, by far the most important of the group, the net barter terms improved from 32 to 119 and the income terms from 13 to 143. By contrast the mineral exporters (Liberia, Mauritania, Niger, Sierra Leone, Togo, Zaire, Zambia) did very well in the 1960s, with an improvement of 6.5 per cent in their barter terms of trade; but these deteriorated by 7.1 per cent in the 1970s and, with declining export volumes, their purchasing power fell by 7.7 per cent. Finally, the majority of African states, as commodity exporters, did reasonably well throughout. Their barter terms of trade improved by an average of 1.0 per cent from 1961 to 1970 and by 2.9 per cent from 1970 to 1979. But, whereas a larger volume of exports increased their purchasing power by an average of 4.9 per cent in the 1960s, a decline in the volume of exports of 2.1 per cent in the 1970s offset the improved barter terms of trade to reduce the rate of increase in the income terms of trade to 1.1 per cent.

Despite these contrasts between types of economy and period, it seems clear that the terms of trade cannot be regarded as a major source of economic weakness for Black Africa as a whole. The worst hit by market fluctuations were the mineral exporters, who built high hopes and contracted heavy overseas obligations on the strength of high prices in the 1960s; for Zambia, Zaire, Mauritania and Liberia in particular this imposed severe limitations on their later development.

Overseas Markets

What, then, of overseas protectionism as a bar to the expansion of export-oriented industries in Africa? There is no doubt that Africa remained very heavily dependent on the markets of the developed countries of the West: in 1969 82 per cent of all sub-Saharan exports were to the West and only 2 per cent to the 'centrally planned economies'. In 1979 the proportions were 78 and 2 per cent.[5] Tariffs, quotas, etc., in the West were, therefore, likely to have a major impact on African production. But how severe were these levels of protection on the three general categories of unprocessed raw materials (including foodstuffs), part-processed commodities and manufactures?

First, raw materials faced zero tariffs in EEC, USA and Japan, except for 1.9 per cent on cotton entering the USA, 55 and 18 per cent respectively on tobacco entering Japan and the USA. There were virtually no quotas limiting these exports to any overseas market. Tariffs on entrance to EEC were, however, significant on some part-processed goods: for example, 2.2 per cent on pig iron, 5.3 per cent on alumina, 5.8 per cent on unwrought aluminium and 3.9 per cent on leather. Such duties imposed a slight deterrent on the processing of commodity exports but were not so large as to inhibit trade. Even on manufactured exports most duties were small: for example, to EEC 10 per cent on cotton fabrics, 13.7 per cent on cotton clothing; and to EEC at least there were no significant quota limitations on the volume of such exports, though there were to some other countries.

There was, however, a latent threat in the Lomé Conventions that EEC might impose quantity restrictions if African exports seriously threatened domestic industries. This may have inhibited some types of investment in export production in Africa and might be significant in the future. But, historically, since most African exports have remained unprocessed or semi-processed commodities, it would be difficult to demonstate that tariffs or quotas have had any significant effect on export performance so far. Conversely, the average preferential margin on imports to EEC from associated countries in Africa – virtually all of Black Africa – is about 16 per cent; and it was estimated in 1974 that a 65 per cent cut in aggregate tariffs and quota restrictions would have increased African exports by only about 1 per cent, or $292m. Indeed, far more important than overseas protection in causing the decline of African overseas earnings was the drop in Africa's share of world trade, which fell from 18 to 9.2 per cent between 1960 and 1978.[6] This had nothing to do with protection, since the African states were generally favoured by the West compared with Asia and

Latin America. It was the consequence of the inability of established African export commodity producers to maintain their volume of exports in an expanding world market.

The Flow of International Resources

Next, there is the question of international financial dealings with Africa. Did the wealthy countries fail to maintain the flow of investment, loans and credit on which many of the assumptions of the development economists and African plans were based? That is, did the West provide the short- and long-term capital, private and public, which would enable the African states to finance the 'big push' to the point at which their accumulation could become self-sustaining? Did rates of interest and the terms of borrowing harden significantly over time, so that the burden of existing debts became intolerable?

In this area there are no certainties. The statistics are highly variable; much depends on definitions; and it is by no means clear what level of foreign transfers might have been necessary to overcome the 'structural' obstacles to growth pinpointed by the economists. But, for what they are worth, the following estimates, mostly from World Bank sources, give some indication of the scale of foreign transfers to sub-Saharan Africa after 1960.

Broadly, transfers took three main forms: direct (equity) investment by foreign private enterprises; long-term loans; and short-term loans or credits, in the last two cases from both public and private agencies. Some idea of the net overall size of these flows is provided by the World Bank's *World Tables* for the years 1965, 1970 and 1977 (see Table 4.1).

Ignoring direct equity investment, which did not constitute foreign debt, another measure of the size of foreign capital flows can be gained from the World Bank's figures for the total outstanding debt of Black Africa in the 1970s.[7] These totals include four main types of loan: bilateral concessional (government to government loans at below commercial rates of interest and repayment); official export credits; concessional and non-concessional multilateral loans from bodies such as IBRD, whose International Development Association (IDA) provided loans at exceptionally favourable rates to poor borrowers; and private loans, both long and short term, some of it backed by public guarantees, some not, and therefore at substantially higher rates of interest. In addition there were substantial grants, mainly from one government to another which, of course, do not show in the totals of outstanding debt. In 1970 the outstanding total of loans of all types ('debt outstanding disbursed' in World Bank terminology which is used in the tables below) stood at $5.7b., of which $3.4b. was from official sources and $2.2b. private. In 1979 the total was $31.8b., of which $17.3b. was public and $14.5b. private. Of total, $12.4b. was at

Table 4.1 *Foreign Capital Flows to Black Africa, 1965–1977 (US$m.)*

	Direct investment	Long-term capital	Short-term loans, etc.
1965	359.2	228.6	74.4
1970	452.6	907.2	339.5
1977	433.7	1911.5	−701.4

Source:

World Bank, *World Tables* (Washington DC, 1980).

'concessional' rates of interest and terms for repayment. Thus in nine years African indebtedness had increased by some $26.1b., or at an average rate of $2.9b. a year.[8]

These global figures have to be related to the realities of African life. How important were such transfers in relation to African incomes, public and private? Taking 1979 as a snapshot year, the World Bank provides the following statistics. The total flow of resources (that is, to offset the deficit on Black Africa's balance of payments) made up of loans, credits and grants of all kinds, amounted to a weighted average of $24.6 per capita, as compared with average per capita incomes of $411, or about 6 per cent.[9] Actual net official aid disbursed that year (i.e. excluding private direct investment and private loans) amounted to $5,940m. or $17.1 per capita. This represented 3.5 per cent of Black Africa's GNP and 20 per cent of gross domestic investment.[10]

These were huge amounts, both relatively and absolutely. Whether they were enough is quite a different question. There were two major constraints on the size of resource flows, one at each end of the system. On the overseas side it was the capacity of investors and governments, given rival claims, to maintain or increase the volume of grants and loans at concessional rates; and the international organizations were perpetually urging governments to increase their aid contribution to at least 1 per cent of GNP. On the African side, unless aid came as an outright grant, the main constraint was ability to service foreign loans. This depended partly on the cost of debt service (payment of interest and repayment of capital), whose severity lay partly out of the control of African governments; this will be discussed in more detail below. But, even if this cost did not increase disproportionately to the size of the foreign debt, ability to meet it depended on Africa's capacity to put borrowed money to good use: that is, increased borrowing should be reflected in increased production.

It is here that a major weakness becomes evident: African production on a per capita basis did not keep pace with either domestic investment or foreign borrowing. The average rate of growth of GNP per capita (since the figure for average production per worker is not available) for the two decades 1960–79 was 1.6 per cent.[11] The median growth rate of gross domestic investment in 1960–70 was 5.7 per cent, and in 1970–79 3.2 per cent.[12] In 1970–79 the trend growth rate of all types of external debt was 22.5 per cent.[13] Meantime, the volume of exports declined by an average of −0.8 per cent a year.[14] These are merely very rough indicators of performance; but they suggest that per capita production did not increase proportionately to domestic investment, still less to foreign borrowing. The probability is, therefore, that a very large proportion of the latter must have been used to finance current consumption (including, of course, the higher costs of foreign debt service and the deficits on the balance of payments which almost every Black African country was running in the 1970s[15]) rather than as capital for productive investment. The World Bank calculated that it would be necessary to double official aid to African countries in the 1980s if any substantial growth was to be achieved;[16] but this implies what may well be an excessively optimistic assessment of the use likely to be made of such aid.

Interest Rates and Debt Repayment

There remains, however, the question of interest rates and the hardening of the terms of borrowing over these two decades. If an African state borrowed heavily to pay for development on certain assumptions about the cost of paying interest and repaying the principal, those assumptions could be made false and the country put into a difficult position if those costs rose substantially as a result of changes in the international economy. How far can exogenous trends of this type be held responsible for the economic problems of Black Africa in the early 1980s?

The essential facts for Black Africa and the developing world as a whole are set out in Tables 4.2–4.7; but the problem is an extremely complex one. Of the increase in debts (expressed in US dollars) there is no doubt. Tables 4.2 and 4.3 show that external public debt of all these countries rose immensely between 1970 and 1982, in some cases by more than ten times. It also shows that for six of these thirteen states the burden of debt service as a proportion of external debt rose substantially. On the other hand for the remaining seven states this ratio changed very little and for them average interest rates also remained virtually constant. This is surprising because, as can be seen from Table 4.4, the average cost of borrowing rose very substantially between 1970 and 1982, though it eased again between 1983 and 1985. Tables 4.5–4.7 also indicate that the ratio between public and private sources of foreign borrowing changed radically in this period. Table 4.5 shows that, whereas in 1970 total outstanding concessional bilateral

Table 4.2 The Burden of Interest and Repayment on External Public Debt for Selected African Countries, 1970 and 1982 (US$m. rounded to nearest million)

Country	A External debt[a] 1970	A External debt[a] 1982	B Debt service[b] 1970	B Debt service[b] 1982	B/A (%) 1970	B/A (%) 1982	C Interest payment on external debt 1970	C Interest payment on external debt 1982	C/A (%) 1970	C/A (%) 1982	B-C/A(%) Repayment Rate 1970	B-C/A(%) Repayment Rate 1982
Mali	238	822	0.7	8	0.3	0.9	n/a	5	n/a	0.6	n/a	0.36
Zaire	311	4,040	36.8	81.2	11.8	2	9	72	2.9	1.8	13.1	0.23
Malawi	122	692	5.9	64.3	4.8	9.2	3	32	2.4	4.6	2.3	4.6
Tanzania	248	1,632	15.7	112.6	6.4	6.9	6	33	2.4	2.0	3.9	4.9
Togo	40	819	2.3	33.7	5.7	4.1	1	22	2.5	2.6	3.2	1.4
Ghana	489	1,116	23.7	65.1	4.8	5.8	12	27	2.4	2.4	2.4	3.4
Kenya	316	2,402	27.4	376.2	8.6	15.6	12	147	3.8	6.1	4.8	9.5
Senegal	98	1,328	6.7	101.9	6.8	7.6	2	64	2.0	4.8	4.8	2.8
Zambia	622	2,381	59	184.3	9.5	7.7	26	88	4.2	3.7	5.3	4.0
Ivory Coast[c]	256	4,537	38.5	996.7	15.0	21.9	11	476	4.3	10.5	10.7	11.5
Nigeria[c]	480	6,085	55.7	1,339.5	11.6	22.0	20	722	4.2	11.8	7.4	10.1
Cameroon	131	1,912	8.6	264.2	6.5	13.8	4	121	3.0	6.3	3.5	7.5
Gabon[c]	91	871	11.3	288.1	12.4	33	3	97	3.3	11.1	9.1	21.9

Notes:
a. External debt = total public and publicly guaranteed debt.
b. Debt service = total interest plus repayments on external debt.
c. Nigeria's ratio of private to public debt in 1982 was $4.9/1.14b., that of Ivory Coast $3.2/1.3b., of Gabon $550/321m.

Source:
World Bank, *Toward Sustained Development in Sub-Saharan Africa* (Washington, 1984), Appendix tables 13, 14.

Table 4.3 *Debt Service as a percentage of GNP and the Export of Goods and Services (EGS) for Selected African and Other Countries, 1970 and 1982*

| | Debt service as a percentage of: | | | |
| | GNP | | EGS | |
Country	1970	1982	1970	1982
Mali	0.2	0.8	1.2	3.5
Zaire	2.1	2.6	4.4	9.1 (1979)
Malawi	2.1	4.5	7.1	22.8
Tanzania	1.2	1.1	4.9	5.1 (1981)
Togo	0.9	4.3	2.9	24.4 (1979)
Ghana	1.1	0.2	5.0	6.8
Kenya	1.8	5.4	5.4	20.3
Senegal	0.8	4.2	2.7	4.2 (1979)
Zambia	3.5	5.1	5.9	17.4
Ivory Coast	2.8	14.9	6.8	36.9
Nigeria	0.6	1.9	4.2	9.5
Cameroon	0.8	3.7	3.1	15.6
Gabon	n/a	10.1	5.5	12.6 (1981)
All Sub-Saharan Africa	1.2	2.7	5.1	12.6
Mexico	2.0	5.5	23.6	29.5
Brazil	0.9	3.5	12.5	42.1
Argentina	2.0	4.4	21.5	24.5
All low-income countries[a]	1.1	1.1	11.3	8.8
All lower middle-income countries[a]	1.6	3.7	9.2	16.8
All upper middle-income countries[a]	1.5	4.4	10.7	16.9

Note:
a. Indicates weighted average for whole world.
Sources:
For Black Africa and all low, lower middle and upper middle-income countries: World Bank, *Toward Sustained Development*, App. 13.
For Latin American Countries: World Bank, *World Development Report, 1984* (Washington DC, 1984), table 16.

Table 4.4 *Average Terms of Borrowing for Sub-Saharan Africa, 1970–1982*

	1970	1971	1972	1973	1974	1975	1976	1977	1978	1979	1980	1981	1982
					Average terms for commitments of public and publicly guaranteed debt								
Total public debt													
Interest rate (per cent)	3.6	4.2	4.4	5.5	5.2	5.6	5.4	5.6	6.6	8.1	7.5	10.5	8.6
Maturity (years)	24.2	22.3	20.5	20.2	19.9	19.9	18.6	18.1	16.5	15.0	18.2	15.5	18.9
Grace period (years)	6.6	6.6	5.8	5.6	6.0	5.2	5.1	4.7	4.7	4.4	4.9	4.3	5.0
Grant element (per cent)	46.1	41.5	37.1	32.0	34.1	30.0	30.3	28.5	23.3	14.6	21.3	4.8	15.2
Total official debt													
Interest rate (per cent)	2.0	3.0	3.1	2.8	3.2	4.1	3.4	4.1	3.8	4.2	3.7	5.1	4.4
Maturity (years)	31.7	27.8	27.7	29.1	25.8	26.4	27.2	24.8	25.0	22.8	25.3	25.3	28.7
Grace period (years)	9.3	8.2	7.8	8.0	7.8	6.7	7.0	6.3	6.5	6.1	6.6	6.1	6.9
Grant element (per cent)	63.9	53.8	52.0	55.4	50.7	43.6	49.6	42.9	44.9	40.2	45.5	36.0	43.5
Bilateral debt													
Interest rate (per cent)	1.3	2.0	2.6	1.8	3.0	3.2	3.3	4.0	4.1	4.8	4.3	4.8	4.4
Maturity (years)	31.3	26.4	23.2	25.6	22.4	23.0	22.5	21.3	22.9	18.2	21.1	20.1	24.8
Grace period (years)	9.7	9.2	7.8	8.1	7.8	6.6	6.7	5.9	6.2	5.4	6.1	5.3	6.4
Grant element (per cent)	69.5	61.0	52.9	60.5	50.3	47.4	47.4	41.1	42.3	32.9	40.0	34.4	41.9
Multilateral debt													
Interest rate (per cent)	4.4	5.0	3.9	4.2	3.7	5.0	3.6	4.2	3.4	3.4	3.1	5.3	4.4
Maturity (years)	33.1	30.4	35.5	34.2	32.7	30.2	33.5	29.4	27.8	28.5	29.6	29.4	32.1
Grace period (years)	7.8	6.5	7.7	7.9	7.8	6.8	7.5	6.7	6.8	6.9	7.0	6.7	7.3
Grant element (per cent)	46.0	39.9	50.4	48.0	51.5	39.4	52.6	45.3	48.6	49.0	51.1	37.3	44.9
Total private debt													
Interest rate (per cent)	6.7	7.3	6.7	8.7	8.7	8.4	7.8	7.8	9.4	11.2	12.6	14.5	12.7
Maturity (years)	10.1	8.5	8.3	9.7	9.5	8.1	8.5	8.6	8.1	8.8	8.5	8.2	9.4
Grace period (years)	1.7	2.4	2.6	2.7	2.9	2.4	2.8	2.6	2.8	3.1	2.7	3.0	3.1
Grant element (per cent)	12.7	10.4	11.9	4.3	4.8	5.5	7.5	8.4	1.7	−5.7	−11.5	−18.8	−12.5

Source: World Bank, *Toward Sustained Development*, App. 17.

Table 4.5 Third World Indebtedness, 1970–1980: Total External Public Debt by Creditor Source, and Private Non-Guaranteed Debt (US$b.)

	1970	1971	1972	1973	1974	1975	1976	1977	1978	1979	1980[a]
Public Debt											
Total concess. bilateral	22.6	27.0	30.1	34.8	40.2	45.5	51.6	59.5	67.5	71.4	78.3
DAC governments	18.0	21.7	24.4	28.0	31.7	34.0	38.0	43.4	49.8	52.0	55.6
OPEC governments	0.4	0.5	0.5	0.8	1.8	4.6	6.3	7.6	8.6	9.8	11.6
CPE governments	3.8	4.5	4.8	5.7	6.1	6.2	6.6	7.6	8.0	8.6	9.9
Other bilateral	0.3	0.3	0.4	0.4	0.6	0.7	0.8	0.9	1.0	1.1	1.3
Total offic. export credits	4.3	4.6	5.3	6.2	8.0	9.4	11.5	13.8	18.3	21.2	23.4
DAC governments	3.9	4.3	4.9	5.7	6.9	7.8	9.2	10.6	14.0	16.6	17.9
OPEC governments	0.0	0.0	0.0	0.1	0.2	0.6	1.0	1.6	2.3	2.6	2.9
CPE governments	0.3	0.1	0.2	0.2	0.3	0.4	0.5	0.5	0.8	0.8	1.1
Other bilateral	0.1	0.1	0.2	0.3	0.5	0.7	0.8	1.0	1.2	1.3	1.5
Total multilateral loans	8.0	9.2	10.8	12.9	15.7	19.3	23.4	29.5	36.4	43.5	51.8
IBRD	4.9	5.6	6.4	7.2	8.3	9.9	11.6	13.4	15.6	18.5	21.9
IDA	1.8	2.1	2.8	3.6	4.5	5.6	6.9	8.0	9.1	10.4	12.1
Regional banks concessional	0.5	0.5	0.6	0.7	0.9	1.0	1.3	1.7	2.3	3.0	3.9
Regional banks non-concessional	0.5	0.7	0.9	1.2	1.6	2.1	2.7	3.4	4.4	5.3	6.4
Other multi-concessional	0.0	0.1	0.1	0.1	0.2	0.3	0.4	1.9	3.6	4.5	5.8
Other multi-non-concessional	0.2	0.2	0.1	0.1	0.2	0.3	0.6	1.1	1.5	1.7	1.7
Total private source loans	17.7	21.2	26.6	35.1	47.2	60.8	80.5	104.9	138.9	169.3	187.3

Suppliers credits	7.0	7.8	9.1	10.1	12.0	13.1	14.6	17.4	21.6	21.5	19.4
Financial markets	9.5	12.3	16.5	23.4	33.5	46.3	64.0	86.0	115.9	146.7	167.2
Financial institutions	6.3	8.7	12.5	18.7	28.4	40.8	57.2	75.4	101.4	131.2	147.9
Bonds	3.2	3.5	4.0	4.7	5.1	5.5	6.8	10.6	14.5	15.5	19.3
Other	1.1	1.1	1.0	1.2	1.7	1.4	2.0	1.6	1.3	1.1	0.7
Total public debt	52.6	62.1	72.8	89.0	111.0	135.0	167.1	207.1	261.1	305.5	340.7
Total private non-guar. debt	11.0	14.2	19.3	25.7	32.2	38.8	45.7	53.4	64.4	73.4	82.5
Total public and private debt	63.5	76.2	92.0	114.8	143.3	173.9	212.9	261.0	325.5	378.8	423.3
of which:											
Total bilateral	26.9	31.7	35.3	41.0	48.1	54.9	63.2	73.3	85.7	92.7	101.7
Total official	34.9	40.9	46.2	54.0	63.8	74.2	86.6	102.8	122.2	136.2	153.5
Total private source	28.6	35.3	45.9	60.8	79.4	99.6	126.3	158.2	203.3	242.6	269.8
Total concessional	24.9	29.8	33.6	39.3	45.8	52.4	60.2	71.1	82.5	89.4	100.1
Total non-concessional	38.6	46.5	58.5	75.5	97.5	121.4	152.6	189.9	243.0	289.4	323.2

Notes:
Figures include all developing countries in the World Development Report (WDR) data base that report to the Debtor Reporting System (DRS) except Iran and Iraq.
DAC: Development Advisory Committee (of the OECD); OPEC: Organization of Oil-Exporting Countries; CPE: centrally planned economy;
IBRD: International Bank for Reconstruction and Development (World Bank); IDA: International Development (of the World Bank).
a. All 1980 data are estimates.
Source: World Bank Staff Working Paper no. 88, *Developments in and Prospects for the External Debt of the Developing Countries: 1970–80 and Beyond* (Washington DC, 1981).

Table 4.6 Growth Rates of Third World Indebtedness, 1970-1980: External Public Debt by Creditor Source, and Private Non-Guaranteed Debt
(annual growth rate, per cent)

	1970	1971	1972	1973	1974	1975	1976	1977	1978	1979	1980[a]	Trend[b] Growth 1970-9
Public Debt												
Total concess. bilateral	14.5	19.7	11.2	15.7	15.4	13.3	13.5	15.3	13.4	5.9	9.7	13.9
DAC governments	15.7	20.5	12.3	15.0	13.0	7.4	11.6	14.3	14.7	4.3	6.9	12.3
OPEC governments	3.1	12.0	5.9	57.0	144.2	150.4	36.2	22.1	13.0	13.4	18.4	53.3
CPE governments	10.7	18.1	6.5	17.0	7.1	1.7	6.9	15.0	6.1	7.0	15.1	8.8
Other bilateral	8.7	1.9	9.1	-5.4	60.8	22.5	14.2	14.2	13.8	7.0	18.2	16.7
Total offic. export credits	15.4	7.5	13.6	18.8	27.5	18.7	22.2	19.3	32.7	16.4	10.4	20.5
DAC governments	17.1	12.1	12.4	17.6	20.2	13.3	18.7	15.2	31.2	18.5	7.8	17.6
OPEC governments	-18.0	-16.2	2.2	122.9	249.4	141.5	80.3	58.9	41.6	12.1	11.5	81.2
CPE governments	-3.5	-56.4	28.2	18.2	79.8	29.1	8.4	16.3	49.9	3.1	37.5	21.6
Other bilateral	26.9	13.0	38.3	33.2	91.2	27.7	22.7	17.1	24.3	8.2	15.4	32.5
Total multilateral loans	12.4	15.2	17.5	19.5	21.5	22.8	21.4	25.9	23.5	19.3	19.1	21.3
IBRD	11.2	12.7	13.9	12.7	16.4	19.1	16.7	15.7	16.2	19.1	18.4	16.0
IDA	10.4	15.1	33.6	28.5	24.7	23.5	23.3	15.8	12.8	15.1	16.3	22.2
Regional banks concessional	23.1	19.5	12.5	23.8	15.5	19.9	24.7	34.3	34.4	28.5	30.0	23.2
Regional banks non-concessional	18.8	30.2	24.6	36.0	34.4	32.1	26.7	27.7	29.5	21.0	20.8	29.8
Other multi-concessional	62.3	24.3	19.1	13.8	136.4	54.2	33.0	361.4	92.0	25.9	28.9	73.0
Other multi-non-concessional	14.2	26.1	-58.7	35.9	61.2	68.2	74.9	87.8	39.2	12.3	0.0	36.9
Total private source loans	27.4	19.9	25.8	31.7	34.6	28.9	32.5	30.2	32.4	21.9	10.6	29.9

Suppliers credits	14.4	11.3	15.9	15.3	15.0	9.4	10.9	19.1	24.5	-0.7	13.9
Financial markets	36.2	29.1	34.7	41.6	43.0	38.2	38.2	34.3	34.8	26.5	37.0
Financial institutions	31.8	38.2	43.1	49.6	51.6	43.9	39.9	31.9	34.5	29.4	41.4
Bonds	45.6	11.0	13.9	16.7	8.5	6.9	24.9	55.0	37.4	6.3	20.0
Other	51.8	-4.7	-4.9	16.0	41.1	-18.7	46.6	-21.5	-14.1	-14.3	3.2
Total public debt	18.2	18.1	17.3	22.4	24.7	21.6	23.8	24.2	25.7	17.0	22.3
Total private non-guar. debt	—	29.2	36.0	33.5	25.3	20.4	17.8	16.7	20.7	13.9	23.4
Total public and private debt of which	—	20.0	20.7	24.7	24.8	21.4	22.4	22.6	24.7	16.4	22.5
Total bilateral	14.6	17.7	11.5	16.2	17.2	14.2	15.0	16.0	17.0	8.1	15.1
Total official	14.1	17.1	12.9	17.0	18.3	16.3	16.6	18.7	18.9	11.4	16.7
Total private source	106.5	23.4	29.9	32.5	30.6	25.5	26.7	25.3	28.5	19.4	27.5
Total concessional	14.4	19.3	12.8	16.9	16.5	14.6	14.9	18.1	15.9	8.4	15.5
Total non-concessional	70.4	20.4	25.8	29.2	29.1	24.6	25.7	24.4	28.0	19.1	25.9

Notes:
Figures include all developing countries in the World Development Report (WDR) data base that report to the Debtor Reporting System (DRS) except Iran and Iraq.
a. All 1980 data are estimates.
b. Growth rates estimated by least-squares regression analysis.
Source: World Bank Staff Working Paper no. 488.

Table 4.7 Sources of Third World External Debts, 1970–1980: External Public Debt by Creditor Source, and Private Non-Guaranteed Debt (shares of total debt, per cent)

	1970	1971	1972	1973	1974	1975	1976	1977	1978	1979	1980[a]
Public Debt											
Total concess. bilateral	35.6	35.5	32.7	30.3	28.0	26.2	24.2	22.8	20.7	18.9	18.5
DAC governments	28.4	28.5	26.5	24.4	22.1	19.6	17.8	16.6	15.3	13.7	13.1
OPEC governments	0.6	0.6	0.5	0.7	1.3	2.6	2.9	2.9	2.7	2.6	2.7
CPE governments	6.0	5.9	5.2	4.9	4.2	3.5	3.1	2.9	2.5	2.3	2.3
Other bilateral	0.5	0.5	0.4	0.3	0.4	0.4	0.4	0.4	0.3	0.3	0.3
Total official export credits	6.8	6.1	5.7	5.4	5.6	5.4	5.4	5.3	5.6	5.6	5.5
DAC governments	6.1	5.7	5.3	5.0	4.8	4.5	4.3	4.1	4.3	4.4	4.2
OPEC governments	0.1	0.0	0.0	0.1	0.2	0.3	0.5	0.6	0.7	0.7	0.7
CPE governments	0.4	0.2	0.2	0.2	0.2	0.2	0.2	0.2	0.2	0.2	0.3
Other bilateral	0.2	0.2	0.2	0.2	0.4	0.4	0.4	0.4	0.4	0.3	0.4
Total multilateral loans	12.6	12.1	11.8	11.3	11.0	11.1	11.0	11.3	11.2	11.5	12.2
IBRD	7.8	7.3	6.9	6.2	5.8	5.7	5.4	5.1	4.8	4.9	5.2
IDA	2.9	2.8	3.1	3.2	3.2	3.2	3.3	3.1	2.8	2.8	2.9
Regional banks concessional	0.7	0.7	0.7	0.7	0.6	0.6	0.6	0.7	0.7	0.8	0.9
Regional banks non-concessional	0.8	0.9	0.9	1.0	1.1	1.2	1.3	1.3	1.4	1.4	1.5
Other multi-concessional	0.1	0.1	0.1	0.1	0.1	0.2	0.2	0.7	1.1	1.2	1.4
Other multi-non-concessional	0.3	0.3	0.1	0.1	0.1	0.2	0.3	0.4	0.5	0.4	0.4
Total private source loans	27.8	27.8	28.9	30.5	32.9	35.0	37.8	40.2	42.7	44.7	44.2

Suppliers credits	11.0	10.3	9.8	9.1	8.4	7.6	6.8	6.7	6.6	5.7	4.6
Financial markets	15.0	16.1	18.0	20.4	23.4	26.6	30.1	32.9	35.6	38.7	39.5
Financial institutions	10.0	11.5	13.6	16.3	19.8	23.5	26.8	28.9	31.1	34.6	34.9
Bonds	5.0	4.7	4.4	4.1	3.6	3.1	3.2	4.1	4.5	4.1	4.6
Other	1.8	1.4	1.1	1.0	1.2	0.8	0.9	0.6	0.4	0.3	0.2
Total public debt	82.7	81.4	79.1	77.6	77.5	77.7	78.5	79.6	80.2	80.6	80.5
Total private non-guar. debt	17.3	18.6	20.9	22.4	22.5	22.3	21.5	20.4	19.8	19.4	19.5
Total public and private debt	100.0	100.0	100.0	100.0	100.0	100.0	100.0	100.0	100.0	100.0	100.0
of which:											
Total bilateral	42.3	41.6	38.4	35.8	33.6	31.6	29.7	28.1	26.3	24.5	24.0
Total official	54.9	53.6	50.1	47.0	44.6	42.7	40.7	39.4	37.5	35.9	36.3
Total private source	45.1	46.4	49.9	53.0	55.4	57.3	59.3	50.6	62.5	64.1	63.7
Total concessional	39.3	39.1	36.5	34.2	32.0	30.2	28.3	27.3	25.3	23.6	23.6
Total non-concessional	60.7	60.9	63.5	65.8	68.0	69.8	71.7	72.7	74.7	76.4	76.4

Notes:
Figures include all developing countries in the World Development Report (WDR) data base that report to the Debtor Reporting System (DRS) except Iran and Iraq.
a. All 1980 data are estimates.
Source: World Bank Staff Working Paper no. 488.

official loans were greater than private source loans, by 1973 the latter were larger and by 1980 were more than twice as large: private source loans were by then 44.2 per cent of the total, concessional bilateral loans only 18.5 per cent. Table 4.6 shows that the trend growth rates of these two sources of capital were 29.9 per cent for private and 13.9 per cent for bilateral loans. Also in 1971 there was an increase in the rate of growth of private non-guaranteed lending (that is, whose capital and interest were not guaranteed by the lending or borrowing state). The growth rate of this most expensive type of borrowing was greatest in 1972, though as a proportion of total debt its peak came in 1974.

We are, then, faced with at least three main questions. Why did the developing countries switch from official to private sources of loans in the early 1970s? Why did interest rates, particularly on private loans, rise so sharply in the late 1970s? Finally, why were some African states much worse affected by hardening borrowing conditions than others?

First, the switch to private borrowing had a number of causes. The amount of money available on official concessionary terms was limited. Many Third World countries wanted or needed more than they could get from official sources to finance development programmes or, increasingly, to meet budget deficits and had to go where money was available. For their part the commercial banks of the West had to handle a huge flow of oil profits deposited by the oil-exporting countries. To match the liabilities represented by these deposits, they sought actively to lend on a major scale; and in carrying out this intermediary role, they have been accused by some of enticing unwary customers into borrowing more than they could afford.

But it is also significant that this new flow of private borrowing coincided with a relative decline in the flow of foreign direct investment to the Third World. The *IMF Survey* of 18 March 1985, based on the Fund's Occasional Paper no. 33, asked the question 'why the upsurge in private capital flows . . . comprised mostly debt-creating flows rather than foreign direct or portfolio equity investment and whether . . . equity capital could have been substituted for the bank credits if different policies had been adopted by capital-exporting and capital-importing countries'. Reviewing past trends, the reports showed that the net flow of foreign direct investment increased about five times from their 1960 level between 1974 and 1982, but that external borrowing, particularly from commercial banks, increased more than tenfold between 1974 and 1982, so that FDI fell from some 50 per cent to *c.*25 per cent of total private capital flows. Given that this trend was reversed between 1981 and 1983, when new foreign direct investment fell by only 29 per cent in the recession compared with 72 per cent, the questions are why its relative importance had declined so sharply in the 1970s and what effect this had on the debt problems of Third World countries.

Reasons for declining rates of foreign direct investment vary from one country to another, but there were some very common explanations. Many governments excluded foreign capital altogether from extractive industries. Many proposed industrial ventures were regarded as non-viable by multinationals. Conversely, foreign direct investment is essentially 'project oriented', whereas Africans normally wanted untied foreign exchange. Much of the capital used by multinationals to establish new ventures in Third World countries consisted of reinvested local profits or locally raised loans, and so made a minimal impact on balance of payments problems. Foreign direct investment did nothing to meet budget deficits or balance private capital outflows. Many states fixed a maximum level of foreign participation in the equity of old and new enterprises, resulting in substantial compulsory disinvestment by foreign owners. Foreigners were excluded from certain areas of production. Restrictions on transfers of dividends and capital deterred some MNCs.

Whatever the reasons, the shift by Third World states from using foreign firms to found and fund new enterprises to establishing state or parastatal enterprises using commercial credit significantly increased their debt problems. The cost of servicing FDI varied with the health of the host economy, so that during a depression foreign transfers were likely to be reduced. States could, in any case, restrict or postpone such transfers. Debt service on other forms of borrowing was inflexible, unless rescheduled, and this imposed a heavy burden on foreign currency earnings during depressions such as those of the 1970s and early 1980s. The IMF found that in twenty-eight developing countries which had to reschedule part of their external debts in 1983, foreign direct investment accounted, on average, for only 14 per cent of their total external liabilities. By contrast, in the forty-nine reporting states which did not have to reschedule debts that year, foreign direct investment represented on average 24 per cent of their external liabilities.

Why, in the second place, did interest rates and the terms of debt repayment harden so markedly late in the 1970s, with such evidently disastrous effects on many Black African countries? The process began in 1973, when interest rates began to rise steadily, but the position deteriorated sharply in 1979–81, which proved the peak. During the earlier years interest rates rose because of international inflationary tendencies; but they did not rise as fast as the rate of inflation in the West or in most African states because there were so many petro-dollars to lend. Furthermore, imports of capital goods from developed countries could be financed on extremely attractive terms, subsidized as they were by the governments of the exporting countries. And as banks competed for international lending assets, their margins (the spread between their cost of funds and the interest they received) were cut and the period of credit offered lengthened. Those Third World countries which imported capital goods and exported commodities therefore enjoyed a boom time.

From 1979, however, this picture changed. A dramatic rise in international interest rates, coming after the second oil price increase, fed through to a seriously high level of real interest rates. Secondly, the subsidization of officially supported interest rates for capital goods export credits was gradually reduced. Finally, banks began to reduce the list of countries to whom they were prepared to lend and also to harden the terms of those loans they did make. So, although (according to the *IMF Survey* of 18 March 1985) the average loan rate from private lenders dropped from 14.3 per cent in 1981 to 10.9 per cent in 1983, reducing the absolute cost of borrowing from private sources by African countries in nominal terms, this was misleading. In fact the simultaneous restriction of access to bank loans and shortening of the periods over which loans were made increased the borrowers' debt service burdens in real terms.

The answer to the third question, why some African states were much worse hit by these international trends than others, must depend on the peculiar mix of their foreign debts. Those with more or less consistently low rates of debt service and low interest payments were, on the whole, those which had borrowed mainly from official or multilateral sources, especially if these debts were contracted before about 1973, when interest rates were low and terms of repayment lenient. Conversely, those states with very heavy debt service burdens had a relatively large proportion of debts to private lenders and had incurred much of their debt when terms were hardest. Another variable was the proportion between different types of loan. From an African standpoint, long-term fixed interest loans, especially if contracted before about 1973, were very favourable, whereas both short-term and variable interest loans left them vulnerable to hardening terms. Thus, of those worst affected, Kenya's private debt rose tenfold from 1970 to 1979, while her official debts rose only fourfold. Ivory Coast's private debt rose from $112m. to $3,193.4m. between 1970 and 1980; that of Nigeria, despite (or perhaps because of) its oil revenues, from $96.2m. to $4,940.7m.; that of Cameroon from $11.6m. to $601m., of Gabon from $24.4m. to $549.9m. By contrast, although Zaire's private debt increased sixfold in this period, its official debt increased twenty-eight-fold, from $95.3m. to $2,750m., most of it on the most favourable concessionary terms. Ironically Ghana, the first really flagrant foreign borrower in Black Africa, had a comparatively modest debt service ratio in 1982 and its average rate of interest was unchanged between 1970 and 1982 at a modest 2.4 per cent.

It must, however, be emphasized that these apparent advantages were relative, not absolute. Limited commercial borrowing was often due to inability to obtain new commercial bank loans; real interest rates rose as the dollar appreciated; and the real debt service burden increased as conditions of repayment hardened. In fact there can be no doubt that increased interest rates in the late 1970s had a serious economic effect on all Black African countries.

The blame cannot, however, be laid entirely on the international economy. The size of the new borrowing was to a large extent the responsibility of African states. Their inability to balance budgets or to maintain a positive balance of payments, their excessive enthusiasm for unproductive forms of public investment and their preference for using fixed-interest loans to pay for new industrial and other enterprises instead of relying on foreign direct investment were all 'policy' factors which contributed to their problems. Before 1970 and for much of that decade most African states got good value from foreign loans. It was only between 1979 and 1981 that the problem became a crisis, with the coincidence of a slump in world commodity prices and a sharp rise in the cost of new private borrowing.

Indeed, the most serious aspect of foreign borrowing was the burden of debt service in relation to the balance of payments and the growth of national income. Table 4.2 shows this problem at its worst by contrasting the position in 1970 with that in 1982. The problem was the combined effect of higher interest payments, a greatly increased public debt and reduced export prices, though it was compounded for some states by a reduced volume of exports which often reflected domestic discouragement of commodity production. The worst year proved to be 1982, when the debt service ratio for all developing countries peaked at 24.4 per cent of exports of goods and services; in 1983 the proportion was down to 22.1, in 1984 to perhaps 21.5 per cent on IMF calculations. This, however, remained very serious. African states were partly responsible for the burden of their indebtedness, but there is no doubt that those which did not export oil had suffered severely from the general rise in international lending rates.

Taking a broad view, it would not, however, seem possible to blame limitations in African development simply on adverse external factors. In some respects the dependence of African economies on the international economy was certainly very high. African states continued to be extremely vulnerable to movements in commodity prices. They relied very heavily on foreign capital and know-how. However much they wanted autonomy and socialism, almost all found it necessary to collaborate with multinationals, which in turn involved substantial transfers of profits as well as foreign capitalist penetration of the economy and society. Their nascent industries, whether or not controlled by foreign firms, used imported capital and intermediate goods very extensively, and this made them vulnerable to the pricing policies of their suppliers and the international market. In short, Africa could develop fast only if international conditions were reasonably favourable.

The essential point, however, is that, for much of the period to the mid-1970s, international conditions were more favourable to African development than, perhaps, ever before. Despite fluctuations, there was no long-run adverse trend in the terms of trade and some export commodities experienced periods of exceptionally high prices. The flow of foreign resources from about 1950 was unprecedented and showed no tendency to dry up. Western governments were anxious to help, both for economic self-interest and increasingly for political reasons, to prevent communist penetration. Private enterprises, attracted by the many new incentives offered by new states in their hurry to industrialize, were more active than during the colonial period, although conditions became adverse in many ways: compulsory dilution of the equity and partnership with indigenous interests, limited transfers of capital and dividends, complex licensing controls on imports, obligatory use of local management, increasingly heavy corporate taxation and the multiple frustrations resulting from inadequate infrastructure, unreliable flows of both imported and locally produced inputs, and political instability. The contrast with the pre-1939 period was total, mirrored in any comparison between post-1950 figures for official and private investment with those calculated by S. H. Frankel for the 1930s.[17]

Thus, even if the international environment was in no sense optimal for Africa, it is difficult to believe that external conditions were likely to be more favourable in any foreseeable future, or that they were so adverse in the decades after independence that they determined Africa's destiny. It is precisely because this has been recognized that analysts from most sectors of the ideological spectrum have increasingly turned to look for the sources of limited development in the internal conditions of African states; and in this we must now follow their example.

Endogenous African Influences on Development

Both of the generalized explanations of limited African development considered so far place the blame on man-made errors – the wilfulness of African rulers or the deficiencies of the international economy. But there is a third approach which tends to play down both these factors, while not denying their potential significance. This takes a rather more deterministic attitude to the whole question of African – and indeed, Third World – economic and social developments, saying in effect that one should rather be surprised that so much growth and development have taken place, given the immense obstacles in their path. At that very general point this approach loses its unity; thereafter any analyst can construct his own list of dragons in the path of Third World development. It is proposed here only to point to three possible, but potentially major, general problems that have been emphasized by one or more recent writers: the generally adverse geo-physical environment; exceptional drought conditions during the two decades after 1960; and African attitudes to economic development.

The Adverse Geo-Physical Environment

The clearest recent restatement of an argument which is as old as European penetration of Africa, but which tended to be overlaid by the universalist enthusiasm of the development economists, is that most parts of sub-Saharan Africa constitute a peculiarly hostile environment for economic growth.[18] Andrew Kamarck points out that all the world's really poor countries lie in the tropics, Black Africa among them. There is no necessary reason why this should be so, but the implication is that tropical conditions may make it much harder to carry out successfully some aspects of economic development which were relatively easy in the areas where 'modern' development originated, the temperate regions. This has nothing to do with the 'racial' characteristics of the inhabitants: Europeans have failed very badly in many tropical ventures. It derives rather from a number of inherent climatic or physical features which may be difficult, expensive or even impossible to overcome.

Kamarck lists and discusses five main problems. First, rainfall: in the tropics there tends to be either too much or too little. Too much results in the proliferation of pests, blights and diseases which are never killed off by frosts that do this outside the tropics; too little results in low yields, soil erosion and starvation. Moreover, since rainfall in many regions is highly variable, continuous agricultural development is very difficult and to offset this by means of water storage or irrigation is very expensive. The economic significance of drought in the period 1960–80 is discussed at greater length below.

Then there are problems with soils. Heat and variable rainfall easily result in erosion and the deterioration of once fertile soil into laterite, which is hard to work, has low yields and leads to protein deficiency. Given such soils, Africa cannot afford the luxury of intensive and recurrent monoculture common in other parts of the world, even with large use of fertilizer.

Thirdly, agriculture faces a wide range of special dangers resulting from climatic conditions: rapidly growing weeds, insects, locusts, trypanosomiasis (carried by the tsetse fly), and so on. These pests can be controlled, but only at high cost in agricultural research and in the probably unpopular administrative means needed to eradicate them in cattle, etc.

Fourthly, Africa, despite the image of a continent rich in gold, diamonds and uranium, is in fact relatively badly off for minerals. Few African countries have had the good luck to be floated into development by gold-strikes, or their equivalent in diamonds, petroleum, etc. Moreover, laterite soils make mineral prospecting difficult. Even where large mineral deposits are found, it may happen (as in Zambia and Zaire) that the costs of transport to the ocean are higher than for most international competitors; and the demand for minerals tends to fluctuate widely on the world market.

Finally there are the basic health hazards of the tropics. They may no longer necessarily be a grave for white or black men, but great heat reduces efficiency; diseases are endemic; and, although the main diseases such as bilharzia, malaria, river blindness, parasitic worms and leprosy can all be countered, the economic cost (which includes pure water supplies and adequate sewerage) is extremely high and must eat into any country's limited development budget. Since very little has so far been done to counter these health problems, the general effect is a debilitated work-force whose capacity for sustained hard work is in many areas substantially lower than that of their equivalents in temperate countries.

Kamarck in effect suggests that the initial cost in capital and human effort needed to overcome these special problems and get a Black African economy on to an upward spiral is much higher than most planners have assumed. It is, therefore, unreasonable to expect that a given quantity of capital and labour will provide anything like the same 'push' against the assumed structural obstacles to development that the same inputs might give elsewhere. Hence one should tend to be impressed by how much has been achieved in the post-1945 era rather than disappointed that it was not greater.

Drought during the Period 1960–80

It is possible to argue that among the endemic obstacles to sustained development in Black Africa the droughts which have affected certain regions, and above all the Sahel, have had far greater economic significance in the two decades after independence than at most other times. Indeed, some have suggested that drought was the most important single factor checking development. Of the fact of these droughts there is no doubt; the problem is to decide how relatively important they were in the context of longer-term trends and in relation to the policies adopted by African governments both before and after independence.[19]

Each zone of Africa has had different periods of serious drought, which can be defined as a significant reduction in rainfall below the long-term mean for a particular area. For the Savanna–Sahel regions of

West Africa there was prolonged drought from the mid-1960s to 1973, with a climax in 1972–3, when the worst-hit areas had only about 50 per cent of average rainfall.[20] In the northern states of Nigeria, where groundnuts were the staple crop, official production dropped from 765,000 tons in 1968/9 to 250,000 tons in 1971/2 and 25,000 tons in 1972/3. In Kano alone the loss in 1973 was estimated at 115,000 tons, valued at naira (N)6m.[21] In East Africa there were comparable disasters during the same decade, continuing in the north-east to the mid-1980s.

The main impact, however, fell on food-grain production and livestock rather than on cash crops. Thus in Senegal the groundnut crop actually increased: in 1973 (the peak year of that period of drought) it rose from 449,000 tons in 1972 to 650,000 tons, largely at the expense of food grains such as millet and rice. This resulted in a very large increase in food-grain imports. In Mali, where some 40 per cent of cattle died and 40 per cent of food production was lost in 1972, groundnut and cotton production was barely affected. In Nigeria food production suffered as well as cash crops. Despite the government's 'Feed the Nation' project of the 1970s, 15 per cent of food-grain consumption had to be imported by 1977/9, representing 17 per cent of the cost of all Nigerian imports.[22]

These, however, are merely random indications of the impact of drought in particular areas; its specific effects varied very greatly. The significant question is how such short-run crises should be related to long-term trends in agriculture and to the effects of government policies. Was the drought itself the consequence of the dangerous extension of agriculture and pastoralism which had the effect of increasing the size of the desert? Should drought be seen as a major reason for the slowing up of economic development or as a marginal factor which merely underlined the frailty of African agricultural systems and the weakness or unwisdom of governmental attempts to deal with them?

On these questions there seems to be a growing consensus. One view of the crises of the early 1970s in West Africa is that these were merely the culmination of a short-run cycle of weather variation from 1962 to 1973, caused by a peculiar conjunction of air masses, which was in no sense the outcome of human interference with the ecosystem. Its effects were patchy: they were restricted to the Savanna–Sahel and did not have significant long-term implications. The 1974 rains put things back to normal.[23] The dominant view, indeed, appears to be that variations in rainfall in the tropics are always a threat. What converted this period of drought into a major crisis, which may have had a significant effect on economic development in the areas affected, was that these societies were already too near the margin of safety, particularly in food production, and that the responsibility, therefore, lies partly with governments which failed to take appropriate precautionary measures.

For this view there is considerable support. Earl Scott, for example, in a general survey of 'Life and Poverty in the Savanna–Sahel Zone',[24] argues that a general agricultural deterioration had set in long before the drought period, especially in food-grain production. With high per capita grain consumption, rapidly rising population, low grain yields per hectare and generally small proportions of total available land under cultivation, consumption was already pressing hard on available supplies of food before the droughts began. In some cases the dependence on imported food grains was caused by over-commitment to cash-crop production for export, most acutely in Senegal and The Gambia. Thus it required only a relatively small reduction in rainfall to create a famine. He concludes that neither the drought of 1968–74, nor the 'encroaching desert' caused the current level of impoverishment in these zones. Current problems were

> the result of a process involving the imposition of a European, extractive economy, the rapid growth in both the cattle and human population, the increasing sedentization of the Fulani nomads, and the establishment of a system of low wage labor, burdensome taxes, and forced labor, which limited or took away entirely the ability of West Africans to obtain food. Over time Savanna–Sahelians lost entitlement to food, specifically through an inability to produce it and to purchase it. This means that the Savanna–Sahelians are the victims of famine, not drought.[25]

This last point is a matter of opinion, reflecting conventional distrust of cash-crop production as a potential means of buying food more cheaply than it could have been produced at home; the same position has been adopted, among others, by Samir Amin. Yet Scott himself argues against Nigerian production of wheat on the ground that it could be imported at about half the price; and Keith Hart makes the point that, 'This argument would be more convincing if it could explain the crass neglect of their own interests exhibited by the peasants themselves in this instance. Why do they use their groundnut sales to buy trinkets, when more food would save them from starvation?'[26]

Scott's argument does, however, support the now widespread assumption that the droughts of the 1960s and early 1970s should be seen as contributory rather than prime causes of the growing shortage of food in Black Africa, and this is borne out by the World Bank's 1984 survey of African economic conditions, *Toward Sustained Development in Sub-Saharan Africa*. This shows that per capita food production in the twenty-four African countries affected by drought during the period 1970–83 had a downward trend of some 2 per cent a year. Actual production deviated slightly above or below the trend line in different years. The trend line passed below the 140 kilograms a year regarded as the minimum necessary for good health in 1975 and was only 135 kilograms in the good year of 1981. Although this is an average figure and individual countries were much more badly affected in particular years, the implication is clearly that, overall, drought had only a marginal effect. Indeed, the same is true for all Black African countries, whose per capita food production has been falling steadily below the 1960–5 average except in the late 1960s.[27]

A tentative conclusion may, therefore, be that the droughts of the 1960s and 1970s were not unique, nor were they a prime cause of decelerating economic development in Black Africa. Their effects were obviously considerable in those Sahelian states in which agriculture was at all times at risk and which had large populations of nomads dependent on marginal grazing. In most other West, Central and East African states, however, drought did not affect all parts of a country or for long periods. It might create short-run food shortages and threaten development projects for a year or two as funds allocated to them had to be to be used to pay for imported food; but it is difficult to see how it can be treated in isolation as a major cause of economic weakness. Ultimately it must be seen as one of the many problems endemic to many parts of Africa, of which the rulers of states have to take account in planning economic policies and which has been made more acute by the policies followed both by post-independence governments and the colonial governments which preceded them.

African Attitudes to Economic Development

A third explanation of limited economic growth has been found in what one can broadly describe as the adverse effects of certain features of Black African society and its attitudes to 'modernization'. Again, there is a long and, at root, racist European tradition that Black Africans were work-shy (high leisure preference, the backward-bending labour supply curve, etc.), dishonest, lacking in the instincts essential to both entrepreneurs and proletarian workers. Such prejudices have been largely discredited; yet, in a non-racist form it is still useful to consider the effects of specifically African cultural and social traditions and the extent to which Africans have absorbed Western education, technology, etc., in relation to the needs of the sort of 'modern' economy most African states have attempted to build. To put it another way, are African 'human resources' well or not so well suited to the development process?

There are, of course, as many answers to these questions as there are writers; but few would now assert African 'human resources' are unequivocally favourable. Kamarck, for example, draws up an interesting balance sheet.[28] On the credit side, Africans have exceptionally few hang-ups: they are peculiarly open to new ideas and to innovation. African society is relatively class-less and has no castes. Africans are basically hedonistic and increasingly acquisitive, and so anxious to work to obtain wants. They are mobile, ready to move to towns and adapt to urban industrial conditions. Most have keen commercial instincts. On the other side of the coin, the so-called extended family, in whatever form, may act as an obstacle to accumulation by its more enterprising members and also imposes the need to provide patronage, so that 'corruption' and favouritism by the successful is expected. Work attitudes may be 'tradition-directed' towards collective rather than individual enterprises and male attitudes to the position and role of women are adverse. From the colonial period Africans have inherited the expectation that the highest-paid posts will be in the public service and that a sufficiency of such jobs for the educated must be a first charge on the economy.

Obviously no precise balance sheet of such plus and minus factors can be drawn up. Most writers on the theme of economic development have tended to concentrate on the qualifications and capacities of Africans as entrepreneurs; and most have emphasized a typical combination of enterprise and enthusiasm with very limited relevant skills or even instincts. The World Bank, for example, in a chapter headed 'Basic Constraints', has a section on 'Underdeveloped Human Resources' as an obstacle to growth. It emphasizes the shortage of adequately trained people to fill senior posts in government, the professions and industry, which it attributes partly to inadequate educational facilities during the colonial period, partly to racist prejudice which inhibited the promotion of blacks in almost all parts of the modern sector.[29] Whatever the causes, most writers seem to agree that contemporary Africans still suffer from a number of handicaps which limit their effectiveness as administrators and large-scale capitalists. Schatz, in his study of Nigerian capitalists,[30] lists some of their limitations. Although there are hundreds of thousands with strong business instincts and ambitions, they find it very difficult to make the vital 'leap' from a small-scale family concern to the next stage, which requires a variety of non-traditional skills. Above all, they expect too much feather-bedding by the government. He calls this 'nurture capitalism'. Though possibly exaggerated, financial irresponsibility is widespread. Schatz concludes that 'Nigerian businessmen are less capable of making the leap than their advanced-economy counterparts. There is an entrepreneurial gap.'[31]

Kilby painted a similar picture of Nigerian businessmen of the 1960s, especially in the small-scale industrial sector from which large-scale indigenous enterprise must be expected to grow to replace foreign firms.[32] The evidence might suggest that the major weakness was lack of education; but Kilby concluded that this was relatively unimportant compared with what he describes as

> traditional socio-cultural factors common to all of Nigeria's ethnic groups. The personality characteristics which these socio-cultural factors tend to produce are manifest in the realm of economic activities not only among entrepreneurs, but among supervisors, civil servants, Nigerian managers in the public sector, etc.[33]

He goes on to analyse the roots of such attitudes, and finds them in the technology of subsistence agriculture,

> which was both simple and static; with every contingency anticipated in accumulated customary practices, technical talents were seldom called upon. Concomitantly a division of labour extending no further than age and sex required only a minimum of organization and supervision. While Yoruba and Ibo patterns of status mobility based on achieved wealth provide a strong incentive to establish a business enterprise as a means of obtaining high social status, once established there are no antecedent roles conferring respect for efficient managerial performance. On the contrary, because conspicuous leisure is the principal manifestation of superior status, the carrying out of supervisory functions (concern with the task performance of subordinates) represents a socially degrading activity.
>
> Because of the universality of organizational requirements in modern economic activities, the overcoming of entrepreneurial deficiencies is likely to occur as a part of a general transformation of traditional social structure which sees changes in the efficiency of human performance in a wide range of productive roles. While economic forces will play an important part in this process, developments in political institutions and ideology, in bureaucratic administration, in education, and in technology will in aggregate probably exert a greater influence. This is but an important instance of the homely truism that economic development involves far more than mere economic change.[34]

Such propositions are not capable of proof, but they appear to be supported by the evidence of all Black African societies. Moreover, they lead on to another variant of the same theme, the concept of 'the uncaptured peasantry', which has been defined and elaborated by Goran Hyden, using mostly Tanzanian evidence, but which appears to be supported by evidence drawn from most other African states.

Hyden's basic idea is, of course, very old: Marx in many of his writings emphasized that the pre-capitalist mode of agricultural production was not progressive because peasants cannot or will not accumulate beyond the level of primitive accumulation. Only by being subordinated to a feudal regime could their surplus value be siphoned off and ultimately made available for capitalist accumulation. Hyden adapts this approach to the African rural producer.[35] His argument, in brief, is that in many parts of Africa the transition from 'primitive cultivation' to 'peasant cultivation', in which the peasant produces partly for the market while remaining primarily a subsistence farmer and retaining control of his own means of production, is still incomplete. Even when it is complete, the peasant mode of production retains essential features of its pre-market history. Its primary aim is family survival. It is 'resource-based', in that its basis is traditional know-how in relation to a given environment. This Hyden calls 'the economy of affection', whose basic motivation is support of family and kin or community. It is concerned with problems of reproduction not production. In fact, it is potentially static unless family and other needs increase.

Hyden holds that this pattern, not capitalism or the machinations of international capital, is the real reason for limited African development. By contrast with many other underdeveloped regions there has been no growth in per capita food production in Africa since 1945 because most peasants find inadequate incentives to increase productivity. Peasants often remain resistant to money incentives to start or expand production for the market, the problem to which colonial governments commonly responded by compulsory production of cash crops. State attempts to stimulate increased productivity by the example of modern state farms or larger capitalist farms or the creation of village settlements have had remarkably little effect because most peasants do not accept that the state has any moral claim to control their pattern of life. Moreover, while most peasants welcome the 'modern' benefits the state can provide (education, water, electricity, roads, etc.), they regard these as luxuries and are not prepared to sacrifice their autonomy to buy them.

To support these generalizations Hyden surveys the various attempts made by the Tanzanian government since independence to stimulate greater agricultural production and extract more surplus for government purposes. These will by examined in Chapter 6. All met with the same negative peasant response. It is true that 'villagization', coupled with good rains, resulted in a substantial increase in food production in 1976–8, but this involved no technical advance and reflected only peasant efforts to counter inflated consumer goods prices, the attraction of higher product prices and the desire for security of food supplies in the new environment. The peasants retained much of their autonomy and could still 'deceive' the petty-bourgeois party agents and bureaucrats who administered the new village system.

But it was not only the rural peasant who remained unreconstructed.

Hyden argues that the same attitudes pervaded the urban environment as peasants brought in their conceptual baggage with them. In 1971 Nyerere attempted to socialize urban enterprises, mostly state-owned, by his so-called *Mwongozo* policy – essentially greater worker participation, though in fact intended to increase TANU control at the expense of the new managerial class. He hoped that greater involvement would increase productivity. In fact it led to endless demands for better conditions and to labour troubles which reflected pre-capitalist preoccupation with family needs rather than the good of the enterprise or the state. Such attitudes permeated all levels of the bureaucracy as well as industry; and Hyden concludes that Tanzania was 'stuck with a bureaucracy . . . that will pose a limit to any productivity gains as long as the pre-capitalist forces are capable of holding capitalist and socialist penetration at bay'.[36]

Hyden clearly admires the capacity of the African peasant to hold to his values and his autonomy; yet he recognizes that, because the peasant is not progressive and cannot produce a sufficient surplus for building a modern socialist economy and society, his independence must somehow be overcome. How this can best be done remains obscure. African socialists cannot, like their Western counterparts, use the work ethic forced on to European peasants by feudalism and capitalism, and now deeply ingrained; it does not exist in Black Africa, except in a very few urban or mining communities. The use of political cadres is unlikely to be effective without the use of force. Peasants may be persuaded to produce more if the state provides more reliable services to back up higher production and treats the peasant as a consumer, tickling his wants. But ultimately force will be necessary. 'Whether the modernizer is capitalist or socialist his task is to impose his *nature artificielle*; to capture everybody in social relations that negate the values of which the peasant mode is the only guarantor. As long as peasants in Africa are able to enjoy the power of small, it can never be beautiful to its rulers.'[37] There can be few clearer statements of the view that the peasant mode of production has been and remains perhaps the main obstacle to accelerated development in Africa.

The evidence and argument of this chapter do not make possible any firm conclusions about how relatively influential 'non-policy' factors were in Black African economic development after independence. They do, however, suggest one broad and obvious inference which can be tested in the case studies of individual countries in Part Three and will be reviewed in the concluding chapter. This is that, whatever policies the new African states chose to adopt, there was no possibility of a quick or easy road to affluence through development. This is evident whether one looks at their situation from a worldwide or domestic standpoint.

International conditions in these two decades were neither uniformly favourable nor unfavourable to Africa; but over time they undoubtedly deteriorated. The 1960s were in most respects (though not for all countries, depending on their mix of commodity exports) a continuation of the prosperous 1950s, and it was then that many states committed themselves to ambitious programmes of development which were contingent on continuing high commodity prices and relatively low costs of foreign borrowing. The turning-point was 1973. The great increase in oil prices then engineered by OPEC had adverse effects on all non-oil-exporting African states. Dearer oil put a severe strain on their balance of payments. World Bank estimates suggest that, for a sample of eight oil importing states, the cost of oil rose from 4.4 per cent of their export earnings before 1973 to 12.5 per cent in 1978 and 23 per cent in 1980. In that year Tanzania's oil-import bill cost 60 per cent of export earnings.[38] The effect was to force states to reduce imports of many essentials and to raise domestic costs and prices. Agriculture was affected by higher fuel and fertilizer costs and by shortages of these and equipment. Industry was similarly affected, many factories operating at low levels for lack of inputs. Inflationary tendencies were increased. Externally the ensuing international depressions of the later 1970s and early 1980s reduced the demand and therefore the price of most commodity exports and greatly increased the cost and burden of foreign borrowing as Western states adopted dear money policies to counter their own inflation. This in turn had very serious consequences for the African balance of payments.

Adverse international trends in the decade after 1973 were thus bound to check the rate of growth of all Black African countries other than the oil exporters; and even these suffered from over-enthusiastic borrowing on the strength of inflated oil revenues, only to find the price of oil declining and the cost of debt service increasing by the early 1980s. Other countries, of course, were badly affected by many of these trends; but African economies were worse affected than those of more developed countries simply because they were in the throes of structural change and exceedingly vulnerable to major fluctuations in the economic environment.

These international trends did not make continued African growth and development impossible, but they certainly made it harder and slower than in the previous two decades. More specifically, increasingly difficult conditions highlighted defects in the development policies adopted by those states which had gambled on perpetually calm seas and were unable to trim their sails in rough weather. For all of them it became essential to review and if necessary change the whole range of policies; and it was inability to do this, rather than the state of the world economy in itself, that created many of the critical problems of the mid-1980s.

Yet, even if the unprecedentedly favourable world conditions of the 1950s and 1960s had continued indefinitely, development, in the sense of sustained growth combined with social and economic restructuring, was at all times bound to be more difficult in tropical Africa than in many other parts of the world. Some of the obvious obstacles have been mentioned above, but there were many others. That they existed should have caused no surprise, since Europeans had been pointing to them from the early days of Western penetration. The really surprising fact was that, in their eagerness to blame colonialism for lagging African development, the early nationalists, backed by some development economists, tended to minimize their importance, proclaiming that, after independence, a sufficiency of good planning and capital investment could eliminate endogenous handicaps. That this could be done was right; the mistake was to think that it could be done cheaply or quickly. It was difficult in the mid-1980s to find grounds for thinking that any African state had made significant headway in neutralizing the adverse features of endogenous African conditions.

Notes

1 Some main examples are listed above in Chapter 1, n. 5. A comment on the relevance of such theories to modern Africa was made in my essay 'Decolonization, Development and Dependence: a Survey of Changing Attitudes', in P. Gifford and W. R. Louis (eds), *The Transfer of Power in Africa. Decolonization, 1940–1960* (New Haven and London, 1982).

2 W. A. Lewis, 'World Production, Prices and Trade, 1870–1960', *The Manchester School of Economics and Social Studies*, vol. 20 (1952), table II, pp. 117–18. These assumptions have, of course, been challenged and effectively refuted by Paul Bairoch in *The Economic Development of the Third World Since 1900* (London, 1975), pp. 112–34. Bairoch points to two main flaws in Lewis's calculations and arguments, which were similar to those previously produced by the League of Nations and the United Nations. First, the price indices of 'world' exports, which showed a substantial price increase, were in fact only those of Britain. If the USA and industrialized Europe are included, the real prices of manufactured exports between 1872 and 1928 were virtually static. Secondly, the prices of raw materials exported from the Third World were calculated on import prices to final markets c.i.f., thus including transport and other costs. But since transport costs fell very considerably during this period, the f.o.b. price may not in fact have dropped and the producer price may actually have risen. Bairoch concludes that, even though precise calculation is impossible, it is likely that 'the terms of trade for primary products improved by between 10 and 25 per cent instead of worsening by about 20 per cent' during the period 1872–1928 (p. 115).

3 On the seminal Kenyan case, see especially N. Swainson, 'State and

Economy in Post-Colonial Kenya, 1963–78', *Canadian Journal of African Studies (CJAS)*, vol. 12, no. 3 (1978) and 'The Rise of a National Bourgeoisie in Kenya', *RAPE*, vol. 8 (1977); Colin Leys, 'Accumulation, Class Formation and Dependency in Kenya', in M. Fransman (ed.), *Industry and Accumulation in Africa* (London, 1982); B. Beckman, 'Imperialism and Capitalist Transformation: A Critique of a Kenyan Debate', *RAPE*, vol. 19 (1980).

4   The following statistics are taken from World Bank, *Accelerated Development in Sub-Saharan Africa (AD)* (Washington DC), table 3.2 and App. 13.

5   *AD* App. 12.

6   *AD* table 3.4.

7   *AD* App. 19.

8   *AD* App. 21.

9   *AD* App. 1, 22.

10 *AD* App. 22.

11 *AD* App. 1.

12 *AD* App. 4.

13 World Bank Staff Working Paper no. 488, table 1.b, reproduced here as Table 4.6.

14 *AD* App. 7.

15 *AD* App. 17.

16 *AD* p. 122.

17 S. H. Frankel, *Capital Investment in Africa* (London, 1938).

18 Based mainly on A. M. Kamarck, *The Economics of African Development* (New York, 1971) and *The Tropics and Economic Development* (Washington DC, 1976). See also S. H. Frankel, *The Economic Impact on Under-Developed Societies* (Oxford, 1953).

19 There is now a large and expanding literature on drought in tropical Africa and elsewhere, some of which is referred to here. The main problem, however, is to related information on variations on rainfall and suggested explanations for this to economic development. The following analysis draws heavily on the following: J. Derrick, 'The Great West African Drought, 1972–74', *African Affairs*, vol. 76, no. 305 (October 1977), pp. 537–86; D. Dalby and R. J. H. Church (eds), *Drought in Africa* (London, 1973) and D. Dalby, R. J. H. Church and F. Bezzaz (eds), *Drought in Africa II* (London, 1977), both of which consist of specialized papers on different aspects of the drought; E. Scott (ed.), *Life Before the Drought* (Boston, 1984), which consists of eight essays on different aspects of drought and its effects on the Savanna–Sahel zone. There is a very sensible short comment on the subject by K. Hart, *The Political Economy of West African Agriculture* (Cambridge, 1982), pp. 126–7. See also R. F. Hopkins, 'Food, Agricultural Policies and Famine: Implications for African International Relations', in R. E. Bissell and M. S. Radu (eds), *Africa in the Post-Decolonization Era* (New Brunswick, US and London, 1984), pp. 59–81.

20 Derrick, p. 546.

21 Dalby, *et al.*, *Drought in Africa II*, p. 121, table 14.1.

22 Derrick, pp. 555–7; Scott, p. 12.

23 Dalby *et al.*, *Drought in Africa II*, pp. 121–7.
24 Scott, 'Life and Poverty in the Savanna–Sahel Zone', in Scott (ed.), *Life Before the Drought*.
25 ibid., pp. 13–16. See also table 1.1, pp. 14–15.
26 Hart, p. 27.
27 World Bank, *Toward Sustained Development*, pp. 13–15 and figs 1.1 and 1.2.
28 In *The Economics of African Development*, ch. 3.
29 *AD* ch. 2.
30 In *Nigerian Capitalism* (Berkeley and Los Angeles, 1977), ch. 5.
31 Schatz, *Nigerian Capitalism*, p. 90.
32 In *Industrialization in an Open Economy* (Cambridge, 1969), ch. 11.
33 Kilby, *Industrialization*, p. 341.
34 ibid., pp. 341–2.
35 In *Beyond Ujamaa in Tanzania* (London, 1980).
36 ibid., p. 176.
37 ibid., p. 234.
38 These were Ethiopia, Ghana, Kenya, Madagascar, Senegal, Sudan, Tanzania and The Gambia. Quoted (without reference) in Overseas Development Institute, *Briefing Paper* no. 2 (London, September 1982), p. 4.

PART THREE

The 'Policy' Explanation in Six African States

5

Anglophone West Africa: Ghana and Nigeria

Ghana

The Ghanaian case is probably the most heavily documented of any Black African state. This is because Ghana was the first to become independent and to adopt a highly structured centralized economic system, and also because Ghana can be presented as a model of the disastrous consequences of such a system. It is obviously central to the present study; but because so much information and interpretation are readily available, this account can be made brief.

The State and the Economy

First, the state's role in the economy. By comparison with other African states, the Ghanaian state's share of total consumption was not particularly large either at the beginning or at the end of the two decades after 1960: 10 per cent in 1960, 9 per cent in 1979.[1] But during the critical 1960s, when the modern Ghanaian economy was created, the state's share rose from 10 per cent in 1958/9 to 15 per cent in 1964/5, with an annual growth rate of 10 per cent, and was still 15 per cent in 1968/9 before declining in the next decade as a result of reformist policies.[2] On the other hand, public employment as a percentage of all 'formal' (that is, paid) employment in the early 1970s was higher than that of any other large African country in the World Bank's list: in 1972 it was 73.9 per cent of those in formal employment, who in turn constituted 10.1 per cent of the working-age population.[3] Here indeed was that largely urban mass of state employees with a vested interest in maintaining high levels of taxation of other groups to maintain their position which Rimmer and others have seen as the root of African government strategies.

This massive expansion of the public sector was coupled with the imposition of the apparatus of a centrally managed economy. The exchange rate was held firm until 1967, after Nkrumah's fall, despite domestic inflation. The result, taken together with the effects of taxation, was to reduce the index of the effective exchange rate from 100 in 1960 to 63 by 1966: that is, it greatly lowered the real price of imports. Conversely, the same factors reduced the effective exchange rate for exports from 100 in 1960 to 33 in 1965, thus providing an immense disincentive to export.[4] Nkrumah attempted to offset these factors by rigid licensing of imports and internal price controls; but, although these probably reduced the size of the adverse balance of payments, they failed to eliminate it, partly due to over-optimistic estimates of export receipts when calculating the total of licences to be issued.[5] Nor were price controls any more effective. Killick estimated that in 1970 the control price was being observed in only 17 per cent of the cases studied, and there was much evasion and a shift to the black market.[6]

The effect of these and other factors, including the decline in world cocoa prices between 1960 and 1966, was seriously to erode Ghana's living standards. Between 1960 (index = 100) and 1966 the real value of the minimum wage, on which many public wages were based, declined to 56; that of monthly earnings in the private sector to 81 and industrial earnings to 75. The incomes of cocoa farmers dropped to 34. Significantly, the terms of trade of food producers improved from 100 to 132 in the same period, as they benefited from shortages and in-elasticity of demand.[7] Ghana's income distribution was at all times more equal than that of most low-income countries, but the effect of these government policies was a marked deterioration: in 1956 the lower 50 per cent of income receivers took 33 per cent of national income, by 1968 only 26 per cent. But the most significant fact was the virtual stagnation of the GNP: at constant (1960) prices it was cedis (₵) 946m. in 1960 and ₵923m. in 1966.[8] Given a rate of population increase of 2.6 per cent, per capita GNP dropped from ₵140.6 in 1960 to ₵115.3 in 1967.[9] Meantime, despite Nkrumah's aim of high savings and rates of investment, gross domestic savings dropped from 19 per cent of GDP in 1959 to 8.3 per cent in 1967, net national capital formation from 14 to 1.9 per cent of net national product and net national savings from 14 to −5.6 per cent of net national product in the same years.[10] It is not surprising that Killick should write that 'By the standards of other low-income countries, the performance of Ghana's economy was appalling'.[11]

Industry and Manufacturing

If we turn to the industrial record, some of the reasons for this disaster become clear. Nkrumah was, of course, committed to rapid indus-trialization, both for what then seemed sound economic reasons[12] and, more importantly, because he believed that industrialization was necessary for making Ghana a truly independent nation. In pursuit of these intrinsically admirable aims, he ignored most of the constraints implicit in a limited local market – shortages of skill, capital and entrepreneurial experience and Ghana's lack of many industrial raw materials – and provided all the stimuli for public and private manufacturing investment that the state could contrive. The irony is that in this he was rejecting the advice of W. A. Lewis, whom he himself had commissioned when he first achieved political power in 1952 to make a report – published in 1953 as an official blue book, *Report on Industrialization and the Gold Coast* (Accra, 1953). Lewis's report was lucid, cautious and also predictive. His main concluding paragraphs were as follows:

252. Measures to increase the manufacture of commodities for the home market deserve support, but are not of number one priority. A small programme is justified, but a major programme in this sphere should wait until the country is better prepared to carry it. The main obstacle is the fact that agricultural productivity per man is stagnant. This has three effects. First, the market for manufactures is small, and is not expanding year by year, except to the extent of population growth; consequently it would take large subsidies to make possible the employment of a large number of people in manufacturing. Secondly, it is not possible to get ever larger savings out of the farmers, year by year, to finance industrialisation, without at the same time reducing their standard of living; hence industrialisation has to depend on foreign capital, and large amounts of capital for this purpose could be attracted only on unfavourable terms. And thirdly, agriculture, because it is stagnant, does not release labour year by year; there is a shortage of labour in the Gold Coast which rapid industrialisation would aggravate.

253. Number one priority is therefore a concentrated attack on the system of growing food in the Gold Coast, so as to set in motion an ever-increasing productivity. This is the way to provide the market, the capital, and the labour for industrialisation.

254. Priority number two is to improve the public services. To do this will reduce the cost of manufacturing in the Gold Coast, and will thus automatically attract new industries, without the government having to offer special favours.

255. Very many years will have elapsed before it becomes economical for the government to transfer any large part of its resources towards industrialisation and away from the more urgent priorities of agricultural productivity and the public services. Meanwhile, it should support such industrialisation as can be established without large or continuing subsidies, and whose

proprietors are willing to train and employ Africans in senior posts. Because industrialisation is a cumulative process (the more industries you have already, the more new industries you attract) it takes time to lay the foundations of industrialisation, and it would be wrong to postpone the establishment of any industry which could flourish after a short teething period . . .

Until 1961 such advice was generally heeded; thereafter it was not. With the dismissal in 1960 of Komla Gbedemah, the minister of finance, who had fought hard and successfully against demands by both Ghanaians and foreign firms for tariff increases, favours, and so on, the dogs were off the leash. I have been unable to find useful statistics for the amount of manufacturing investment in Ghana in the 1960s and 1970s, nor for the growth of industrial production. Rimmer puts manufacturing at 10 per cent of GDP in 1960 but has no figure for 1979;[13] but in a separate table he gives the manufacturing percentage of GDP for 1977 as 10.8 per cent, which gives the impression that there had been no sustained sectoral shift into manufacturing.[14] Yet the growth of industrial capacity in the 1960s was undoubtedly rapid. W. F. Steel calculated in 1970 that 78 per cent of his sample of Ghanaian industries came into production during that decade; and Killick estimated that 'of the 43 import items having a value of ₵1m. or more in 1960, only 11 were then also being produced in Ghana in significant quantities: by 1970 . . . 33 of these same items were locally produced, most of the remainder being machinery and transport equipment'.[15] Between 1960 and 1969 the ratio of imported consumer goods to private consumption of these goods dropped from 32.2 to 21.3 per cent.[16]

This implies a very large degree of import substitution. Moreover, the Ghanaian share of the ownership of manufacturing, measured by output, rose substantially. The percentage attributable to firms under total Ghanaian ownership, private and public, rose from 24.8 to 29.2 per cent from 1962 to 1966 and of mixed Ghanaian/foreign firms from 11.9 to 21.4 per cent. Meantime total foreign ownership declined from 63.2 to 48.3 per cent. By 1970, while totally owned Ghanaian production was down to 21.6 per cent, foreign-owned was also down to 40.8 per cent. The major increases lay in state ownership (from 11.8 per cent of Ghanaian ownership in 1962 to 15.6 per cent in 1970), and in joint state/foreign firms, from 7.1 to 17.3 per cent; and also in joint private Ghanaian/foreign firms, which rose from 4.8 to 20.9 per cent in the same period. It is, nevertheless, significant that, if one adds the total of partially and completely foreign-controlled production, it was 75.1 per cent in 1962 and 78.4 per cent in 1970; that is, foreign capital had actually increased its share in production, even though part of its ownership had been diluted by obligatory or tactical partnerships with the Ghanaian state and individuals.[17]

There may have been some benefits from this expansion, but there can be no doubt that, in terms of the efficient use of national resources, Nkrumah's strategy was a disaster. Since most industry could operate only behind high protective walls, much of it was 'inefficient' in the sense that it did not save foreign exchange. Steel calculated that in 1967–8 only 13.5 per cent of total manufacturing output was an efficient saver of foreign exchange at the official exchange rate of ₵1.02 = $1.00, though this was greatly over-valued. A further 19.2 per cent of output was efficient at exchange rates between ₵1.02 and ₵1.53 (allowing for a 50 per cent devaluation), while 43.3 per cent was inefficient at above ₵1.53 and 24 per cent would be inefficient at any conceivable exchange rate.[18] This inefficiency was due partly to the high cost of importing capital and other goods, partly to the low utilization of productive capacity, which itself was caused by a variety of factors: excessive installed capacity in relation to the market, due often to the minimum size of modern capital-intensive equipment; shortage of inputs due to licensing restrictions, shortage of foreign exchange, etc.; and sheer inefficiency in maintaining plant and operating it. For 1967–8 it was estimated that Ghana was using only 34.8 of manufacturing capacity, as compared with levels of utilization between 62.3 and 73.8 per cent in a range of semi-industrialized countries – Argentina, India, West Pakistan and Taiwan – in the mid-1960s.[19]

Industrialization, moreover, did not make any substantial contribution to the rest of the Ghanaian economy; indeed, as the scale of manufacturing grew, these linkages weakened. Killick estimates that between 1960 and 1968 purchases from other sectors of the local economy as a percentage of total material inputs declined from 65 to 46 per cent.[20] Nor did manufacturing create much employment. While the 'industrial' labour force increased from 14 to 20 per cent of the labour force from 1960 to 1979,[21] and the urban population from 23 to 36 of total population,[22] in 1970 only 1.6 per cent of the total labour force was in 'large-scale' manufacturing, which nevertheless contributed some 10 per cent of GDP.[23]

Within the general area of manufacturing, moreover, state-owned industry, the main beneficiary of Nkrumah's policies, was notably less efficient than private. In 1964/5 state industrial enterprises made an overall accounting loss of ₵1.5m., in 1969/70 of ₵9.6m.[24] A better measure of profitability in state monopolistic concerns setting their own price levels was, however, the value added per worker; and this was always much lower than in joint or private enterprises. In 1965/6, for example, value added per worker in private industries averaged ₵1,775; in joint state/private firms, ₵4,415; in state enterprises ₵690. Total wages and salaries as a percentage of total value added in that year were 23.4, 13.5 and 46.1 per cent respectively.[25] The obvious conclusions are that most state enterprises were unprofitable by any domestic or foreign criterion (though there was some improvement after 1966, with the wages/value added ratio down to 30.6 per cent in 1969/70); and also that joint state/private enterprises, mostly involving foreign firms as managers, were significantly more efficient than private Ghanaian firms. In short, foreign participation was an essential element in relative efficiency and Nkrumah's aim of industrial autonomy was not within sight. Much of the manufacturing project was, in fact, in Killick's words, 'a high-cost way of providing what were, in effect, unemployment benefits'.[26]

In one respect, however, the industrialization strategy had some success. As has been seen above, it is a much-debated issue whether, under conditions of artificially created import-substitution industrialization, a genuine class of indigenous capitalists can emerge. For Ghana Paul Kennedy has argued that a genuine capitalist class in manufacturing did indeed evolve after the 1950s. Basing his study on a survey of 126 manufacturing firms, 25 building contractors and 35 traders with permanent shops in 1968–70, he found that most had been in some sort of business before going into manufacturing and had had some capital: about 50 per cent had £100 or less, 25 per cent between £100 and £500. Most aimed at accumulation and expansion, even if many failed. Success was related to education or business training, especially with foreign firms, though most lacked these advantages. Accumulation and expansion were helped by factors such as 'lucky breaks' (e.g. government contracts or contacts or help from foreign firms) but these were not essential. Before 1970 government provision of capital to small firms was very limited, since Nkrumah feared the growth of an independent capitalist class; and it was only in 1970 that Busia's government restricted certain sectors of the economy to native Ghanaians and in 1976 that the Investment Policy decrees compelled foreign enterprises to take Ghanaian partners. Thus Kennedy decided that 'In only a few cases does politics appear to have been a crucial variable that made all the difference between success and failure'. Nor was the link with foreign capital very important, except in terms of business training and example. Foreign investment was seen as a danger or rival by most Ghanaian businessmen, few of them depended on current joint ventures, and few acted as 'front men' for foreign firms. Kennedy concludes that Ghana possessed a genuine indigenous manufacturing bourgeoisie which might grow if it could develop export markets.[27]

Agriculture

This may have been some compensation for Ghana's immense losses under the policy of industrialization. What of agriculture? Here we are dealing with three main sectors: the export commodity producers, mainly cocoa farmers; the state farms; and peasant food producers. The first two can only be described as disaster areas after 1960, while the third prospered up to a point. The question is how far these failures and successes were the result of public policy.

Too much has been written about the fate of Ghanaian cocoa for more than a short summary to be necessary.[28] Cocoa production dropped from a peak of 560,000 tons in 1965 to 249,000 tons in 1979; and Ghana's share of world production shrank from about a third to a sixth in the same period.[29] Although world prices for cocoa dropped in the mid-1960s, this had little direct effect on cocoa production, since the state cocoa marketing board stood between producers and international market. As has been seen, it was deliberate state policy to milk the cocoa farmers as the main source of domestically generated government revenues and public investment. This was done in two ways: by widening the existing margin between the f.o.b. export price and the price paid to producers; and by manipulating exchange rates so as further to reduce farmers' incomes. The results speak for themselves. The index of real producer prices and the index of real value of total payments to cocoa producers both fell from 100 in 1960 to 37 in 1965. The former stood at 64 in 1970, the latter at 60. Meantime, government payments to cocoa farmers as a percentage of total export receipts for cocoa fell from 72 in 1960 to 41 in 1965 and were 37 in 1970: significantly a large margin of state profit existed even before the new economic policy of the 1960s. To make matters worse, the real value of budgeted government expenditure on the industry fell from 100 in 1960 to 16 in 1962, then slowly increased to 41 in 1970. The index of quantity of insecticide sales to cocoa farmers fell from 100 in 1960 to 2 in 1965, but had risen to 118 in 1970.[30] Given such hostile discrimination, cocoa farmers reacted by not planting new trees, selling cocoa illegally across the borders, where prices were much higher, or going in for food production on the side. Seldom has official policy been so evidently successful in partially strangling an economically golden goose.

Equally disastrous was the essay in large-scale state farming in the 1960s, which Nkrumah saw as a means of applying modern methods to an otherwise unprogressive peasant industry. Between 1962 and 1966 these farms received c.90 per cent of the total agricultural development budget and a large injection of equipment, seeds and fertilizer.[31] The total spent in the years 1963–5 alone was ₵19.8m. in subsidies, concentrated on some 19,845 ha (by 1970). The yield in 1970 was a mere 0.5 tons/ha, compared with 2.32 tons/ha on peasant holdings; and labour productivity was 0.59 tons per worker as compared with 3.33 tons.[32] Large private farms, mostly in the northern savannah, which were favoured by later governments for the same reasons as state farms, did little better, though these were the beneficiaries of post-Nkrumah regimes. In 1975/6, 75 per cent of imported fertilizers and almost all improved seeds went to these farms, though they constituted less than 23 per cent of agricultural holdings and produced less than 20 per cent of total Ghanaian agricultural output. In 1974, 56.3 per cent of credit provided by the Agricultural Development Bank went to 3.5 per cent of farmers, who were allowed to borrow at low rates of repayment; and there was clear evidence tht political contacts were a significant factor here.[33] Clearly the state's preference for the big in agriculture survived Nkrumah.

State help to agriculture thus changed its character with the regime of the moment, from state farms (most of which eventually decayed or ceased to operate) to a few relatively rich farmers. Either way this use of resources was largely futile in relation to food production. Such mechanized farming, in fact, made a very small contribution to Ghana's food needs. This fact was shown by increasing imports of food aid in the 1970s, reaching a peak of 88,700 tons (8.1 kg a head) in 1978, which reflected a negative annual rate of growth of production of -3.1 a head from 1969–71 to 1977–9.[34] Significantly the only relatively bright spot in this story was the response of peasant food producers to increasing demand. Denied any significant help, since the state did little to provide improved irrigation or transport and the extension services were so heavily politicized as to be virtually useless, and discouraged by low official buying prices for staple foods, the peasants nevertheless found their own way of responding to market forces. It has been seen that, despite government price controls, food prices rose faster than the general price index and that the terms of trade for food farmers also improved steadily. Food production became very much more attractive than cocoa farming: the index of their respective terms of trade rose from 100 to 388 between 1960 and 1966.[35] Peasants responded in many ways: by diversifying cocoa production and food crops, using additional land and making more intensive use of their family (especially female) labour: the growth rate of female agricultural labour from 1960 to 1970 was 2.9 per cent a year, as against 0.4 per cent for men.

This was, in Hyden's terms, one 'exit' for the peasant from the constraints of a state-managed economy: he produced a bit more food and sold it if possible on the unofficial market, thus offsetting the price of what he bought. Yet it is important not to overstate the case. Peasant food production, with so many handicaps, could not keep up with the growth of population, which averaged 3.0 per cent in the 1970s.[36] From 1969–71 to 1977–9 alone the index of per capita food production dropped from 100 to 82;[37] and, with food aid imports included, the World Bank calculated that in 1977 the daily supply of calories per capita was only 86 per cent of total requirements.[38] If the conservative view is correct, a sufficient price incentive should result in increased production to meet the needs of the market. Ghanaian peasant farmers received virtually no state help in this period, so it is difficult to guess how much better their performance might have been with more fertilizer, better infrastructure, a really efficient extension service, and so on. Yet the suspicion remains that the basket of factors which limited the production of Hyden's 'uncaptured peasants' in Tanzania and made them inadequate as the basis for national accumulation, operated in much the same way in Ghana. The food-producing peasantry survived Nkrumahism better than the cocoa farmers, but they could not and did not offer an alternative route to national affluence.

Public Debt

Yet perhaps the most striking and symbolic feature of the Nkrumah period from 1957 to 1966 was the staggering increase in the public debt and the burden of debt service which accompanied it. The main facts are set out in Tables 5.1–5.3.

It was seen in Chapter 2 that on the eve of independence, in 1955, Ghana's total public debt, domestic and foreign, was only £22.1m. In 1959 it was still only £24.9m., of which £8.6m. was external debt, including £7.2m. in commercial suppliers' credits. That marked the end of the conservative public borrowing characteristic of the colonial era. In the next five years Nkrumah went on an incredible borrowing spree; the results are shown in Table 5.1. In the five years 1959–64 he increased Ghana's total debts by £301.2m. and in addition used up £129.2m. of foreign reserves – a total of £430.4m. During this period for the first time suppliers' credits became a main source of development capital, rising from £13.8m. to £156.9m. between 1960 and 1964. Much of this was done by the President rather than through the normal government machinery; and the *Report of the Auditor General on the Accounts of Ghana for the Financial Year ended 30 June 1961* (Accra, 1962) commented (pp. 10–11) that in that year the government had for the first time entered into twenty-two credit agreements with foreign firms and governments for supplies and credits totalling £33.6m., with interest increased from 2.5 to 6.25 per cent. 'In many instances the Auditor-General's office have not been able to obtain sight of the agreements nor has it been possible to obtain satisfaction that goods have been received and work carried out in accordance with the agreements.'

That clearly marked the end of conservative public financial management; for Ghana, decolonization meant, among other things, unbridled foreign borrowing. The result, made worse by the temporary drop in cocoa export prices in the mid-1960s, was virtual bankruptcy

Table 5.1   Ghana's Public Debt, 1959–1964 (£m.)

	1959	1960	1961	1962[a]	1963	1964
Total debt of which:	24.9	55.6	82.7	153.4	267.3	326.1
domestic	16.8	38.6	44.0	80.7	133.1	142.2
foreign	8.1	17.0	38.7	72.7	134.2	183.9
suppliers' credits	7.2	13.8	28.4	60.8	117.3	156.9
Revenue	67.0	70.2	83.3	97.2	84.6	122.6
Liquidity	180.4	161.6	79.5	81.6	50.8	51.2

Note:
a. For 15 months ending September 1962.
Source:
UN Statistical Yearbook 1965 (New York, 1966), tables 187, 192.

Table 5.2   Ghana's External Debt and Debt Service, 1967–1982 (US$m.)

	A Total outstanding	B Debt service	C Export of goods and services	B/C (%)	A/C (%)
1967	526.6	22.4	311.4	7.2	169.1
1970	489.4	23.7	472.4	5.0	103.6
1973	703.7	23.7	647.0	3.6	108.7
1977	785.0	37.2	1,017.8	3.6	77.1
1979	986.9	54.6	1,186.8	4.6 [4.2]	83.1
1982	1,115.6	65.1	964.1	6.8	115.7

Sources:
1967: World bank, World Tables (Washington DC, 1976), p. 318
1970–77: World Bank, World Tables (Washington DC, 1980), p. 298
1979, Columns A and B: World Bank, Accelerated Development in Sub-Saharan Africa (Washington DC, 1981), Appendix tables 17, 18
1982, Columns A and B: World Bank, Toward Sustained Development in Sub-Saharan Africa (Washington DC, 1984), table 14.
1979 and 1982, column C: IMF, International Financial Statistics Yearbook (New York, 1984). For 1979 the ratio B/C is slightly different from that given by Accelerated Development, which does not give the figure for EGS on which it must be based.

Table 5.3   *The Relationship between Ghana's External Public Debt and GDP, 1960–1979 (US$m.)*

	A External public Debt	B GDP	A/B (%)
1960	40.8	1,216.2	3.3
1962	174.5	1,380.8	12.6
1964	441.4	1,437.7	30.7
1967	526.6	1,474.2	35.7
1970	489.3	2,213.4	22.1
1975	672.1	5,018.3	13.4
1977	785.0	14,327.0	5.5
1979	986.9	10,160.0	9.7

Sources:
1960–4: UN, *Statistical Yearbook 1965*, table 192.
1967–77: World Bank, *World Tables* (Washington DC, 1976 and 1980).
1979: World Bank, *Accelerated Development*, Appendix tables 3, 18.

from which the country had not fully recovered by the mid-1980s. Successive regimes after Nkrumah had virtually to stop foreign borrowing and to cut imports to the bone to service this debt. Table 5.2 indicates the main trends from 1967 to 1982. The rate of new borrowing was effectively checked after 1966 and, with higher export prices, the burden of external debt service could gradually be got under control, at least until the crisis of 1979–82 forced Ghana to increase foreign borrowing at very much higher rates of interest. Meantime Ghana was unable to raise new capital to keep the development process going and the strain on foreign currency earnings meant that both agriculture and industry were starved of necessary inputs.

But perhaps the most significant change was in the ratio between Ghana's external public debt and GDP, shown in Table 5.3, because this is a rough measure of the extent to which this new foreign borrowing resulted in economic growth. The critical decade was the 1960s, when external public debt rose at one point to over a third of the domestic product. It was not until 1975, after a decade of enforced public abstinence, that the ratio of 1962 was nearly regained; and in 1979 the ratio had again risen to 10 per cent. The implications are important. The huge borrowing in which Ghana indulged during the first decade of independence had a disproportionately small effect on the growth of the economy. Borrowing on such a scale was, admittedly, a gamble on the expectation that it would provide the big push to take Ghana over the magic threshold of sustained accumulation. Ghana was the first African state to make this gamble, the true symbol of economic decolonization. Its failure should have been a warning to other states that such indiscriminate borrowing was unlikely to pay off; but few were prepared to heed it.

Any conclusion on Ghana must be qualified. On the one hand the conservative consensus is right in believing that the over-ambitious and badly executed policies of the post-1961 governments – all governments, in fact, despite changes of style and direction after 1966 – almost certainly did more harm than good to the economy. Ghana would probably be a much more prosperous country now if the moderate policies recommended by Lewis in 1953, and to some extent followed for the rest of that decade, had been continued. There would have been no great leap forward, but equally many of the structural problems of the 1980s would probably not have developed. Conversely, it would be simplistic to argue that a simple return to market mechanisms would make Ghana affluent. The underlying structural problems remain, and an unreconstructed peasantry is one of them.

Nigeria

Post-independence Nigerian economic history has three main features which distinguish it from that of all other Black African countries. First, Nigeria's population was very large, estimated in 1979 (probably very inaccurately) at 82.6m., as contrasted with 11.3m. for Ghana, 15.3m. for Kenya and 18.0m. for Tanzania.[39] Secondly, Nigeria was a federal state in which the distribution of powers between federal and state governments (and indeed the increasing number of states) varied from time to time. While this left macro-economic control with the centre, it also resulted in a far greater dispersal of development funds and enterprises than might have been the case in a unitary state. Finally, and above all, Nigeria was one of the very few Black African countries to benefit from the equivalent of a major gold-strike. The immense rise in the price of petroleum from 1973 made it worth while for the international oil companies to increase levels of production from 152.4 million barrels in 1966 to a peak of 823.3 million in 1974. Meantime the average price per barrel rose from $2.17 in 1966 to $14.69 in 1974: the average export value in 1976–8 was $10,984m.[40]

Although much of the profit from oil went to the oil firms, the federal government did extremely well. From 1974 oil revenues averaged over 75 per cent of total federal revenues, in that year and again in 1979 rising to over 80 per cent.[41] Public consumption grew at 10.0 per cent in the 1960s and 12.4 per cent in the 1970s, but large revenues enabled it to take a relatively low 10 per cent of GDP in 1979.[42] In the later 1970s Nigeria had a massively favourable balance of payments, though this was reversed when declining oil revenues coincided with huge overseas commitments in the early 1980s. External debt service was light: 0.4 per cent of GNP, 1.5 per cent of the value of exported goods and services in 1979.[43] While the national product in 1982 was still low in per capita terms – $860 – its growth rate from 1960 to 1982 averaged 3.7 per cent and per capita GDP had risen from $105.5 to $791 in the same years.[44] In short, from being one of the poorest countries in Black Africa, Nigeria had become one of the richest. Here at least one would have expected to see a substantial increase in affluence and welfare. The main interest of the Nigerian experience is how little good use was made of this unique opportunity by successive governments, civilian and military, and how small the benefit that accrued to the mass of the population.

Government here means the central government for, despite various constitutional changes which increased the number of components from the original three regions to nineteen states by 1975, and although from 1981 44 per cent of centrally collected revenue was distributed among the states, the central government never lost control over economic policy. The basic fact is that, although in some sense Nigeria remained an open economy, its economic strategy was typical of that of most of post-independence African states. That is, Lagos, exactly like Accra, aimed to concentrate the largest possible share of the national product in its own hands, to expand the public sector and to develop import-substituting industry by means of tariffs, import licensing and other stimuli. At the same time agricultural prices were to be kept down by marketing boards to benefit both industry and the urban consumer and to provide government income. Let us examine the effects of these conventional strategies in turn as they affected public and private consumption, industry and agriculture.

Public and Private Consumption

One very striking feature of Nigerian economic history is the contrast between incomes, consumption and output. Between 1950–3 and 1974–7 (at 1962 prices) the four-yearly average of per capita income rose from naira ₦58.1 to ₦116; per capita output grew from ₦50.1 to ₦92.0; but consumption rose only from ₦45.2 to ₦56.5. Within this period there were contrasting trends. From 1950 to 1957 all these measures grew at about the same rate. From 1958 to 1965 consumption grew at 1.3 per cent, income at 0.9 per cent and output at 2.8 per cent. but from 1970 to 1977 these rates were 0.3, 9.9 and 3.3 per cent respectively. Over the whole period the growth rate of consumption averaged 0.9, income 2.8 and output 2.4 per cent.[45] The significance of this is that, in the booming 1970s, the average Nigerian's consumption grew very little, less fast than it had done in the 1950s; indeed, his best period was 1950–7, under colonial rule and long before oil revenues became significant. The main reason for this paradox was that, in a country in which 82 per cent of the population was still rural in 1978 and 55 per cent of the labour force still in agriculture, the index of real rural wages declined over the period (at constant 1962 prices) from ₦157.1 in 1954–7 to ₦78.5 in 1970–3, rising only to ₦108.6 in 1974–7. Meanwhile the index of real urban wages had risen from ₦59.7 in 1950–3 to ₦126.1 in 1974–7.[46]

The clear implication of these statistics is that the state greatly increased its share of the national income: between 1960 and 1979 government consumption of GDP increased from 6 to 10 per cent, gross domestic investment (much of it on government account) rose from 13 to 31 per cent, while private consumption dropped from 87 to 58 per cent.[47] Thus the state, and through the state the urban worker, were the main beneficiaries of increased national wealth, while the bulk of the rural population became poorer than it had been in the 1950s. These are the hallmarks of a state-centred economy in which private welfare suffers from inefficient state consumption and policies which benefit the urban economy at the expense of the countryside.

Industry and Manufacturing

To pursue this issue one stage further and to look at the purposes for which the government used its revenues is to turn to the second feature of Nigerian policy, import-substituting industrialization. Nigeria's industrialization policy began in the mid-1950s, but the major state-support system only began after independence in 1960 and the subsequent high tariffs on manufactured imports came in about 1965. From the early 1970s money from oil and the consequential inflation further stimulated demand for consumer products. The result was a substantial increase in manufactured output, both in absolute and relative terms. At constant (1962) prices manufacturing output increased from an average of ₦52.9m. in 1954–7 to ₦79.6m. in 1962–5; then from ₦369.2m. in 1970–3 to ₦614.8m. in 1974–7. In those two decades manufacturing grew from 2.7 to 10.0 per cent of GDP, at an average rate of growth of 10.7 per cent.[48]

The record of industrialization, however, falls into three fairly distinct periods: the late colonial era; the early 1960s; and from the early 1970s. In the colonial period and down to the early 1960s most of the industrial investment was by foreign firms, so that, in 1963, 68 per cent of the ownership of large-scale industry was foreign, 10 per cent private Nigerian, 3 per cent federal government and 19 per cent regional governments.[49] Most of this development took place in the main urban areas – Lagos, Kano/Kaduna and Port Harcourt/Aba. Much of it resulted from established firms such as UAC and John Holt diversifying out of the import–export trade into manufacturing, often in partnership with other foreign firms who provided the technology and know-how. Kilby argues that most of this investment was defensive – to protect shares of the Nigerian market at a time of rapidly growing demand when new firms might otherwise have stepped in. Tariff protection was low and government help unimportant, though these firms may well have expected adequate protection once they were established. Indeed, there were many outsiders anxious to get in on these expanding opportunities: large firms looking for new investment opportunities (such as Aluminium Ltd, Alcan and Pfizer), individual entrepreneurs, manufacturers seeking a use for redundant machinery, manufacturers of capital equipment ready to co-operate with the state, even second-hand machinery merchants.[50]

These industries were established under fairly strictly free trade conditions and depended mainly on natural protection for their viability. It was in the second period, between independence in 1960 and about 1965, that both the federal and regional governments began to subsidize industries by loans, provision of infrastructure, fiscal incentives, tariffs and licensing, and these policies became the basis of the next stage and type of Nigerian industrial development. In the 1960s the state was mainly concerned to encourage large-scale foreign industry; but a third phase began in the early 1970s when the federal government increasingly reserved sections of the Nigerian economy for Nigerians. Heavy industry, or at least a majority of the equity in such manufacturing industries as gas liquefaction, iron and steel-making, petrochemicals and fertilizers, was to be held by the state. From 1972, under the Nigerian Enterprises Promotion Decree, foreign businesses in a number of specified fields had to transfer part or all of their equity to private Nigerian investors or businessmen (though in fact the state often bought such shares). Twenty-two activities were scheduled to become the preserve of Nigerian nationals and in another thirty-three foreign enterprises were to be excluded unless above a specified size and with at least 40 per cent Nigerian ownership of the equity.

These restrictions were extended in 1977 both in the range of types of manufacture covered and in the proportion of the equity to be held by Nigerians. In all unlisted activities Nigerians were to hold a minimum of 40 per cent of the equity. Indigenization had thus become a primary aim of government policy, made possible only by its ability to funnel oil revenues through new credit agencies to state holding companies and to favoured individuals. In this way the government was able to use its wealth to the greatest possible political effect.[51] Meantime schemes that had begun in a small way in the 1940s for providing credit and facilities to small-scale Nigerian entrepreneurs continued, particularly the Approved Manufacturers Scheme begun in 1955, and the provision of industrial estates to give a start to would-be entrepreneurs with little capital.[52]

These policies certainly increased manufacturing production. As a proportion of GDP manufacturing remained constant at 5 per cent in 1960 and 1979; but its gross output increased in that period from $157.5m. to $3,758.5m.; and between 1964 and 1976 the number employed in manufacturing rose from 64,965 to 214,280.[53] But this was achieved at a very high economic and social cost. This can best be studied under two heads: the relative efficiency of industries which developed under state protection and help during and after the 1960s; and the ability of industry to respond to the stimulus of oil revenues during the 1970s.

Kilby's case studies of four major industries in the 1960s – tobacco and cigarettes, beer, cement and cotton textiles – demonstrated how expensive large-scale industrialization with considerable state help could be.[54] Tobacco received tariff protection of between 100 and 200 per cent, and this subsidy exceeded the domestic value added by more than 50 per cent. In the mid-1960s some 64 per cent of the income of these firms went to the government through various forms of tax and duty, and almost all the profits to Britain, to the parent companies of these firms. The only significant benefit to Nigeria was demand for local tobacco – worth £1.3m. in 1961. Beer had effective protection from transport costs of 40 per cent, to which rising import duties added c.18 per cent in 1948 and 65 per cent in 1964/5, giving effective protection of about 100 per cent. High profits were thus possible with little value added at international prices, and there were few linkages since most raw materials required were not produced in Nigeria.

Cement was an exception. Most of its protection came from the cost of overseas transport (c.70 per cent of value), plus 20 per cent per 160 km of inland carriage, so that the 20 per cent protective import duty was unimportant. Given the huge demand, large-scale production at several places was possible, and there were many linkages backward into raw materials, coal and oil, and forward into the construction industry. Conversely, cotton textiles were a classic case of misdirected state stimulation. Nigeria produced about 50,000 tons of raw cotton a year, but, as this was mostly exported, there was no natural incentive to manufacture locally. The Northern and Western Regions, however, were anxious to stimulate manufacture and offered substantial incentives to foreign firms. By 1965 there were seventeen plants, some owned by Nigerians, with 12,117 employees. Sales were worth £20.8m. and value added £9.8m. But protection was excessive. In 1961 value added on imported 'grey' cloth was 7.7d per 0.91m (a yard); on Nigerian cloth, including the tariff, it was 19.7d The margin of 12d (representing effective protection of 155 per cent) provided for both inefficiency in management and high profits at the cost of the Nigerian consumers. The greatest amount of effective protection was provided for the bleaching and printing of imported cottons, which were given effective protection of 191 per cent and whose raw material import costs were greater than the cost at which the finished product might have been imported. Such inefficiency increased over time as protection grew: for 1968 Rimmer calculated that the effective protection cost (the proportion by which domestic value added is allowed to exceed the value added on the same goods at the point of importation) was 2.2 for textiles, 2.43 for metal goods and 3 for glass, radios and television assembly, among other things.[55]

Many of these benefits went to foreign firms which set up subsidiaries; but how greatly did indigenous Nigerians benefit, apart from those enabled to buy equity in foreign enterprises? Did an 'autonomous' indigenous class of entrepreneurs emerge? Both Kilby and Schatz give depressing answers.[56] Schatz argues that most positive actions to develop the modern manufacturing sector were taken by foreign firms with encouragement from the Nigerian government. These firms set the terms of the economic environment and made it difficult for Nigerians to compete, however enterprising they might be. In particular, such enterprises found it very difficult to make the 'leap' from the small family firm to a corporate structure and from local sales to large-scale distribution. The Approved Manufacturers Scheme ran into bureaucratic and regional problems; the industrial estates failed. The Loans Board programme was heavily politicized, administratively inefficient and in the end helped only a very few successful ventures at huge cost. Schatz concluded that, given certain features of foreign direct investment and the apparent inability of Nigerians to compete on a large scale, the best future for Nigeria lay in the public corporation; though he seems to overlook the fact that the administrative incompetence and political corruption which he sees at the root of most failures to help individual businessmen would probably have equally bad effects on public corporations.

The main test of the efficiency and potentiality of Nigerian manufacturing came when oil revenues greatly increased demands for its products after 1973 and the evidence suggests that it failed this test. In his book published in 1977 Schatz described the pattern of state-supported indigenous private enterprise as it developed in the 1960s as 'nurture capitalism', which he defined as a capitalist system in which the government provided the infrastructure, helped indigenous capitalists in every possible way and adopted a nationalist standpoint which enabled Africans to buy a shareholding in foreign companies and provided them with a guaranteed share of markets and economic opportunities. In a subsequent article, published in 1984, he reviewed developments since the great increase in oil revenues began in 1973 and its impact on Nigerian industries.[57] The salient points are as follows.

Between 1973/4 and 1977/8 Nigerian GDP, excluding oil, grew (at constant prices) at an annual rate of 7.4 per cent, while the average annual increase in government oil revenues was 80.2 per cent – eleven times that of the rest of the economy. Meantime manufacturing grew at 12.0 per cent from 1970 to 1982, faster than its 9 per cent rate of increase during the 1960s and faster than the rest of the economy, but not nearly as fast as oil revenues.[58] This poses the question why the economy as a whole and the manufacturing sector in particular responded so relatively sluggishly to this unprecedented stimulus of government revenues which, including oil, rose from ₦633m. in 1970 to ₦15,812m. in 1980, before dipping to ₦10,204m. in 1982.

Schatz's explanation adds up to the proposition that the economy could not respond because it was 'inert': the non-oil economy had insufficient dynamism. The government, the main initial beneficiary of the oil price increase, spent a large proportion of its revenues abroad, either on goods and services, or on servicing new foreign loans. It did so, despite its commitment to Nigerian industrial growth, because the domestic economy could not provide the goods which the government and private consumers demanded. Thus the main domestic effect was not manufacturing growth but inflation. Schatz shows (Table 3) that from 1973/4 to 1981, while in current prices non-oil GDP increased by an average of 18.5 a year, in constant prices the rate of growth was only 4.1 per cent. Thus the increased production represented only 22 per cent of aggregate demand, as against an inflation of 78 per cent. Indeed, at constant prices the rate of growth of non-oil GDP actually declined from an average of 7.4 per cent in 1974/5–1977/8 to 0.7 per cent between 1978 and 1982.

This in turn poses the question why the domestic economy, and primarily industry, could not respond. Schatz argues that the indigenous capitalist sector was already accustomed before 1973 to depending almost entirely on the continued growth of government spending; there was almost no other endogenous stimulus to investment. In the decade after 1973 rising government revenues should have provided an additional stimulus; but its effects were muffled by a number of characteristic Nigerian obstacles. As before, the real block to new industrial investment was not capital but the shortage of viable investment opportunities and lack of entrepreneurs able and willing to find them. Environmental problems, including inadequate infrastructure, such as power supplies, and excessive bureaucratic controls, acted as a deterrent. An over-valued exchange rate discouraged enterprise. It discouraged industry by making imports comparatively cheap. It also discouraged agricultural production because commodities sold abroad at world prices, which were then translated into inflated nairas. The effect was to reduce the real price farmers received, adversely affecting their terms of trade with the rest of the domestic economy. A possible third factor was rising wage costs per unit, though it is also possible that wages merely rose in line with inflation. Finally, since the government was the conduit through which oil revenues had to flow into the rest of the economy, waste, corruption and ill-advised allocation of resources further reduced the growth potential of public wealth.

The result Schatz describes as 'pirate capitalism', a qualitative change from 'nurture capitalism' in that the productive effect of capitalism had virtually disappeared, to be replaced by almost total dependence on government and what oil revenues would buy. He concludes: 'In Nigeria manipulation has taken the place of monopoly as the inimical alternative [sc. to the market economy]. The predominance of such widespread manipulation signifies pirate capitalism, and is a major factor in the emergence of the inert economy.'[59]

The evidence therefore suggests that the growth of manufacturing in Nigeria was as inefficient as that in Ghana, not in this case because of the predominance of state or parastatal enterprises, but mostly because the federal and regional governments put 'nationalist' objectives before economic considerations. The price, of course, was paid by the mass of the rural population, both as consumers and as producers subsidizing urban enterprises; and the agricultural achievement is as depressing as that of Ghana.

Agriculture

Nigeria's agricultural record falls into two parts: export commodity production and food production. At constant (1962) prices, commercial crops outgrew for each period from 1950–3 to 1962–5, from ₦108.8m. to ₦194.1m. It was down to ₦151.0m. in 1970–3 and to ₦88.5m. in 1974–7. From 1970 to 1977 the growth rate was − 13.3 per cent a year. By 1980 cocoa alone retained a significant share of total exports − 2.2 per cent. Groundnuts and their derivatives, palm oil, cotton and timber, had ceased to be exported in significant quantities and palm kernels were down to 0.1 per cent of total exports.[60] Nigeria had effectively destroyed its commodity exports, apart from oil.

Part of this decline of exports was, of course, the result of higher domestic consumption; even so, the performance was appalling and was due almost entirely to the low prices paid by state marketing boards, which, until the civil war, were run by the regions. For the decade 1964/5 to 1976/7 the annual average of producer prices as a percentage of gross f.o.b. price was as follows: cocoa 55 per cent, groundnuts 53 per cent, palm kernels 62 per cent, palm oil 61 per cent.[61] For none of these main crops was the real price in 1977 as high as it had been in the later 1950s. The bottom had been reached at different times for different crops: for cocoa from 1962–5 to 1970–3; for cotton 1962–5; for groundnuts 1970–3; for palm oil and palm kernels 1970–3. By the latter 1970s there had been a partial recovery in prices as the government used oil revenues to pay a slightly higher rate, and to some extent producers responded. Real incomes of cocoa, groundnut and cotton producers were above their 1954–7 averages in 1974–7, but those of palm-oil producers were still well down.[62] Overall, the growth of real incomes in agriculture was only 0.3 per cent between 1950 and 1977.

As for food production, since much of this was not marketed, useful data are scarce. As a percentage of total imports food was the same (14 per cent) in 1960 and 1978, but, since the volume of imports had increased immensely, this implied a considerable absolute increase. Much of this consisted of 'luxury' goods – sugar, wheat and flour, rice and convenience foods. According to the World Bank, wheat and flour imports grew from 400,000 tons to 1.3m. tons between 1971 and 1978, and were estimated to be 1.0m. tons in 1980. Rice imports rose from 50,000 tons to over 550,000 tons, stimulated by major reductions in import duties from 66.6 per cent to 10 per cent *ad valorem* between 1974 and 1975. From 1978 controls were imposed to limit these imports.[63] It was the policy of Nigerian governments from the early 1970s to increase food production, despite the relative inefficiency of producing most crops of these types in Nigeria. Thus the World Bank calculated that in 1979 the domestic resource costs per unit of foreign exchange for some main foods produced in Nigeria were: groundnuts 1.40; maize 1.76; millet 1.21; rice 2.55; sorghum 1.66. That is, it would be cheaper to import these things, given Nigerian domestic costs. By contrast, the DRC of palm oil was 0.39.[64] Nevertheless governments used large sums to increase food production.

As defined by Tina Wallace, they adopted three basic methods of approach.[65] The first was to carry out two large-scale projects: irrigation schemes in the north, aiming at 274,000 hectares by 1990, mostly to grow wheat; and integrated rural development schemes financed by the World Bank, which provided a complex of extension services, fertilizers, ploughs, etc., in select areas. These projects were very expensive. The World Bank made large claims for the integrated schemes,[66] but Wallace claims that both were largely ineffective in increasing production. Northern irrigation had little effect because of farmer resistance (due to high costs of labour and other inputs), the uncertainty of wheat production on marginal land, and the low price paid for wheat by the government because of the lower cost of imported wheat. Integrated rural development schemes seem to have benefited mainly a minority of richer farmers.

The second strategy was to provide improved inputs to farmers in general under the National Accelerated Food Production Programme of 1975–80, which aimed at a 'green revolution'. Most of these funds were, however, absorbed by the bureaucracy. This was followed by the

'Operation Feed the Nation' of 1976, under which fertilizers were distributed direct to farmers to avoid bureaucratic obstacles; but again the effects were limited. Most fertilizer went to farms with easy transport access and was taken over by rich farmers, village headmen, etc. The third major strategy was to provide easier credit through the Agricultural Bank; but again this was administered by the states for approved schemes only and proved very ineffective.

Wallace concludes that the main weakness of all these schemes was that everyone assumed that only the larger farmers could use improved inputs efficiently. No serious attempts were made to help smaller farmers by provision of better roads, fertilizers, markets or health facilities, nor by raising controlled prices. So again we have the phenomenon of the state ignoring the obvious device for increasing food as well as commodity production, by offering higher prices to the mass of the peasantry. Faced by declining real incomes, the peasant increasingly drifted to the towns; and Teal regards this as a major reason for the lag in food production and the rapid growth of urbanization.[67]

In Nigeria, as in Ghana, the record of public policy as an instrument of economic development, therefore, seems very poor. Although there were marked sectoral shifts to industry and the towns, as the national plans intended, the effects were generally unfortunate. Industry was for the most part extremely inefficient. Agriculture experienced virtually no growth. A huge increase in the national income, due to higher oil prices and larger oil exports, was converted into a minute increase in per capita consumption. The balance of national income was largely absorbed by the state apparatus, increasingly politicized and linked to private interests,[68] by conspicuous public consumption and by import-substituting industrialization, involving the investment of huge sums with little real return. That Nigeria was able to sustain these policies so long without the disastrous consequences faced by Ghana, Tanzania and many other African states was simply and solely because of the life-raft of oil revenues.

The supreme irony of Nigerian economic development, however, is that, despite the flow of oil wealth, by 1982 the country was more heavily burdened by debt than at any previous time. Table 5.4 summarizes the main facts. Until the flow of oil money began, debt service stood at a conventional African level of about 4.0 per cent of export of goods and services. In the 1970s the great expansion of exports allowed this burden to be substantially reduced; but, despite the second oil price increase of 1979, between then and 1982 external debts increased by about a third and the burden of debt service rose almost to its highest previous level. In 1979 Nigeria had a favourable trade balance of $1,429m. and gross international reserves of $5,870m. By 1982 she had a balance of payments deficit of $7,324m. and gross

Table 5.4 Nigeria's External Public Debt
and Debt Service, 1959–1982 (US$m.)

	A Debt out-standing	B Debt service	C EGS	A/C (%)	B/C (%)
1959	49.2	n/a	458[a]	10.7	n/a
1964	97.9	n/a	601	16.3	n/a
1967	382.4	36.2	729.1	52.4	4.9
1970	478.1	55.7	1,331.0	35.9	4.1
1973	1,155.9	150.5	3,738.5	30.9	4.0
1975	1,085.2	246.5	8,629.0	12.5	2.8
1979	3,969.1	341.0	18,068.0	21.9	1.8
1982	6,084.7	1,339.5	13,979.0	43.5	9.5

Note:
a. for 1960.
Sources:
1959, 1964: UN, *A Survey of Economic Conditions in Africa, 1960–1964* (New York, 1968), table 16.
1967–1975: World Bank, *World Tables* (Washington DC, 1976 and 1980).
1979: World Bank, *Accelerated Development*, App. 7, 17, 18.
1982: World Bank, *Toward Sustained Development*, Apps. 7, 13, 14.
1979 and 1982 column C: IMF, *International Financial Statistics Yearbook* (1984).

international reserves were down to $1,927m., about one month's coverage. While this position resulted largely from the drop in oil prices after 1980, it also reflects the excessive dependence of the economy on oil and the extraordinary lack of wisdom on the part of a federal government which had gambled on the continuation of high oil prices in undertaking huge foreign borrowing and committing itself to equally large imports. The parallel with Ghana's gamble on cocoa prices in the early 1960s is obvious.

Notes

1 World Bank, *Accelerated Development in Sub-Saharan Africa* (*AD*) (Washington DC) App. 5.
2 T. Killick, *Development Economics in Action* (London, 1978), table 4.1.
3 *AD* table 4.1.
4 Killick, *Development Economics*, table 5.5.
5 ibid., ch. 10.
6 ibid., p. 288.
7 ibid., table 4.10.
8 ibid., table 4.2. The cedi was then worth half the pound sterling.
9 ibid., table 4.4.
10 ibid., table 4.B.

11 ibid., p. 83.
12 See, for example, R. Prebisch, *The Economic Development of Latin America and its Principal Problems* (New York, 1950); A. O. Hirschman, *The Strategy of Economic Development* (New Haven, 1958); A. Singh, 'Industrialization in Africa: a Structuralist View' and F. Nixson, 'Import-Substituting Industrialization' both in M. Fransman (ed.), *Industry and Accumulation in Africa* (London, 1982) for a summary of the main arguments then regarded as conclusive.
13 D. Rimmer, *The Economies of West Africa* (London, 1984), table 4.
14 ibid., table 3.
15 W. F. Steel, 'Import Substitution Policy in Ghana in the 1960s', PhD dissertation, MIT, 1970, quoted by Killick, *Development Economics*, p. 168.
16 Killick, *Development Economics*, table 5.8.
17 ibid., table 5.7.
18 ibid., table 8.1.
19 ibid., table 8.3.
20 ibid., table 8.5.
21 *AD* App. 35.
22 *AD* App. 36.
23 Killick, *Development Economics*, p. 187.
24 ibid., table 9.1.
25 ibid., table 9.2.
26 ibid., p. 239.
27 Paul Kennedy, 'Indigenous Capitalism in Ghana', *RAPE*, vol. 8 (1977).
28 See in particular R. H. Bates, *Markets and States in Tropical Africa* (Berkeley and Los Angeles, 1981); Killick, *Development Economics*; Rimmer, *The Economies of West Africa*; K. Hart, *The Political Economy of West African Agriculture* (Cambridge, 1982).
29 *AD* p. 26, Box A.
30 Killick, *Development Economics*, table 5.6.
31 Bates, *Markets and States*, p. 46.
32 Killick, *Development Economics*, table 4D.
33 Bates, *Markets and States*, pp. 57–9.
34 *AD* App. 24, 25.
35 Killick, *Development Economics*, table 4.D.
36 *AD* App. 33.
37 *AD* App. 1.
38 *AD* App. 37.
39 *AD* App. 1.
40 A. Kirk-Greene and D. Rimmer, *Nigeria Since 1970* (London, 1981), table 11; *AD* App. 10.
41 S. P. Schatz, 'Pirate Capitalism and the Inert Economy of Nigeria', *JMAS*, vol. 22, no. 1 (1984), table 1; Rimmer, *The Economies of West Africa*, table 22 and p. 163.
42 *AD* App. 17.
43 *AD* App. 17; World Bank, *Toward Sustained Development in Sub-Saharan Africa (TSD)* (Washington, 1984), App. 13.
44 *TSD* App. 1; GDP from UN *Survey of Economic Conditions in Africa, 1973* (New York, 1974), *TSD* App. 1, 3.

45   F. Teal, 'The Objectives of Development Policy in Nigeria and the Growth of the Economy since 1950', paper given at a conference on 'The Fate of Post-Colonial Economies in West Africa', SOAS, July 1983, table 2.2.
46   Teal, table 2.3.
47   Rimmer, *The Economies of West Africa*, table 6.
48   Teal, table 2.1
49   Tom Forrest, 'Recent Developments in Nigerian Industrialization', in Fransman (ed.), *Industry and Accumulation in Africa*, ch. 16.
50   Peter Kilby, *Industrialization in an Open Economy* (Cambridge, 1969), chs. 1–3.
51   Kirk-Greene and Rimmer, ch. 8; R. A. Joseph, 'Affluence and Under-development: the Nigerian Experience', *JMAS*, vol. 16, no. 2 (1978).
52   For details of these schemes see S. P. Schatz, *Nigerian Capitalism* (Berkeley and Los Angeles, 1977), especially chs. 10–13.
53   Rimmer, *West African Economies*, table 4; *AD* App. 3; J. O. C. Onyemelukwe, *Industrialization in West Africa* (London, 1984), table 7.10.
54   Kilby, *Industrialization in an Open Economy*, ch. 4.
55   Rimmer, *The Economies of West Africa*, p. 235.
56   Kilby, *Industrialization*, pp. 333–42.
57   Schatz, 'Pirate Capitalism'.
58   *TSD* App. 2.
59   Schatz, 'Pirate Capitalism', p. 56.
60   Rimmer, *The Economies of West Africa*, table 15.
61   ibid., table 23.
62   Teal, table 2.4.
63   *AD* App, 9; p. 57, Box E.
64   *AD* p. 65, Box G.
65   Tina Wallace, 'The Challenge of Food: Nigeria's Approach to Agriculture 1975–80', *CJAS*, vol. 15, no. 2 (1981).
66   *AD* App. 7, 3, 14.
67   Teal, *passim*.
68   See P. Koehn, 'The Role of Public Administrators in Public Policy Making: Practice and Prospects in Nigeria', *Public Administration and Development*, vol. 3, no. 1 (1983), pp. 1–26, for a general study of the changing role of senior public servants in Nigeria, and in particular the growing importance of political pressures and private relationships on their policy formulation.

6

Anglophone East Africa: Kenya and Tanzania

Kenya

Kenya is perhaps the most controversial of all post-colonial Black African states. Born shortly after the Mau Mau struggle, one of the very few serious domestic crises experienced by African colonies between 1914 and the 1960s and which at the time was inaccurately regarded as a rising against white domination, Kenya nevertheless became the only Black African state (except the later Zimbabwe) in which a substantial white settler population remained and played an active role in economic and public life. Despite some early rhetoric, Kenya made little pretence of socialism. Africans, led by the new political elite, bought and ran large one-time settler farms, collaborated with foreign capital and established capitalist enterprises. Kenya remained to a large extent an open economy, heavily dependent on a limited range of commodity exports. In 1979 exports represented 26.6 per cent of GDP (compared with 10.8 per cent for Ghana in 1978/9), and the percentage share of the three major exports increased from 34.2 to 52.2 between 1961 and 1976–8.[1] Monetary policy was based on pegging the Kenyan pound successively to the pound sterling, the dollar and (from 1975) International Monetary Fund Special Drawing Rights. The Foreign Investment Protection Act of 1966, even as modified in 1976, guaranteed ownership and the right to remit dividends, royalties and capital to foreign investors. To those who believe that socialism and autonomy should be the aims of all Black African countries, a successful Kenya would, therefore, be an embarrassment.

Yet, with virtually no mineral endowment and as perhaps the only significant African country in which land is in short supply, Kenya's economic performance has been better than most. The annual average growth rate of per capita incomes in 1960–79 was 2.7 per cent and the growth rate of GDP was 6.0 per cent in the 1960s and 6.5 per cent in the 1970s, well above the average for middle-income oil importers (3.4 and 4.6 per cent in each period).[2] If there was little change in the sectoral distribution of the domestic product from 1960 to 1979 (agriculture down only from 38 to 34 per cent, industry up from 18 to 21 per cent), the quantity index of manufacturing production increased from 100 in 1963 to 345 in 1977. In 1977, 118,000 were employed in manufacture, 13 per cent of total wage employment. Moreover, in 1978, 13 per cent of merchandise exports were manufactures, and this total might have been much larger had it not been for the break up of the East African Common Market.[3] Kenya also become more self-sufficient over time. The ratio of imports to GDP (at constant prices) declined from 43.2 per cent in 1964 to 28.1 per cent in 1976, and, as a proportion of the total supply of manufactures, imported goods declined from 42.6 per cent in 1964 to 30.8 per cent in 1975.[4] Imports of consumer goods as a percentage of total imports dropped from 33 to 24.4 per cent from 1964 to 1975.[5] While not staggering, these were comparatively impressive achievements. Do they imply that Kenyan government policies were substantially different from and much wiser than those of other Black African states? Let us consider the same three major problems: the role of the state in the economy; industry and manufacturing; and agriculture.

The State and the Economy

It would certainly not be true to say that Kenya was an unmanaged economy or that the state's role was small. As a proportion of GDP, the state's share increased from 11 to 20 per cent from 1960 to 1979, while private consumption decreased from 72 to 65 per cent.[6] Between 1964 and 1977 public employment rose from 32 to 42 per cent of total wage employment. It is not known what proportion of manufacturing output was in the public sector after 1967, but at that date the few but large government establishments (only 2 per cent of the total number) employed 20 per cent of manufacturing workers and were responsible for 15 per cent of the gross product (value added).[7] Through the Industrial and Commerical Development Corporation, the successor to the Industrial Development Corporation of 1950 and its various subsidiaries, the state invested heavily in both indigenous and foreign-owned enterprises. In 1977 its assets were nearly K£31m., of which 45 per cent was in loans and advance, 27 per cent in equity and 24 per cent in subsidies.[8]

The state also took a controlling position in agriculture. The Maize and Produce Board had a theoretical monopoly of buying and selling maize, though in fact, because of private consumption and illegal sales at higher prices, it handled a small proportion of the total output. The Kenya Tea Development Authority, the Kenya Meat Commission (with a monopoly of the urban, but not the rural, meat trade) and organizations for coffee and other cash crops, performed the same functions as marketing boards in other African states. From the start, also, Kenya produced overall national plans and adopted conventional protection by means of tariffs and licensing of imports and productive capacity. In form, at least, Kenya therefore adopted much the same state-centred approach to development as most other African countries. How did the state use these powers and what effects had they on manufacturing and agriculture?

Industry and Manufacturing

The main debate over the state's policy towards manufacturing turns on its encouragement of foreign direct investment, the 'appropriateness' of methods of production and the goods produced, and the position of indigenous Kenyan capitalists. Of the importance of foreign ownership there can be no doubt. In 1967, 57 per cent of the gross product (value added) was foreign owned; in 1972 it was 59 per cent.[9] Kenya did not go to the same extremes as some other states to attract multinationals; there were no tax holidays and permitted rates of depreciation were not generous. Moreover, there was considerable pressure on multinationals to employ Kenyans in management and on their boards, and to sell shares in the equity to the state and private Kenyans. From 1971 multinationals had to obtain permission to raise finance locally, to issue shares and to develop new lines of production.[10] On the other hand, the government generally tried to help multinationals, for example, by providing effective protection on demand. Langdon's sample showed that more than 75 per cent of all domestic manufacturing firms had protection and 79 per cent of their requests had been sucessful; the larger the firm, the more probable its success would be.[11] For their part multinationals' motives were, of course, mixed; but the predominant aim was to safeguard existing product markets created by exports against other multinationals and indigenous competition.[12] Langdon argues that, from their viewpoint, the results were satisfactory: his sample indicated that average after-tax profits and fees were about 23 per cent of capital employed, dividends taking some 65 per cent of profit, most of them repatriated.[13]

Kenyan government industrialization strategy thus in many ways resembled that of Nigeria, and one must ask the same basic questions: how efficient was this import-substituting strategy as an alternative to importing the same goods; did it lay foundations for continued development of manufacturing to replace the import of intermediate and capital goods; what linkages were there with the rest of the economy; what effect did it have on the growth of an indigenous bourgeoisie?

I have been unable to find estimates of the efficiency of Kenyan industry, measured by international prices, comparable to those available for other countries, though it is likely that excessive protection again resulted in negative value added in some areas.[14] It is, however, true that the value added in manufacturing was low compared with that in more developed countries; the value added in all Kenyan manufacturing declined from 28.6 per cent of output in 1963 to 22.4 per cent in 1975, compared with 38.6 per cent in the United Kingdom; but the decline is probably attributable largely to the rise in the cost of raw materials in the petroleum and chemicals industries after 1973.[15] This suggests that, if Kenyan industry was not merely a 'finishing touch' affair, it was not very far off it.

This leads to the second question: how progressive was industrialization in Kenya? The answer seems clear. There was no significant increase in the extent to which manufacturing produced its own requirements of intermediate and capital goods.[16] The end-use of the gross product of manufacturing hardly changed from 1963 to 1975, with consumer goods static at 56 per cent, intermediate goods rising only from 12 to 15 per cent and capital goods dropping from 32 to 29 per cent. More significant, only 8.8 per cent of manufacturing output went into manufacturing.[17] On the other hand, linkages with other sectors of the Kenyan economy were quite significant. In 1971 domestic inputs to industry from non-manufacturing sectors amounted to 28 per cent of the value of output, compared with 29.6 per cent of imported inputs, of which 15.6 per cent was from domestic agriculture. Conversely, 22.9 per cent of manufactured output went downstream to other domestic sectors: for example, 16 per cent of the beverages and tobacco industries went to the Kenyan hotel and restaurant trade, 27 per cent of sawmill production into building and construction.[18] Thus, whether processing local raw materials for home consumption or export, or providing goods for other sectors of the domestic economy, Kenyan manufacturing was in no sense an insulated enclave; which in turn suggests an economy capable of expanding to provide the needs and consume the products of local industry.

Finally there is the question of the growth of indigenous capitalism and a bourgeoisie capable eventually of replacing foreign capital as a source of investment and entrepreneurship. On this opinions are strongly divided, and a non-contestant is wise merely to record the main contrasting positions. The first, broadly, is that, in a 'peripheral' economy such as that of Kenya, there is no possibility of a genuinely autonomous bourgeoisie developing, that is, a class which owns the means of production and accumulation. Thus Colin Leys in 1975, followed by Stephen Langdon in 1975 and again in 1981, supported by Kaplinsky in a survey article published in 1981, have all, from varying standpoints, held that, since the multinationals dominate the industrial world, it is almost impossible for indigenous capitalists to compete with them or to establish genuinely autonomous enterprises.[19]

Rather, a minority of Kenyans, who can be described as members of the petty bourgeoisie, uses state backing to acquire senior positions in multinational subsidiaries, partnerships with multinationals or small businesses dependent on multinational purchases or financial backing. Kaplinsky in particular argues that the apparent shift of ownership in manufacturing to Kenyans represented only the sale of minority holdings in foreign subsidiaries to both private capitalists and parastatal organizations, together with the creation of a few smaller firms or acquisitions from foreign firms and Asians. In his view this was not genuine capital formation by indigenous Africans.

The contrary view was stated by Leys himself in a later article, by Nicola Swainson and others.[20] Leys there argued that even before 1960 Kenya had a considerable capitalist class of Africans, initially formed by the accumulation of land capital. After 1955 these were able to expand by starting to take over land and engage in production previously monopolized by Europeans. After independence the state helped these Africans, especially the Kikuyu bourgeoisie, to expand the range of their enterprises, so that by 1977 only construction, financial services, insurance, mining and manufacturing were still predominantly in foreign hands. By 1975 a third of the total operating surplus (c. K£180m.) belonged to Africans and was available for accumulation. In this process the state was neither 'neutral' nor against foreign capital, but was 'the register of the leading edge of indigenous capital in its assault on those barriers' (*sc.* capital, scale and technology) which hindered African progress.

Such trends were possible in Kenya, though not necessarily in other parts of Black Africa, for two reasons: African accumulation was in progress in Central Province long before independence; and the white settlers had created the basis of a locally owned capitalist economy before the multinationals became important. Conversely, the indefinite extension of African bourgeois wealth and the expansion of capitalism were threatened by three factors: the limitations of the internal and regional markets; the limited growth of production by the 'middle peasants', who were politically important but had a declining productivity trend; and the class interests of the capitalists themselves, who wanted economic 'freedom' for themselves but not for the masses or for foreign capital. This argument is supported with detailed studies of the growth of Black Kenyan enterprises, their penetration of foreign enterprises and the emergence of a few really large-scale African entrepreneurs, able to compete with the multinationals.

No firm conclusion on this debate seems possible at present; only the future will show whether the Kenyan government's strategy of import-substituting manufacture and support for both foreign and indigenous capital will result in a genuinely autonomous growth of capitalism; Bjorn Beckman at least has suggested that the antithesis drawn in this debate is unreal.[21] We are, therefore, left with the general conclusion that in Kenya state support for industrialization appears not to have had as disastrous economic effect as in Ghana, nor to have done as little to encourage genuine indigenous capitalism as in Nigeria. On the other hand, there was little evidence by the early 1980s that Kenyan industry was capable of moving beyond the first stage of an import-substituting strategy; and it was clear that what had been achieved was at a high cost in terms of dependence on foreign capital and of government borrowing overseas to finance indigenous investment (through state credit agencies) and the acquisition of foreign assets.

Agriculture

What of agriculture? Kenyan government policies have generally been praised on the ground that the state was far more favourable to a prosperous indigenous agriculture and sustained commodity exports than most other African governments. Thus the nominal protection coefficients of the main export crops (the price paid to the producer divided by the net world market price; the higher the more favourable) were generally quite reasonable. During the period 1971–5 these were: coffee 0.94;. cotton 1.07; maize 0.96; tea 0.89. In the later 1970s maize and wheat did even better.[22] Moreover, Kenya has been credited with an imaginative policy of replacing white settlers by substantial African farmers, thus preserving mixed and grade cattle farming, as well as establishing a class of medium and small farmers geared to the market. Certainly, agriculture could boast some impressive results. The annual growth rate in the 1970s (there are no comparable figures for the 1960s) was 5.4 per cent; and, although from 1969–71 to 1977–9 there was a small negative trend in per capita food production, the growth of non-food production was sufficient to make Kenya one of the very few Black African states with a positive per capita growth of agricultural production in that decade.[23] Between 1970 and 1977, and at current prices, the gross marketed production of crops and livestock (that is, excluding subsistence production) rose from K£85m. to K£415m.; and of this coffee, the boom crop, increased from K£22.1m. to K£190m., tea from K£13.6m. to K£91.3m.[24] On the other hand, it is impossible to value the greater proportion of the product of Kenyan agriculture, since most of it was not marketed; one has, therefore, no information on whether total agricultural production was increasing at anything like the same rate as the major cash crops, and very little on the production or productivity of the majority of small farmers who did not enter the cash economy.

In fact, the main controversy over Kenyan agricultural performance turns on the differentiation between large and small, cash and subsistence farming. The distinctive feature of Kenyan land and agricultural policy was the individualization of ownership, through registration of tenures, as contrasted with the informal or group ownership and largely private use characteristic of most African peasant societies. This was the result of large-scale European land ownership, the commercialization of a significant part of agricultural production, which encouraged Africans to consolidate their holdings, and the process by which land was transferred from European to Black African ownership from the mid-1950s. By 1977 a very large proportion of usable land in the most productive areas had been registered or was under adjudication: 99.3 per cent in Central, 64.1 per cent in Rift Valley, 82.7 per cent in Nyanza and 92.5 per cent in Western.[25] It is over the effects of this creation of an African land-owning class that the main debate about Kenyan agricultural policy turns.

The process began officially in 1955 and was virtually complete in Central Province before independence. Equally important was the simultaneous removal of all previous limitations on the commercial crops Africans were permitted to grow, which had been restricted in the interests of European settlers, since this provided the incentive for Africans to invest in European land. The transfer of ownership was lubricated first by the Land Transfer Programme financed by Britain under the CD&W Acts, then in 1961 by a scheme funded by the World Bank and the Colonial Development Corporation and run by the Kenya Land Development and Settlement Board. Settler land was to be bought and divided into relatively large farms (intended to produce 1,800 'yeoman' farmers with 20 ha or more and 6,000 'peasant' farms of 6 ha or more). Since large down payments were needed, all these settlers would have to be men of substance.

In fact the scheme failed and was replaced by the Million Acre Scheme (405, 000 ha), intended to provide smallholdings for landless people. Official reasons for the change, which resulted in some 35,000 holdings averaging only 13.4 ha, included lack of suitable land, the cost of buying unwanted settler assets such as large farmhouses, and lack of suitable settlers willing to leave their tribal areas. Christopher Leo, however, argues that the main reason was probably that settlers preferred to sell their land above the 1959 assessed value offered under the scheme and that Africans were able to afford to buy land (many borrowing from state credit organizations), so avoiding supervision by the LDSB. The result was that more land (some 600,000 ha) was acquired by Africans privately, much of it in relatively large units, as compared with some 470,000 ha sold under the scheme. In addition a large number of smallholdings, averaging 7.5 ha, were created under the Haraka Scheme, mainly for squatters on settler land; and under the Shirika Scheme of 1971 for co-operative farming on large estates workers were allocated one hectare per family for their own use.[26]

Kenya thus emerged with a uniquely large number of African landowning peasants, but also with an exceptional differentiation between large and small farmers. In 1976 there were some 3,273 'large' farms, occupying some 2.5m. ha averaging 777.5 ha, and perhaps 1.7m. smallholdings, of which about a third were under 0.5 ha and a half under 1 ha. For most of the small farmers an income outside their farming was clearly necessary.[27] In addition there may have been 400,000 landless people, dependent on paid work on farms or in the towns. There had clearly been a process of class formation in which a relatively small number of Black Africans were able, through their own savings or through access to public credit, to take over the assets and dominant position once held by white settlers. This was un-doubtedly supported, if not entirely brought about, by public policy, first that of the colonial state, then of the Kenyatta regime. The question is whether the result was an agricultural revolution which increased productivity and could provide the fuel for Kenyan economic development.

So far as the limited evidence goes, the answer seems to be that it was not.[28] The main positive development was the growth of cash crop production by the larger smallholders, which some have taken to constitute an 'agrarian revolution'. Gross farm revenues of smallholders rose from K£8m. to K£34m. from 1958 to 1968, an increase of 435 per cent, led by coffee, pyrethrum, tea, grade cattle and improved maize. Sugar developed fast in the 1970s: by 1977 smallholders produced 1m. tons of cane, a third of the country's total production.[29] This increase was greatly helped by government research and extension services and, in the case of sugar, by the very successful Mumias nucleus estate scheme in Western Province.[30] At constant (1956) prices, cash revenues to smallholders rose from K£5.8m. in 1956 to K£23.8m. in 1967.[31] At current prices, they were K£24.7m. in 1964 and K£211m. in 1977.[32]

Yet these impressive figures may be misleading, since they relate only to a small proportion of total smallholder production and sales. Hazlewood calculates that in 1974/5 only about 9 per cent of smallholder output was of the main export crops in which this impressive growth had occurred, plus 20 per cent of food-crop sales and 16 per cent of livestock and milk sales. In addition, 38 per cent of production was food and 17 per cent livestock and milk for family consumption.[33] Thus some 33 per cent of smallholder output consisted of livestock and milk; and Kitching estimates that in the later 1960s beef sales alone constituted 25 per cent of farm revenues. Since most of these cattle were unaffected by technical improvements and the prices paid by the Kenya Meat Commission were low, this implied that the mass of smallholders were still heavily dependent on an un-improved product. Kitching, moreover, estimates that less than 12 per cent of cropped land in peasant hands was in high value crops or in improved varieties of maize, so that 'the vast majority of smallholder land was still being used, as it had been used in 1952, for the rearing of basic food crops and the pasturage of animals'.[34] Or, to put it another way, only some 350,000 out of 1.2m. smallholders had been affected by the agrarian revolution. There were two hallmarks of these beneficiaries: they held not less than 1.25 ha; and they had off-farm incomes which enabled them to buy land, employ labour and invest in new crops, particularly those which, like coffee, involved a period of waiting for trees to reach maturity. Smallholders entirely dependent on smaller amounts of land could not afford to set aside enough to grow cash crops; and in areas where non-farm incomes were less easily available, as in the Rift Valley, much more than 1.25 ha were necessary to go in for modern cash farming.

The conclusion must be that, despite improvements in the position of a minority of Kenyan smallholders and the relatively generous prices paid by the state marketing authorities, Kenyan agriculture developed very little in the two decades after the mid-1950s. It is true that productivity (value added) per worker in agriculture increased by 243 per cent from 1955 to 1970, though average farm earnings increased by only 93 per cent, which should have benefited and stimulated the larger farmers.[35] Yet Leo claims that, at least on the Million Acre scheme, the 'progressive', low-density large farms were barely, if at all, more efficient than the small, high-density farms.[36]

Why was the overall agricultural performance so limited? One answer must be lack of potentially agricultural land in relation to population, which limited most holdings to a size too small for progressive production. A possible palliative might have been to divide more of the large farms, on the principle that smallholders work and produce more intensively; in 1976 only 19 per cent of the total area of the large farms was under crops. But in many places this was due to limited rainfall and poor soils and many of the large farms were large simply because they were only suited to pastoralism.[37] Ultimately the explanation must be low agricultural productivity; and Kitching concludes that the solution must lie in

> an increase in the quantity and complexity of the commodities produced in Kenya by means of capital investment. At the level of economic logic, at least, the solution to Kenya's problem is nothing less than industrialisation – the industrialisation of agriculture and the raising of labour productivity outside of agriculture by increased capital intensity of non-agricultural production.[38]

The record of public policy in Kenya, therefore, is mixed. Moderate compared with many other African states, it was far less prone to waste resources on conspicuous public consumption, inefficient state farms

Table 6.1   Kenya's External Public Debt
and Debt Service, 1959–1982 (US$m.)

	A Debt outstanding	B Debt service	C EGS	A/C (%)	B/C (%)
1959	82.9	n/a	107.0	77.5	n/a
1963	142.4	n/a	142.0	100.2	n/a
1967	219.6	19.9	368.2	59.6	5.4
1970	312.8	27.0	468.7	66.7	5.7
1973	433.2	29.6	675.4	64.1	4.3
1977	821.4	54.1	1,570.0	52.3	3.4
1979	1,885.7	235.6	1,629.4	115.7	14.4 [7.5[a]]
1982	2,401.6	376.2	1,598.4	150.2	23.5 [20.3[b]]

Note:
The ratios marked a and b are given in *Accelerated Development* and *Toward Sustained Development* respectively. In neither case is the basis of the calculation clear, since no total is given for EGS.

1959, 1963: UN, *Statistical Yearbook 1965*, tables 148, 192.
1967: World Bank, *World Tables* (Washington DC, 1976).
1970–7: World Bank, *World Tables* (Washington DC, 1980).
1979: World Bank, *Accelerated Development*, App. 7, 17, 18.
1982: World Bank, *Toward Sustained Development*, Apps. 7, 13, 14.
1979 and 1982 column C: IMF, *International Financial Statistics Yearbook* (1984).

and manufactures; relatively generous to producers of cash crops; rational in its treatment of foreign investment. On the other hand, it adopted conventional protectionist policies for industry, provided state support to enable a small wealthy minority to engross land and establish private industrial enterprises, and accepted growing social inequality. It came increasingly to depend on foreign loans and investments to sustain the expanding modern sector and offset deficits in its balance of payments. The pattern of accelerating indebtedness and of its consequences is clear from Table 6.1.

These figures show that, although the total debt increased considerably between 1959 and 1977, its burden was kept down by a parallel expansion of exports and by continuing easy terms of debt service. Thereafter the oil price increase and a sudden rise in rates of interest – which increased from an average rate of 3.8 per cent in 1970 to 6.1 per cent in 1982 – made debt service very onerous indeed. It therefore became a major question in the 1980s whether Kenya could sustain the level of dependence on foreign capital and, if not, what would become of its capitalist economy and social structure.

Once again, then, we have a Black African state in which a thriving modern urban sector and a prosperous modern agriculture were built on a peasant agricultural base which, for a number of reasons, did not develop to provide the market, the jobs or the savings the modern state required. It is difficult to see how either the *laissez-faire* prescription of the conservative consensus or the egalitarian and autarkic proposals of the left could have solved these problems.

Tanzania

If Kenya has encouraged the ideological right, Tanzania has in turn been the hope and the disappointment of those who look for socialist solutions in Black Africa. From independence in 1961 Julius Nyerere, first as Prime Minister, then as President, proclaimed socialist goals. His Arusha Declaration of 1967 was a clarion call to reject capitalist and also urban values and to adopt 'ujamaa' as an idealized version of traditional (but not historical) 'African socialism'. Thereafter Tanzania took more positive steps to break capitalist control, both foreign and indigenous, of the economy and society than possibly any other modern African state. By the later 1970s even rural society had been reconstructed by an unprecedented movement of peasants to state-controlled and conceptually socialist villages.

All this stimulated great expectations among anti-imperialists and the international left. Here at least was one African state which was making a reality of independence. Yet the results have been almost uniformly disappointing. There were substantial achievements in welfare: by the later 1970s some 70 per cent of the age-group was enrolled in primary schools, 19 per cent in secondary schools.[39] Health was improved: life expectancy at birth rose from 42 to 52 between 1960 and 1979. Water supplies were substantially improved.[40] But almost every other indicator suggested very limited success before 1973 and a considerable decline thereafter, with 1967 as a visible watershed. The government claimed a growth rate in the gross material product of 4.3 per cent from 1965 to 1971 and 4.4 per cent from 1971 to 1977; but the credibility of the second figure depended very heavily on an alleged growth rate of 6.5 per cent in subsistence agriculture, which was almost certainly guesswork and highly improbable, since Tanzania imported vast amounts of food in the mid-1970s.[41] More realistic figures would be those for the growth of monetized gross material product: 5.2 per cent from 1965 to 1971, only 2.0 per cent from 1971 to 1977. For the same periods GDP rose at 5.6 and then fell at −4.8 per cent.[42] With population growing at 2.7 per cent in the 1960s and 3.4 per cent in the 1970s, this implied a substantial decline in real incomes after 1971. Indeed, Andrew Coulson calculates that the index of the standard of living of minimum wage-earners in Dar es Salaam (1966 = 100) rose from 99 in 1965 to a peak of 118 in 1974, then dropped to 53 in 1978. In rural areas the index dropped from 100 in 1966/7 to 65.6 in 1974/5, rising to 72.8 in 1978/9.[43]

In agriculture, production of most major export crops declined after 1966/7, especially cotton and sisal, though with slight increases in coffee, tobacco and tea, which resulted in very heavy deficits in the balance of payments by the mid-1970s.[44] Despite the commitment to 'self-reliance', Tanzania had to rely very heavily on foreign aid and investment in the 1970s; thus in 1975 there was a trade deficit of 2,990m. shillings (sh.), or US$418.6m., offset by overseas loans, investment, etc., of 2126m. sh. ($297.6m.).[45] Industrial growth, which had been quite considerable from the mid-1950s, checked in the early 1970s. There was much spare manufacturing capacity: a survey of thirty-nine firms in 1974 showed that 38 per cent of them were using less than half their capacity while, of the 80 per cent of firms affected by input shortages, 60 per cent imported 80 per cent or more of their material inputs. Labour productivity in manufacturing declined by about 3 per cent a year from 1969 to 1974, and the ratio between new investment and output deteriorated from 3:6 to 6:6 from 1968 to 1973.[46]

All these are indicators of an economy which had appeared to be developing soundly in the 1950s and early 1960s but which seemed to have ground to a halt and be in decline from the early 1970s. While adverse trends in terms of trade from the early 1970s and drought in the middle of that decade may have been partially responsible for this downturn, these are clearly not a sufficient explanation. Since the turning-point appears to have come after 1967, when Nyerere explicitly rejected the conventional and moderate policies inherited from the colonial state — the analogy with Nkrumah's new course of 1961 is obvious — it seems reasonable once again to look for explanations in the policies adopted by the state and the way in which these were implemented.

The State and the Economy

Of the state's dominant and increasing role there can be no doubt; indeed, one of Nyerere's 'Principles of Socialism' was 'That it is the responsibility of the state to intervene actively in the economic life of the nation so as to ensure the well-being of all citizens . . .'.[47] After 1967 the state became predominant in all spheres. Central government income (excluding receipts from parastatals) rose from 18.5 per cent of GDP in 1967/8 to 30.5 per cent in 1973/4, though it dropped to 25 per cent in 1976/7.[48] In the modern sector, after 1967 the state took over all commercial banks, insurance companies, grain mills, and the main import–export firms and acquired a controlling interest in the major MNC subsidiaries and the sisal industry. Subsequently the state undertook all importing and exporting through the State Trading Corporation, expropriated all buildings worth more than 100,000 sh. (excluding private residences), took over many small businesses and replaced all co-operative unions by government corporations. Foreign enterprise continued to operate in manufacturing, but only in partnership with the state, as a minority holder of the equity. Trade unions were effectively suppressed in 1962 and replaced by a single national union in 1964 as a branch of TANU, itself the ruling and by then the only legal political party. Most aspects of the modern economy came to be controlled by parastatals (64 in 1967, 139 in 1974, and still increasing), which acted both as holding companies and as business organizations. The state fixed minimum wages, provided all credit and set prices for traded agricultural produce. From 1964 five-year plans were used to allocate resources and control patterns of development. In the rural sector successive policies (which are outlined below) were adopted whose aim was to extend state control over the peasantry. Virtually all political power and economic control were vested in the President, TANU and the bureaucracy. In short, Tanzania ceased, at least in principle, to be an open economy or a liberal democracy. Perhaps nowhere else in Africa was engrossment of power by the state taken further. What were the consequences and who the beneficiaries?

Industry and Manufacturing

In manufacturing at least it is clear that the results were generally unsatisfactory and that the main beneficiaries of state power were the managers of parastatals and individual factories; certainly not the industrial workers nor the mass of rural consumers. The pattern of post-independence industrialization falls into two halves. Before the 1950s there was almost no manufacturing in Tanganyika, apart from some processing. Import-substituting manufacturing, however, began to develop in the later 1950s, before independence, and there were, perhaps, five main reasons for this.[49] The government was now prepared to provide substantial protection to firms which asked for and could put up a good case for it. Asian traders, stimulated by the Aga Khan, began to go into manufacturing as a safeguard against their possible exclusion from trade, some of them coming from Uganda and Kenya. Some foreign companies in Kenya started up subsidiaries in Tanzania as a hedge against a possible break-up of the East African Common Market, though Unilever, interestingly, decided against building a factory for non-soapy detergents at Dar es Salaam in 1964

on the converse ground that, without the Common Market, there
would be inadequate demand for the smallest viable enterprise.[50]
Some outside firms, notably Italian, were attracted by possibilities in
oil refining and provision of pipe-lines and transport. Finally, the
government sponsored the processing of coffee and cashew-nuts.

Until the later 1960s this resulted in a typical pattern of import-
substituting industrialization. Most manufacturing was by foreign
firms. Most products were previously imported consumer goods.
There was a rapid growth of enterprises and production. In 1960–6
value added in manufacturing rose from 109m. sh. to 271m.[51] Cotton
textiles increased from 5.2m. to 28.8m. sq. metres between 1963 and
1968, paints from 432,250 to 1,442,350 litres, sisal rope from nothing
to 16,454 tons, cement to 153,894 tons.[52] Rweyemamu argues that
this expansion was primarily the result of high levels of effective
protection on manufactured consumer imports, coupled with zero
duties and few restrictions on imported capital and other inputs.[53] He
also suggests (elsewhere) that these industries were generally very
profitable to their owners and that the outflow of dividends and other
forms of profit between 1961 and 1968 was far greater at 8577.2m. sh.
than net capital inflow on account of the multinationals of 484m. sh.
– though this is to fall into the trap of confusing current with capital
accounts and to ignore the income-generating potential of imported
capital, technology and know-how.[54] However, these industries
undoubtedly had many of the common features of import-substituting
industrialization in Third World countries. There were very few
backward linkages into other sectors of the Tanganyikan/Tanzanian
economy, except from those firms which processed coffee and sisal.
They were capital intensive: between 1958 and 1966 employment in
manufacturing rose only from 20,000 to 30,000 (i.e. by 50 per cent)
although value added increased by a factor of 2.7.[55] From all this
Rweyemamu concluded that this was 'perverse capitalist industrial
development', as defined by current dependency theory.[56]

That book was written (as a PhD thesis) before it was possible to
discern whether industrialization in the later (and in principle
'socialist') period was equally 'perverse'. The main innovation was, of
course, that the state now owned all or the majority of the equity in
all significant industrial enterprises through its parastatals. Some
factories were run entirely by these state corporations, others by
MNCs as managers and owners of a minority of the equity. The other
main innovation was that in 1971 workers' councils were set up in
factories under the *Mwongozo* (or TANU Guidelines) which, for a
couple of years, seriously disrupted production in a number of factories
until they were brought under control by TANU. This was certainly
socialist industrialization of a sort; did it have better results than the
capitalist industrialization which preceded it?

The evidence is not quite conclusive. Down to the early 1970s the manufacturing sector continued to expand satisfactorily. By 1971 about half the value of total parastatal assets in manufacturing was in new companies formed since 1964,[57] which suggests continued expansion. Output in the major industries – cotton textiles, cement and petroleum refining – continued to expand until 1973/4, after which it became static or declined. Beer, iron sheets, sisal ropes and wheat-flour milling all grew down to at least the later 1970s. A number of new products were introduced from the later 1960s, including electric batteries, shoes and rolled steel. Between 1967 and 1977 there was a significant decline, from 36 to 19 per cent, in the share of consumer goods in total imports and of 14 to 5 per cent in imports of building and other construction goods, while imports of intermediate goods and spare parts rose from 27 to 40 per cent.[58] Bienefeld, who takes a fairly favourable view of Tanzania's performance, estimates that there was a rising trend of productivity in manufacturing from 1965 to 1972, after which it fell back to the 1968 level by 1976, with the main sustained gains in the more dynamic industries.[59]

The initial picture, then, is of continued growth in manufacturing until the early 1970s, with increased employment and some improvement in productivity not, in general, bought at the price of a significant increase in capital investment per worker. Thereafter, however, the picture becomes less favourable. From 1973/4 there was a marked increase in incremental capital output ratios in general, though for parastatals a slight decrease from their previous very high ratios from 1972.[60] The operating surplus of industry was fairly constant at about 24–5 per cent from 1965 to 1975, though this was, of course, determined by levels of effective protection and monopolistic price-fixing.[61] From this Bienefeld concludes that the Tanzanian case is not entirely adverse to the argument for economic growth through industrialization under state control.

On the other hand, there were some serious limitations in this performance, particularly in exclusively state-run enterprises. From 1967 new state enterprises became more capital intensive than private or jointly owned firms and more dependent on imports: 74 per cent of their inputs were imported compared with 30 per cent for older firms, and each unit of labour contributed only half as much to production in these new enterprises as in older firms.[62] Moreover, in about 1973 the newer firms generated domestic savings valued at only 4 per cent of their capital stock, compared with 32 per cent from firms established before 1967, retaining only 50 per cent of value added in Tanzania as against nearly 80 per cent.[63] Detailed studies of individual new plants quoted by Coulson suggest bad planning, excessive use of capital equipment and heavy dependence on imported intermediates. These in turn reflected both the incompetence of the management who planned and ran these new parastatal enterprises, and also the inability of the central grovernment to exert effective control over state managers.

An additional factor was that growing dependence on foreign aid in the 1970s to provide new industrial investment (since foreign capital was largely excluded on dogmatic grounds and Tanzania could not afford the foreign exchange necessary to finance her capital imports) meant that new factories tended to come as packages which reflected industrial conditions in the European or American country of origin. Tanzania, in fact, took what was offered. Significantly, perhaps the most efficient of the new textile mills came from China, cost only about 60 per cent of a similar but capital-intensive mill designed by a French company, produced more fabric in 1975, employed twice as many Tanzanians and made a larger profit.[64]

The general record of manufacturing in Tanzania is, therefore, in line with that in most other African states, despite its increasingly 'socialist' character. Import-substituting industrialization failed to generate significant production of intermediate or capital goods and became increasingly dependent on imported inputs, whose supply became more uncertain as the country experienced serious balance of payments problems. Linkages to the domestic economy remained weak, except in processing. Factory employment rose only from 4 to 6 per cent of the labour force and industrial production from 11 to 13 per cent of GDP between 1960 and 1979.[65] There is, in fact, no evidence that the industrializing process had in any sense taken off; rather it was an expensive nationalistic method of replacing imported consumer goods which would otherwise have come mainly from Kenya. The cost, as always, was met by the general, and particularly the rural, consumer, who had to pay much more for a range of goods which were often inferior in quality and efficiency to what might otherwise have been imported. By the later 1970s Tanzania was in no sense 'independent' in industrial terms; indeed, its dependence on the capitalist world had, if anything, been increased by its need to pay for imports of most of the capital and intermediate goods needed to keep its industry operating.

Agriculture

It was, however, in agriculture that the Tanzanian experience was exceptional, both in the approach evolved by the state over time and in its adverse consequences. The salient facts are well known and have been widely discussed. Nyerere inherited what was in many ways a typical Black African agricultural economy of the mid-twentieth century. While predominantly 'peasant' and 'subsistence', it included an important plantation industry, mainly producing sisal for export, a substantial number of white farmers producing coffee and other export crops on a large scale, and a growing class of small to medium African farmers increasingly active in cash-crop production. Independence led to a large-scale evacuation by white farmers, but African farmers rapidly expanded production of cotton, coffee and cashew-nuts between 1960–2 and 1966–8, with annual growth rates ranging from 8 to 13 per cent.[66] Nyerere did not, on principle, approve of capitalist farming any more than capitalist industry, whether white or black; but he did believe in modernization, and in the 1960s experimented with various methods to improve production and productivity. Existing co-operatives were given a monopoly of buying and selling and were put under state control. Extension services, already well developed under the 'improvement' scheme, were further expanded. The so-called 'transformation approach' was used to establish new settlements on unused land, initially that left over from the Groundnut Scheme, with a considerable investment in irrigation and equipment. In short, there was no significant break in government policy between the later colonial period and the mid-1960s.

Why, then, did a break come in 1967, with the Arusha Declaration?[67] One main and stated aim of the Declaration was to emphasize the role of agriculture and rural development, as contrasted with that of industry and the towns, as part of the new policy of 'self-reliance'. In the context of African thinking on development in the 1960s, this was exceptional and potentially very constructive. Seen in this light previous agricultural policies were clearly inadequate because they had made little impact on peasant methods of cultivation and their inefficiency, apart from the minority of relatively affluent farmers. The co-operatives, given more power and bureaucratized, proved corrupt, undemocratic and incompetent. The extension/improvement policy had very little impact on peasants, partly because the officials were often too rigid in their prescriptions, partly because the material benefits were monopolized by the minority of more successful and influential farmers. The transformation schemes had been expensive failures, mainly because the equipment and techniques were unsuited to both the land and the crops grown. Moreover, while commodity production grew, due mainly to the enterprise of a small minority of large producers and growing production for the market by small-holders, subsistence agriculture grew faster; between 1960 and 1968 subsistence (that is, non-marketed) production increased from 55 to 71 per cent of total agricultural output. Meantime agriculture as a whole declined from 60.9 to 41 per cent of GDP.[68]

The conclusion has to be that agriculture was not developing as fast as the rest of the economy and that subsistence production, implicitly non-progressive, was becoming preponderant. All this provided good grounds for Nyerere to look for a radical new departure in agricultural policy. But an additional consideration may have been what Hyden calls the growth of 'patronage politics' in rural areas, in which party members and bureaucrats created private fiefs and in turn were influenced by the demands of their peasant clients. If peasant resistance to economic change was an economic obstacle to modernization, such a socio-political system was a threat to the power of TANU as the dominant influence in a centralized socialist state.[69]

The Arusha Declaration, therefore, can be seen as Nyerere's response to both problems. By adopting the concept of ujamaa, he attempted to invoke an idealized version of the mutual self-help of the peasant household as the basis for a socialist work ethic. By replacing capitalism with this 'socialist' concept, he could legitimize intrusive action by the state to obtain higher levels of production. At the same time, he could neutralize the political influence of the rural petty bourgeoisie, and this may well have been a primary motive.[70] It remained to be seen how this mix of potentially constructive economic ideas, socialist dogma and political realism would work out.

In practice the new economic course again changed direction in about 1973. During the first six years the emphasis was on collective and communal production and the elimination of capitalist farming. In the second respect at least it was successful: most sisal estates were nationalized, many of the large grain farms were expropriated and became state farms or were handed over to be operated by ujamaa villages. Larger African farmers were forced to give up much of their land. On the other side, some success was achieved in concentrating peasants into villages, which was done to make communal production under official supervision possible. Between 1970 and 1974 the number of people living in ujamaa villages increased from 531,200 to 2,560,472; but in 1972 perhaps only half of the Tanzanian population lived in villages, by no means all of which were organized under the new ujamaa system.[71]

The economic effects of this policy were very unsatisfactory. At constant (1966) prices monetized output grew at 3.9 per cent from 1965 to 1971. Subsistence was estimated to have grown at 3.1 per cent; but in the three years after the new policy took effect, from 1968 to 1971, subsistence production was virtually static and monetized production grew by only about 5 per cent.[72] Meantime the major export crops were in serious decline. Between 1966/7–1967/8 and 1971/2–1972/3 cotton production dropped by 3,695 tons, sisal by 53,612 tons, pyrethrum from 5,558 to 3,962 tons, and coffee production was almost static. Only cashew-nuts and tea grew significantly. Nor were the social effects satisfactory. Apart from the few highly successful voluntary ujamaa villages, such as the famous Ruvuma Development Association (later to be closed down because too independent), peasants found that they could take little active part in planning collective activities, which were in the hands of the civil servants, nor was there much advantage for them in taking part in collective production.

How does one account for this evident failure of the early ujamaa experiment? Hyden explains it mainly in terms of peasant resistance or indifference to policies imposed on them by bureaucrats and party agents in which they could see no benefit for themselves nor any of the moral obligations of the peasant ethic.[73] They were offered no new tools or other aids except as bribes to work on communal land. Communal work was seen as marginal to work on their own land and was refused if it coincided with critical moments in their own cycle of production, such as periods of rainfall. Declining payments for their marketed produce discouraged increased effort: their terms of trade deteriorated by some 30 per cent between 1965 and 1974. Above all, as Hyden puts it, 'the material base of the peasant mode was too narrow for a rapid socialist transformation'.[74]

The outcome of failure in this idealistic venture was Nyerere's adoption of a new and much more brutal technique of state control of the peasantry in 1973. All rural inhabitants were to be compulsorily 'villagized' by 1976, so that they could no longer escape effective control. This announcement coincided with both the drought and a policy of decentralizing the bureaucracy so that it could control the peasantry more effectively: there would be more administration at village level. Even the surviving co-operative villages were to be broken up because they were too independent.

The effects of this policy are not yet clear. By the later 1970s it was claimed that some 13 million people were living in villages, defined as having at least 250 families, which included pre-1967 communal survivals, old villages and the largely new settlements created under the new policy. This must rate as one of the largest enforced population movements of modern history. In the short term, from 1974 to 1976, there was a major drop in agricultural production, which was possibly intensified by drought. In the period from 1971/2–1972/3 to 1976/7–1977/8 cotton production declined from 71,296 to 65,199 tons, sisal from 168,977 to 105,009 tons, cashew-nuts from 121,750 to 82,404 tons.[75] Food crops also suffered, as reflected in an increase of grain imports from 11,600 tons in 1970/71 to 413,200 tons in 1974/5.[76] On the other hand, food production recovered in the years of good rainfall 1976–8, when peasants had settled into their new villages, and food imports declined rapidly to 45,000 tons in 1977. There was also some recovery in commodity production. The government responded to the food crisis in various ways. Some state farms were started with expatriate machines and technicians, sometimes under foreign aid schemes. Heavily subsidized fertilizer was made available to peasants. The prices paid by the National Milling

Corporation were raised from about 300sh. to 800sh. a ton. There was less insistence on communal farming but more intimidation of the peasants. The overall effect, therefore, seems to have been that peasant production of food recovered quickly from the trauma of removal but that cash-crop production did not.

There was, therefore, no great disaster. On the other hand there was no real success in raising agricultural productivity or production. No technical changes were introduced and few new inputs were provided. Peasants may have understood their new ecological environment less well than the old, and nucleated settlements were more prone to crop and livestock disease than dispersed farms. Despite the more intensive pressure now put on them by the bureaucrats, peasants, according to Hyden, retained much of their autonomy: they could still 'deceive' their petty-bourgeois administrators. In short, a decade of new socialist agricultural courses had seriously weakened Tanzania's commodity exports without radically changing the nature of agriculture or transforming it into a provider of surplus for national economic development.

The Tanzanian record, therefore, differs very little from that of the other African states, despite its avowed ideological character and the undoubtedly imaginative and disinterested policies of Nyerere. Relative failure had many possible explanations. In the last years before 1982 adverse exogenous factors included a rapid decline in Tanzania's terms of trade (1980 = 100) from 105 in 1979 to 86 in 1981 and a substantial increase in the burden of its considerable external public debt (shown in Table 6.2), made worse by the decline in the volume as well as the value of commodity exports.[77] But so far as the failure of state public policy-making and execution is concerned, the current consensus seems to be that the main weakness lay in the ability and attitudes of the political and administrative elite. All the main studies emphasize the incompetence of most civil servants to run the complex apparatus of the state and economy and their inability, as members of a predominantly urban petty bourgeoisie, to understand and lead the peasantry. Those writers involved in the highly theoretical debate over the nature of class differentiation in post-colonial Africa agree that, despite the genuine socialist idealism of TANU, the bulk of its members and the civil service were part of the petty bourgeoisie, who saw the state and its policies primarily as a means of enabling them to stand up to the 'metropolitan bourgeoisie' (foreign capital) in the control of the industrial system and also of extracting value from the peasantry.[78] Given such self-interested motives among those who alone could carry out public policy, it is not surprising that there was an unbridgeable gap between imaginative plans and sustained economic development.

Table 6.2 *Tanzania's External Public Debt and Debt Service, 1962–1982 (US$m.)*

	A Debt out- standing	B Debt service	C EGS	A/C (%)	B/C (%)
1962	48	n/a	158.7	30.2	n/a
1967	139.9	7.3	270.3	51.7	2.7
1970	248.5	15.7	308.0	80.7	8.2
1973	463.7	31.9	418.4	110.8	7.6
1977	1,005.0	33.2	686.4	146.4	4.8
1979	1,213.4	59.8	697.2	174.0	8.5 [7.4[a]]
1982	1,631.6	46.4	908.6	179.6	5.1

Note:
a. The ratio marked a is given in *Accelerated Development*. The basis of the calculation is not clear, since no total is given for EGS.
Sources:
1962: UN, *A Survey of Economic Conditions in Africa, 1960–1964*, table 16 and Appendix table 1.
1967: World Bank, *World Tables* (Washington DC, 1976).
1970–7: World Bank, *World Tables* (Washington DC, 1980).
1979: World Bank, *Accelerated Development*, App. 7, 17, 18.
1982: World Bank, *Toward Sustained Development*, App. 7, 13, 14.
1979 and 1982 column C: IMF, *International Financial Statistics Yearbook* (1984).

Notes

1 World Bank, *Accelerated Development in Sub-Saharan Africa (AD)* (Washington DC, 1981), App. 7, 3, 14.
2 *AD* App. 1, 2.
3 *AD* App. 8; A. Hazlewood, *The Economy of Kenya. The Kenyatta Era* (Oxford, 1979).
4 Hazlewood, tables 5.12, 5.13.
5 Hazlewood, table 5.15.
6 *AD* App. 5.
7 Hazlewood, tables 3.10, 5.3.
8 Hazlewood, p. 160.
9 Hazlewood, table 5.5.
10 S. W. Langdon, *Multinational Corporations in the Political Economy of Kenya* (London, 1981), pp. 36–7.
11 Langdon, *Multinational Corporations*, p. 42.
12 ibid., ch. 3.
13 ibid., ch. 5.
14 See R. Kaplinsky, 'Capital Accumulation in the Periphery: Kenya', in M. Fransman (ed.), *Industry and Accumulation in Africa* (London 1982), p. 201.

15 Hazlewood, table 5.11.
16 Hazlewood, p. 66.
17 Hazlewood, tables 5.7, 5.9.
18 Hazlewood, pp. 70, 67.
19 See C. Leys, *Underdevelopment in Kenya* (London, 1975); Langdon, 'Multinational Corporations, Taste Transfer and Underdevelopment: A Case Study from Kenya', *RAPE*, vol. 2 (1975) and *Multinational Corporations*; Kaplinsky, 'Capital Accumulations'; Gavin Kitching, *Class and Economic Change in Kenya* (New Haven, 1975), especially chs 12 and 13.
20 C. Leys, 'Accumulation, Class Formation and Dependency in Kenya', in Fransman (ed.) *Industry and Accumulation*; N. Swainson, 'The Rise of a National Bourgeoisie in Kenya', *RAPE*, vol. 8 (1977) and 'State and Economy in Post-Colonial Kenya, 1963–78', *CJAS*, vol. 12, no. 3 (1978).
21 B. Beckman, 'Imperialism and Capitalist Transformation: A Critique of a Kenyan Debate', *RAPE*, vol. 19 (1980).
22 *AD* p. 56, Box D.
23 *AD* App. 2, 5.
24 Hazlewood, table 4.7.
25 Hazlewood, table 4.6.
26 C. Leo, 'Who benefited from the Million-Acre Scheme? Towards a Class Analysis of Kenya's Transition to Independence', *CJAS*, vol. 15, no. 2 (1981). See also his *Land and Class in Kenya* (Toronto, 1984), which examines these issues in greater detail.
27 Hazlewood, tables 4.18, 4.9.
28 The following argument is based mainly on Kitching, chs. 11 and 12; C. Leo, 'The Failure of the "Progressive Farmer" in Kenya's Million-Acre Settlement Scheme', *JMAS*, vol. 16, no. 4 (1978) and his *Land and Class in Kenya*; Hazlewood.
29 Hazlewood, table 4.17.
30 For details of this scheme, see E. Graham with Ingrid Floering, *The Modern Plantation in the Third World* (London, 1984), ch. 7 (by Floering).
31 Kitching, table 11.2.
32 Hazlewood, table 4.8.
33 Hazlewood, table 4.11.
34 Kitching, p. 329.
35 Kitching, tables 11.2, 11.3.
36 Leo, 'The Failure', table 1.3.
37 Hazlewood, table 4.20.
38 Kitching, p. 428.
39 *AD* App. 38.
40 *AD* App. 34, 37; A. Coulson, *Tanzania. A Political Economy* (Oxford, 1982), ch. 21
41 Coulson, table 20.3.
42 Coulson, tables 20.3, 20.4.
43 Coulson, tables 20.10, 20.12.
44 Coulson, tables 20.5, 20.1.
45 Coulson, table 20.2. The dollar exchange rate of the shilling was about 7.142sh. = $1 from 1960 to 1975, after which it was gradually devalued to stand at 13.041sh. = $1 in 1983.

46 Coulson, table 20.6.
47 Coulson, p. 176.
48 Coulson, table 20.8. *AD* App. 5 has lower figures for 'public consumption', but still shows an increase from 9 to 16 per cent of GDP from 1960 to 1979.
49 This argument is based mainly on Coulson, ch. 18; J. Rweyemamu, *Underdevelopment and Industrialization in Tanzania. A Study of Perverse Capitalist Industrialist Development* (Nairobi, 1973; references are to the 1978 edn.).
50 See D. K. Fieldhouse, *Unilever Overseas. The Anatomy of a Multinational, 1895–1965* (London, 1978), p. 417.
51 Coulson, p. 173.
52 Rweyemamu, *Underdevelopment and Industrialization*, table 4.5.
53 ibid., tables 4.8, 4.9, 4.10.
54 J. Rweyemamu, 'The Political Economy of Foreign Investment in the Underdeveloped Countries', *African Review*, vol. 1, no. 1 (1971), p. 115.
55 Coulson, p. 173.
56 Rweyemamu, *Underdevelopment and Industrialization*, chs. 3 and 5.
57 Coulson, table 23.1.
58 Coulson, table 20.7.
59 M. Bienefeld, 'Evaluating Tanzanian Industrial Development', in Fransman (ed.) *Industry and Accumulation*, table 6.9, fig. 6.4(a), table 6.11.
60 Bienefeld, p. 128.
61 Bienefeld, table 6.12.
62 Coulson, p. 280, quoting W. E. Clark, *Socialist Development and Public Investment in Tanzania, 1964–73* (Toronto, 1978), pp. 117, 135–6 and ch. 20.
63 Coulson, p. 280, quoting C. Barker *et al.*, 'Industrial Production and Transfer of Technology in Tanzania: The Political Economy of Tanzanian Industrial Enterprises', Mimeo, Institute of Development Studies, Dar es Salaam, 1976.
64 Coulson, table 23.3.
65 *AD* App. 35, 3.
66 Coulson, table 17.1.
67 Based on Coulson, ch. 17; G. Hyden, *Beyond Ujamaa in Tanzania* (London, 1980), chs 3 and 4.
68 Hyden, table 3.1.
69 Hyden, pp. 86–92.
70 Hyden, p. 105.
71 Hyden, table 4.1.
72 Coulson, table 20.3.
73 Hyden, pp. 105–15.
74 Hyden, p. 124.
75 Coulson, table 20.5; Hyden, table 5.1.
76 See Linda Freeman, 'CIDA Wheat and Rural Development in Tanzania', *CJAS*, vol. 16, no. 3 (1982).
77 World Bank, *Toward Sustained Development in Sub-Saharan Africa* (Washington DC, 1984), App. 11 and Table 6.2 in this chapter.

78 See, for example, M. von Freyhold, 'The Post-Colonial State and its Tanzanian Version', *RAPE*, vol. 8 (1977); S. D. Mueller, 'The Historical Origins of Tanzania's Ruling Class', *CJAS*, vol. 15, no. 3 (1981).

7

Francophone West Africa: Ivory Coast

Almost alone among Black African states, Ivory Coast stands in the literature as a story of apparent success after decolonization. At least down to 1979 (the second rise in petroleum prices, coupled with a dramatic drop in export commodity prices) virtually every economic indicator was favourable. In 1979 GNP per capita at $1,040 was second only to that of oil-rich Gabon at $3,280.[1] The average per capita rate of growth of GNP for 1960–79 was 2.4 per cent, despite very high rates of population growth (3.7 per cent in the 1960s, 5.5 per cent in the 1970s) which was due to part in a huge influx of Africans from other states.[2] The GDP grew at 8.0 per cent in the 1960s, 6.7 per cent in the 1970s; agricultural production at 4.2 per cent and 3.4 per cent respectively, industrial production at 11.5 and 10.5 per cent.[3] In terms of sectoral shares, agriculture declined from 43 to 26 per cent of GDP, industry increased from 14 to 23 per cent and services from 43 to 51 per cent. The volume of exports grew by 8.8 per cent in the 1960s, and by 5.2 per cent in the 1970s, imports by 9.7 and 10.1 per cent in these decades. In 1979 the merchandise trade was virtually balanced.[4] This performance was greatly helped by favourable terms of trade. The net barter terms of trade (1975 = 100) improved from 113 in 1960 to 129 in 1979, the income terms of trade from 31 to 138.[5] Dependence on the three principal exports (cocoa, coffee, timber) declined from 81.2 per cent in 1961 to 68.1 per cent average in 1976–8.[6] The proportion of export trade with France declined from 51 per cent to 26 per cent in 1960–74 and the import trade from 65 to 39 per cent, though trade with EEC as a whole changed less: exports from 66 to 62 per cent, imports from 75 to 57 per cent.[7]

That is the substance of the success story; but there were some less satisfactory aspects. One was a growing deficit on trade and the balance of payments, coupled with a rapidly mounting external debt and increasingly onerous burden of debt service. By 1979 the adverse balance of payments (before debt service) on current account was $560m., compared with $26m. in 1970. Total external debt had risen from $256.1m. in 1970 to $3,942.7m. in 1979, and $4,537.3m. in

1982; the debt service from $38.5m. to $737.1m. and then $996.7m. As a percentage of GNP debt service had risen from 2.8 to 6.0 per cent between 1970 and 1979, as a proportion of the export of goods and services from 6.8 to 15.2 per cent, and stood at 36.9 per cent in 1982.[8] A dramatic decline in the export price of cocoa and coffee was partly responsible for the deteriorating position in the later years. Between 1977 and 1981 cocoa prices fell from 1,714 francs CFA (hereafter FCFA) to 413, coffee from 1,270 to 550. Since these together represented about 55 per cent of the value of Ivory Coast exports, the result was an unprecedented adverse balance of merchandise trade in 1980 and a rise in the debt service ratio to 29 per cent of the value of the export of goods and services in 1981.[9] This might be seen as a transient consequence of a temporary drop in the previously very high price of these commodities, but its effects pointed to the fact that this 'Ivorian miracle' was in some sense a gamble on the ability to sustain very high levels of commodity exports at reasonable prices. Or, to put it another way, by the later 1970s the country had reduced its safety margin as a commodity exporter dependent on the international market by very heavy overseas borrowing.

It is this fact which calls into question the basic strategy adopted by Ivory Coast. The crisis (if indeed it was a crisis rather than a temporary fluctuation) was precisely what critics of the country had been predicting for a decade and a half. It is, indeed, a special feature of Ivory Coast that, instead of explaining post-colonial failure, analysts, particularly on the left, had been discounting success. The basic reason was ideological. Since the 1960s opponents of capitalism had been denouncing strategies of Third World countries which maintained the 'colonial' emphasis on commodity production for export to capitalist countries on the ground that this implied continued 'dependence' on the West, and which encouraged and relied on a large influx of foreign direct investment. Such strategies, it was alleged, must perpetuate a 'neo-colonial' relationship with the ex-colonial powers and, even if they generated wealth in the short term, were certain to result in 'growth without development', or, in A. G. Frank's later term, 'the development of underdevelopment'. This hypothesis was probably first put forward for Ivory Coast by Samir Amin in his seminal study *Le Développement du capitalisme en Côte d'Ivoire*, first published in 1967, which was based on evidence from 1950 to 1965.[10]

Amin's argument was that since about 1950 the 'miracle' of economic growth in Ivory Coast was the product of a favourable but essentially transient situation. In 1950 the colony was 'in the state of a colonial "reserve", where development had not yet begun'.[11] It had ample undeveloped land suitable for commodity production, a large supply of cheap labour, reinforced by immigrants from neighbouring states, virtually no industry (so considerable scope for import substitution once the break up of the French West African common market and independence made protection possible), a favourable international market for staple exports, and access on good terms to the international capital market. These factors, helped by a liberal economic regime and stable (though less liberal) government, provided all the ingredients for rapid economic growth.

Yet Amin predicted that this growth would be limited both in time and economic significance. Historically it would be analogous to, but must faster than, the expansion of commodity production in other regions of West Africa in the past, notably Senegal and Ghana. As in these countries, expansion would ultimately be checked by shortage of fertile new land and the limited overseas market for their products. Internally industrial import substitution would be checked by the restricted domestic market, and the new industries would strike no firm roots in the domestic economy: they would not stimulate upstream production of intermediate and capital goods, but would rely on imports. Meantime a large proportion of the profits of both agriculture and industry would be siphoned abroad by foreign investors and owners of the means of production. Once economic growth slowed down, the strain on society and government would become intense. Social cohesion would be endangered by growing inequality between more and less favoured regions and between ethnic groups and there would be dangerous competition for jobs between indigenous and immigrant workers. This in turn would probably discredit a dictatorial and elitist political system, whose main asset was continuous growth. Then the economic miracle would grind to a halt and the economic strategy underlying it would be discredited.

When Amin wrote this in the mid-1960s there was little enough empirical evidence to support his pessimism; and in the next two decades those who shared his basic assumptions waited for the day of reckoning to come. It is not proposed here – nor would it be possible yet – to determine whether the 'crisis' of the early 1980s constituted this apocalypse. Rather the same issues will be examined for Ivory Coast as for the other states included in this study: the role of the state as policy-maker in the economy and, in particular, its contribution to the growth of industry and agriculture. But in this case the question is reversed: how far was the state and its strategies responsible for the very solid success of the Ivory Coast until at least the late 1970s and what evidence was there by about 1980 that Amin's doom-laden forecasts were correct?

The State and the Economy

There is a paradox at the heart of any study of the economic role of the state in post-independence Ivory Coast. On the one hand, and central to public rhetoric, was the claim that the state saw its job as creating conditions conducive to economic growth, and not as a prime economic actor. It made no pretence at creating a socialist order and relied on private enterprise, much of it foreign, to undertake development. State enterprise was therefore the exception, not the norm, as in Ghana. Yet, on the other side, the Ivorian state took a very positive role in planning, in the provision of infrastructure, in the extraction of surplus from the domestic economy and in investment. It was also increasingly a minority shareholder in private productive enterprises. In short, while the economic role of the state was very different from that in Ghana, Tanzania or Senegal, the contrast was not between inertia and involvement but between different types of state initiative and action.

Consider first the positive aspects of state intervention in the economy. Between 1960 and 1970 the growth rate of public consumption was 11.8 per cent, compared with 8.0 per cent for private consumption; in the 1970s the rates were 10.0 and 7.3 per cent respectively.[12] In 1960 public consumption was 10 per cent of GDP; in 1979 it was 17 per cent, while private consumption had fallen from 73 to 56 per cent.[13] These proportions for private consumption were among the lowest listed by the World Bank for Black Africa; the explanation lies in the relatively high level of gross domestic saving, which was 17 per cent in 1960 and 27 per cent in 1979. Since most of this saving was made by the state rather than by private citizens, and took the form of compulsory levies of various kinds on the productive sector of the economy, it must be regarded as part of the state's economic activity. Thus, if one combines public consumption and domestic saving, the state was absorbing 44 per cent of the domestic product in 1979. The comparable figure for Kenya in the same year was 35 per cent, for Ghana 14 per cent and for Tanzania 24 per cent. Clearly the Ivory Coast government was a dominant user of national resources.

The point, clearly, is that, while the Ivorian state from the start adopted a 'liberal' economic strategy, in an African context it was essential for the state to play a very much more positive role than had been possible in the liberal economies of Europe and North America in their periods of economic liberalism. The broad pattern, moreover, suggests a gradual movement away from dogmatic *laissez-faire* to unadmitted but increasingly direct state intervention. At independence Houphouet-Boigny deliberately chose to gamble the future economic development of his country on the maintenance of the existing very close relationship with France, which had been largely responsible for its very rapid economic growth since 1945. Since a large part of development capital came from France through FIDES, and as France then took 51 per cent of exports and provided 65 per cent of imports[14] and since most of the import–export trade was in the hands of a small group of French trading companies (SCOA, CFAO, etc.), this was, so critics have alleged, merely to prolong colonialism under the guise of independence. Ivory Coast had no wish to alienate its paymaster.[15] Yet this is too simple: other French territories were in the same position, yet chose not to adopt economic liberalism. Houphouet-Boigny's choice was a positive one, related to the position and needs of Ivory Coast as he saw them.

Liberalism, moreover, certainly did not imply state inertia. From the start the government took positive measures to develop the economy within the desired 'open' framework. The Investment Code of 1959 offered major attractions to foreign direct investment: a five-year tax-holiday, ten years' exemption from import duties on capital goods, no limit to repatriation of profits on capital. For better or worse, those rules, though modified in the 1970s, were the basis of the Ivory Coast's investment bonanza. Also important was adhesion to the franc zone. In 1962 Ivory Coast joined the Union Monitaire Oust'Africaine, which shared a single central bank, a single currency (the CFA franc at 50 FCFA = 1 French franc), paid all foreign currency earnings into the account in Paris and had unlimited convertibility into foreign currencies. These, together with acceptance of the Yaoundé Agreements of 1964 and 1969, which rationalised Francophone Africa's economic relations with EEC, committed Ivory Coast to a particular pattern of economic development, based on maximum international specialization and exchange and virtually free access for foreign capital on the most favourable terms.

Yet, from the start, economic liberalism was coupled with increasingly intensive protectionism and economic management. Admittedly there were no import duties on raw materials or capital goods, and duties on most other imports were relatively low, with a preference in favour of EEC products and quotas on some goods from elsewhere. But over time, as import-substituting industrial production grew, quotas, absolute bans or duties were imposed on competing imports. Equally significant, and characteristic of other African states, were measures taken to extract funds for investment from the domestic economy. There were three main sources: from general taxation, from a levy on business profits, and from a levy on agricultural production.

From the start Ivory Coast had two distinct budgets: the ordinary budget for current government expenditure, and an investment budget – BSIE – which in turn had two parts.[16] BSIE-Trésor was financed by a surplus on the ordinary budget, by a levy on business profits and by a levy on farm incomes. The other – BSIE-CAA – was financed by foreign borrowing. In addition, there was public investment outside these budgets, by public enterprises and other extrabudgetary programmes. Over time the ratio between these changed. In the early

1960s net public savings were 60 per cent of public investment; by 1975 they were down to 37 per cent. Thus the levy on agriculture became the main domestic (as distinct from foreign) source of new public investment capital.

In 1960 Ivory Coast had no marketing board of the type inherited by most new Anglophone African states. In that year a non-state organization, the Caisse de Stablisation et de Soutien des Prix des Productions Agricoles (hereafter Caisse), was set up to equalize prices between good and bad years. Inevitably, in 1966, it became a state enterprise (though by contrast with Anglophone countries, buying and selling of commodities was left to the foreign-owned trading enterprises) whose function was to fix producer prices, operate a reserve stabilization fund and extract profits for the state. Until the later 1970s cocoa and coffee producers were usually given about 50 per cent of the f.o.b. price of their product, while traders and transporters took 12–15 per cent. The government export tax was fixed at 22.5 per cent of the posted price to the early 1970s, then 23 per cent. The balance went to the stabilization fund which could be used by the government as a source of investment capital. Since, however, the government in practice paid the producers fixed prices which rose very slowly, fluctuations in world commodity prices mainly affected the stabilization fund. Thus in the boom year 1977 the producers got only about 25 per cent of the world price and the government take amounted to more than 50 per cent of the total national investment for the year. In 1980 the Caisse was responsible for 51.5 per cent of planned public investment, most of the rest coming from foreign sources on the security of the foreign exchange earnings of cocoa and coffee.[17]

The effects of this system on the rural producers of cocoa and coffee will be considered later. The present point is that, so far as possible, the Ivory Coast state initially attempted to finance a very ambitious plan of public investment, much of it on infrastructure, mainly from compulsory public savings, and this was one of the state's most positive economic functions in the 1960s. In the 1970s, however, state economic intervention became more direct and intense and Ivory Coast moved closer to the pattern found in most other African states. There was no sudden change of stated policy from liberalism to intervention, but one can point to a number of factors which seem likely to have had this result. These included growing disparities between the poorer north and the richer east and south, increasing dependence on imported food, the desire to diversify out of excessive dependence on cocoa and coffee, a growing labour force, especially in the towns, nationalist desire to reduce the dominance of foreign capital, and the need to provide goods and services not provided by the state or by private enterprise.

Increased state activity took a number of forms, among them much greater direct public control and stimulation of production. By 1979 thirty-three state enterprises (SODE—autonomous parastatal societies for development) had started. Among the largest and best run was SODESUCRE, set up in 1974 to stimulate cane-sugar production and refining in the north, whose aim was both to increase employment and wealth in a poor area and to create a very large industry capable not only to replace imports of refined sugar but even to export 200,000 tons in the 1980s. Another was SODERIZ, set up in 1971, to increase rice production from 300,000 to 400,000 tons, again mainly in the north, and so to eliminate imports. SODELPALM was created to increase palm-oil and coconut-oil production.[18]

These agro-business parastatals constituted a turning-point in the character of Ivory Coast economic history. Most of them developed the same basic faults and problems as were found in other African state enterprises. They became private fiefs of the managing elite. They were largely autonomous, so were able to fix wages and borrow money with almost no governmental control: between 1975 and 1977 60 per cent of the increase in external debt (from 142b. to 354b. FCFA) was attributable to twelve of those SODES. Their production fell well below expectation, and their production costs were so high that the prices they charged were well above world prices. Thus between 1975 and 1980 the price of refined sugar rose from 95 to 300 FCFA per kilo, three times the world price; and rice cost twice the world price. In each case the government had to subsidize the domestic price. By the later 1970s the situation was so bad that reforms were undertaken. Seven SODES survived as parastatals, nine were transferred into public industrial and commercial enterprises, three became part of the public administration and fourteen were abolished. But much damage had been done, in particular to the country's debt position and its liability to sustain loss-making enterprises.

The other important increase in state economic involvement consisted in growing public shareholding in private (mostly foreign) owned enterprises through the Societé Nationale de Financement (SONAFI), set up in 1962. Funds were raised in two ways: by issuing bonds (which could also be acquired by established business undertakings in exchange for obligatory retention of 10 per cent of profits by industrial enterprises); and from endowment funds provided by the government out of its ordinary revenues. SONAFI's aims were partly to help Ivory Coast nationals to establish enterprises or to take a share in existing foreign enterprises; partly to buy a share for the state in the latter. By 1974 SONAFI owned some 7 per cent of total capital and the state owned some 23 per cent of the capital of all industrial undertakings. Although there was no compulsory sale of equity by foreign firms, as in most other African states, by 1978 some 58 per cent of capital in the modern sector was owned by Ivory Coast citizens or the state.

Thus, by the later 1970s the Ivory Coast state had partially discarded its non-interventionist policy; it was increasingly active in the economy. Yet, by the standards of most African societies its direct involvement in the productive sector remained small. Most existing state or parastatal enterprises were concerned with infrastructure or special agricultural enterprises; industry remained in private, mostly foreign, hands, the state buying a minority but never a controlling interest. Even so, the costs of increased state intervention had proved very high and Ivory Coast was facing declining returns on new investment. In 1965–70 the incremental capital-output ratio was 2.7; in 1970–5 it had risen to 4.1.[19] This suggested that the policy of artificially stimulating new investment in the 1970s was endangering the economic growth of the Ivory Coast, and in particular that industrial expansion was being bought at an increasingly high and potentially dangerous cost.

Industry and Manufacturing

In 1960 Ivory Coast had almost no industrial activities.[20] Most manufactures were imported from France or Dakar, the industrial centre for French West Africa. Virtually all Ivory Coast agricultural products were exported unprocessed – coffee and cocoa beans, untreated timber. In 1960 'manufacturing' (which consisted mainly of processing raw materials) was estimated at 4.0 per cent of GDP, as against 43 per cent for agriculture. Yet by 1972 manufacturing had risen to 12.7 per cent and agriculture was down to 25.5 per cent.[21] By a different measure, 'industry' (which included 'mining', 'crafts' and 'construction' as well as 'manufacturing') grew from 14 to 23 per cent of GDP between 1960 and 1979;[22] but as the shares of mining and crafts had declined and that of construction increased only by 1.3 per cent, the major increase was in large-scale manufacturing.

Within these totals a contrast can be seen in the dynamics of the two main elements in 'manufacturing': agro-industries (processing local raw materials, much of them for export) and 'import based industries', whose inputs came largely from overseas and which were producing consumer goods for the local market. From 1965 to 1972 the two categories developed at the same rate; but from 1972 agro-industries grew at about twice the rate of import-based industries.[23] One other major feature, which made industrial development exceptional in Black Africa, was the relatively high proportion of manufactures that were exported: in 1974, 32.2 per cent of total exports by value, mostly processed agricultural and sylvan products.[24]

What are the implications of these statistics? Do they imply a successful state policy of industrialization which was capable of indefinite progress and generating sufficient savings to ensure continuous growth of the economy? The first point to consider is why industrialization on such a scale took place at all, given the government's commitment to a liberal economic system, concentration on the production and export of agricultural commodities, and close trading links with Europe.

The general explanation lies in the conventional Third World compound of concessions to attract private foreign capital and effective protection to ensure that its operations were profitable. As has been seen, the Investment Charter of 1959 provided very attractive conditions for all types of foreign investment. For the most part this consisted in overseas firms which had previously exported their goods from France (or Dakar) setting up local factories in Ivory Coast in order to maintain markets against potential competitors. The list of such products was standard: textiles, footwear, petroleum refining, chemical products, rubber goods, building materials, transport equipment and mechanical and electrical products. Their average domestic resource cost coefficient was 1.34 – implying that production costs on average were above international prices at the fixed rate; and the effective protection coefficient averaged 1.42, low by the standards of many other Third World countries but implying that local production of these things was considerably more expensive then imported goods.[25] There were, however, some exceptions, including beer and soft drinks, which had natural protection, board and paper articles. Another almost universal factor was the high import content of most of these industries. The share of imported inputs in total inputs used by industry was 56 per cent in 1961, 63 per cent in 1966 and 58 per cent in 1971. Conversely, only 17 per cent of domestically purchased industrial inputs in 1971 came from the Ivory Coast's industrial sector, though this had risen to 30 per cent in 1973.[26]

Another measure of the importance of industry to the economy is the proportion of the domestic market which it satisfies. Taking 'industry' in the broad sense, the national accounts suggest that between 1970 and 1973 the percentage of domestic consumption provided by domestic production increased from 45 to 52.5 per cent; that domestic industry provided from 51.5 to 52.4 of the demand for industrial products by agriculture, forestry and fisheries; but that it provided only 8.0 to 14.9 per cent of the demand for capital goods.[27] Another set of calculations, more precisely related to manufacturing rather than to industry as a whole, shows that the import of manufactured products in 1974 amounted to 62.7 per cent of total manufacturing production in Ivory Coast, or 94.6 per cent after deduction of exported manufactures.[28] If this average figure is broken down by category of products, standard light consumer goods – the typical first products of import substitution, such as processed products of grain and flour, canned and processed foods, drinks and ices, edible fats, textile products, leather and footwear – were either not imported at all or, in the last case, only to the extent of 76.7 per cent of domestic manufacture. Conversely, more of the intermediate and capital goods required by industry were imported than were produced locally. The coefficient of chemical industry imports was 1.291, of rubber 1.003, building materials and glass 1.065, crude metals 3.911, construction and repairs of transport 1.210, and mechanical and electrical industries not included elsewhere 2.860.[29]

Perhaps more important than the proportion of the market served by local manufacturing is the ratio of imported inputs they used, since this measures the extent to which these enterprises were merely finishing off imported intermediate products. If the value of imported inputs is measured against value added in Ivory Coast (the higher the less value added), the highest were petroleum products (11.224), building materials and glass (2.117), miscellaneous industries (1.587) and grain and flour products (1.583). Those with low coefficients, using mainly local materials, included edible fats (0.032), timber products (0.034) and rubber (0.061). In between were food preserves and preparations (0.822) and textiles (0.505).[30]

Manufacturing also showed a close correlation between four factors: the import coefficients of industrial inputs, capital intensity, capital productivity and foreign ownership of capital. Broadly, though not uniformly, high levels of foreign ownership of the equity were associated with high importation of inputs, high capital intensity, lower capital productivity and high labour productivity. Typical of the highest capital intensity was petroleum, 91.31 per cent foreign owned in 1974, with a capital intensity of 45.4, employing only 335 people, with a labour productivity of 7.9m. FCFA but a capital productivity of only 0.6 and an import coefficient of 11.2. At the other extreme was the rubber-products industry, only 46 per cent foreign owned and with a low capital intensity of 1.5, employing 4,680 people, with a capital intensity of 1.5, a capital productivity of 0.3, a labour productivity of 0.5m. FCFA and a low import coefficient of 0.061.[31]

These statistics seem to support most of the standard criticisms of allowing or encouraging foreign enterprise to undertake import-substitution for domestic consumption. Foreign firms were attracted by liberal rules and incentives, a domestic market apparently expanding rapidly with the growth of an export-oriented agriculture, an adequate state-financed infrastructure, the convertibility of the FCFA and political stability. But they only invested if the size of the market justified setting up a unit of minimal size for using more or less their accustomed capital-intensive technology. The result was a considerable, though only partial, degree of import substitution; there were still large imports of goods which it was not profitable by these criteria to make in Ivory Coast.The economic cost was considerable: relatively few jobs for local citizens, high dependence on imported inputs, and an accelerating outflow of dividends, fees, etc., all of which put an increasing strain on foreign exchange earnings and so mortgaged the future of the economy. In all this Ivory Coast was clearly in little better condition by the later 1970s than most other African states.

But industrialization in Ivory Coast had one unusually favourable aspect: its growing emphasis on manufactured exports. As has been seen, the agro-based industries, mostly the canning of fruit or processing coffee, cocoa and timber, expanded very fast, especially after about 1970, with a growth rate of 36.2 per cent for non-wood and 37.6 per cent for timber-based products, though the second was due more to price increases than to increased volume of production.[32] Industrial exports grew slightly faster than the value of industrial production from 1965 to 1973 and increased as a percentage of total exports from 16.3 in 1965 to 30 per cent in 1974.[33] In 1974 the four main industrial branches which were concerned with the valorization of exports coming from primary production in Ivory Coast – canning and processing of foodstuffs, edible fat foodstuffs, rubber products and timber derivatives – represented 31.5 per cent of value added in all manufacturing and had very low import coefficients.[34] In that year agricultural foodstuffs represented 42.6 per cent of total manufacturing turnover, 47.5 per cent of value added and 62.2 per cent of total exports of manufactured products, though their imported inputs were only 17.7 per cent of total imports of inputs for manufacturing industry.[35] Thus the processing industries had the double merit of earning foreign exchange and providing links with the agricultural sector of the economy. On the other hand foreign capital played a large role in these enterprises: in 1974 foreigners owned 77.9 per cent of the capital employed in them.

Ivory Coast had three other main exporting industries. The textile industry, exporting mostly ginned cotton, grew very fast in the 1970s and provided 11.2 per cent of industrial exports in 1974, most of them to other West African states. Petroleum products, a by-product of the import-substituting refinery, provided 9.8 per cent of industrial exports and were increasing rapidly. Wood products (mainly sawn lumber and veneers) represented 14.5 per cent of industrial exports.[36]

This development of processed exports was a satisfactory aspect of industrialization; against it has to be set the very high proportion of foreign ownership in this as in most sectors of manufacturing. It was also significant for the growth of autonomous capitalism that almost all indigenous capital in manufacturing consisted of state holdings of the equity of foreign enterprises. Official figures show that the share of private Ivory Coast capital in the capital of the modern sector actually declined between 1974 and 1978, from 13.5 to 7.3 per cent, the index

of capital owned rising only from 100 to 143, while total capital
employed rose from 100 to 263.[37] A closer investigation shows that
the larger the capital of a firm, the smaller the proportion owned by
Ivorians; and that enterprises in which Ivorians held a majority of the
capital were mostly very small: more than three-quarters of these had
a capital of less than 50m. FCFA (c.£100,000).[38] Clearly Ivorian
entrepreneurs were mostly to be found in the small and middling
enterprises; and it seems clear that the rate of return on most of these
was substantially lower than on foreign-owned and state enterprises.[39]
De Miras concludes that there was, in the 1970s, no real Ivory Coast
entrepreneurial class. The majority were engaged in agriculture or in
small, artisan-type enterprises which offered very little opportunity for
accumulation. The small minority who owned all or part of enterprises
in the modern sector did so by virtue of being able to save or borrow
sufficient money to buy into foreign enterprises or to own plantations
by being members of the administrative elite or privileged managers of
foreign-owned enterprises.[40]

Seen in the broad, the industrialization strategy of the Ivory Coast
government cannot, therefore, be regarded as part of an 'economic
miracle', except for that part of it which processed local agricultural
and sylvan exports. From the start Ivory Coast had adopted an import-
substituting strategy which closely resembled that of other African
states in its welcome for foreign capital. The predictable result was the
proliferation of subsidiaries of European (mostly French) companies,
most of which merely replaced the import of finished goods by the
import of intermediates in order to take advantage of the various
incentives offered. What were the measurable effects on Ivorian growth
and prospects?

The measurable beneficial effects were small. Little new capital was
brought in: according to one estimate only 44.7m. FCFA between 1967
and 1974, which was about half the repatriated net return. Apart from
the processing plants, industry provided few up- or downstream
linkages. The employment effects were limited, since these were
mostly capital-intensive enterprises. Technological transfer was very
small, since technology came packaged, though there was some value
in the training of senior staff in managerial and technical skills.
Ivorians showed very little enthusiasm for establishing competing
enterprises or taking an active share in foreign enterprises, as happened
in Kenya; private Ivorian shareholders were strictly rentiers. Finally,
the balance of payments effects were increasingly serious by the later
1970s, as the volume of repatriated profits, etc., increased, while export
earnings declined with the price of commodities.

That is the negative side of the picture, but a different case can be
put. Given limiting local factors, especially the almost total absence of
an indigenous bourgeoisie with industrial experience, the alternative

would have been either complete dependence on imported goods or the creation of state-owned enterprises. For consumer goods it would have been cheaper and possibly better to import finished articles on the colonial pattern. But there were many other spheres in which local production – even if only at the finishing level – had advantages: for example, putting together cans for the export of food products from flattened sheet tin, because of the exorbitant cost of transporting ready-made cans. This largely justified the presence of SIEM, subsidiary of the French firm CARNAUD, whose cans were essential to the production of canned pineapple. SIVOA, a subsidiary of Air Liquide, made essential industrial gases for a wide range of mechanical and industrial activities.[41] Local production at least provided a tax benefit to Ivory Coast: in 1975 SIEM paid 117.6m. FCFA in taxes and repatriated 66.3m. FCFA in profits, while SIVOA paid 217.1m. FCFA in taxes, repatriating 39.2m. FCFA in profits.[42] Other subsidiaries were even more useful. CAPRAL, for example, Nestlé's subsidiary, initially made only instant coffee, but later added convenience packet soups. It started in 1959 as apparently a pure prestige enterprise, since there was almost no internal market for Nescafe; but it proved to have very valuable economic effects. Almost all its raw materials were local, including otherwise unsaleable coffee-bean fragments. By the mid-1970s most of its production of Nescafe was exported, with beneficial balance of payments effects. In 1975 the company paid 980.9m. FCFA in taxes.[43] If similar studies of other subsidiaries were available, much the same mixture of positive and negative economic consequences of FDI would probably be found.

It is, therefore, unwise to be dogmatic about industrialization in Ivory Coast. At one level this was clearly industrialization of the most 'dependent' kind, almost entirely generated by foreign capital, which showed very little sign during the first twenty years of evolving an 'autonomous' capital goods or intermediate goods sector. On the other hand Ivory Coast received a number of benefits. Many industries consumed local raw materials, especially those that were export-oriented; and some was essential to other industrial and commercial activities. Although the government spent a great deal on providing essential infrastructure, it also received a substantial tax and was able to buy on average about a quarter of the equity in foreign firms by the later 1970s. Above all the marked shift from the later 1960s to export-oriented industries was clearly beneficial both to the agricultural and sylvan sectors and to the balance of payments. At least Ivory Coast was not saddled with a huge burden of external public debt which had been incurred to establish state-owned industries by many other African governments, on which interest had to be paid whatever their profitability.

Agriculture

If there was in fact an Ivory Coast 'miracle', it was clearly to be found in the expansion of agricultural production and exports. The bare figures are staggering. Cocoa production grew from 94,000 tons in 1960/1 to 242,000 tons in 1974/5, the cultivated area for cocoa from 243,000 ha to 481,000 ha, implying a substantial increase in productivity, and exports from 94,000 to 237,000 tons. Coffee production increased from 178,000 to 270,000 tons, the area used from 534,000 to 760,000 ha. Cotton, the third though much smaller small man's cash crop, grew from 8,000 tons in 1966/7 to 58,000 tons, 14,000 tons of it exported.[44] These were the backbone of agricultural exports: as a percentage of total exports by value, coffee beans were 49 per cent in 1960, 22 per cent in 1974 (plus 1 per cent processed coffee). Cocoa beans were 23 and 21 per cent in the same years, with processed cocoa an additional 5 per cent in 1974. Timber was the other main export commodity, earning from 15 to 18 per cent of total exports receipts between 1960 and 1974, with processed timber at 5 per cent of exports in 1974.[45]

Nor did food production lag, despite this huge increase of export cash-crop production. Of the three main food-grain crops, paddy increased from 250,000 tons to over 400,000 tons 1965–75, though in 1974 73,000 tons of rice were still imported; maize from 200,000 to 280,000 tons.[46] Perhaps the least impressive performance was in the lower quality food products, though, since much of this was not marketed, figures are dubious. Yams increased from 1.3m. tons to 1.75m. tons, cassava from 500,000 to 650,000 tons, plantains from 600,000 to 780,000 tons.[47] In terms of growth (at constant (1973) prices), while all the main industrial crops grew at an average of 5.3 per cent from 1965 to 1970 and 4.7 per cent from 1970 to 1975, the figures for the main food crops were 3.5 per cent and 4.0 per cent respectively.[48] Ivory Coast was one of the very few African states in which average food production per capita was higher in 1979 than in 1969–71.[49]

How was this agricultural growth achieved? None of the main export or food crops was new after independence, nor was there significant change in methods or units of production. The huge expansion was achieved by a combination of factors: great extension of cultivated land, a huge immigrant labour force (in 1974, 81.8 per cent of those employed in the primary sector were non-Ivorian Africans),[50] relatively high wages (though much lower than average national wages), a great improvement in transport facilities, and applied crop research on techniques in cash-crop, but not in food, production. But perhaps the most significant incentive for cash-crop producers was the relatively high price set by the Caisse for payments to producers. On average cocoa and coffee producers were paid 50 per cent of the f.o.b.

price of their products, well above what was common in most African states,[51] despite the very large levy imposed by the state as the basis of its investment programme. In this way Ivory Coast avoided the mistake made by Ghana and others of virtually killing the golden goose on which the whole development of the economy depended.

The prosperity of the peasant farmer should not, however, be exaggerated. Robert M. Hecht has shown that between 1960 and 1979 prices paid to cocoa producers rose by 368 per cent, while the retail price index rose by 360 per cent. Average real prices were, therefore, virtually static over twenty years, but average real incomes rose slightly because the size of farms grew from an average of 4.66 to 5.38 ha between 1954 and 1977, and cultivation became more intensive. Hecht calculated that between 1950 and 1977 average real incomes of peasants producing coffee increased by between 1.3 and 2.3 per cent a year; for cocoa by 2.3 to 3.3 per cent, with a weighted average of 1.7 to 2.7 per cent. But from 1967 to 1977 the figures were much less satisfactory, with coffee incomes changing in the bracket −0.3 to +0.7, cocoa rising from 2.1 to 3.1, with a weighted average of 1.1–2.1, whereas in this period GDP grew at an average of 3.4 per cent.[52] Thus, while farmers did reasonably well, they did not do as well as people in other sectors.

Why, then, were they apparently contented? Hecht suggests a variety of reasons. Producers had the impression that prices paid more than kept up with the cost of their purchases. The rural/urban terms of trade did not deteriorate. The more efficient were given bonuses for improved production methods. There was a plentiful supply of foreign workers at relatively low wage levels. Land tenures were open and secure, with full security for those who brought new land into production. Buying was done by a number of competing private firms, not by a monopolistic state agency.

Such things kept the Ivorian peasant reasonably content. Yet Hecht also points to limitations in the evolution of cash-crop production. In 1975 there were about 450,000 peasant producers of cocoa and coffee in south-eastern Ivory Coast. Of these 98 per cent had less than 20 ha under cultivation, with an average of 5.4 ha per family. The size of farm units had increased very little, the main obstacle being lack of good new potential land. Nor was there much technical progress. Production methods remained labour intensive and very few farmers could afford loans to pay for higher yield trees, spraying equipment and extra labour.

Amin and Campbell are, moreover, clearly wrong in claiming that there was 'a veritable bourgeoisie of planters'.[53] In fact only 2.1 per cent of cocoa or coffee producers had more than 20 ha, and of these 1.6 per cent had 20–30 ha and only 0.4 per cent 30–40 ha. In 1975 per capita incomes from the 20–30 ha farms averaged $601–901, rising to

$902–1,203 for the top 1,792 families. But, as average GDP was $600 in 1978, very few even of the richest farming families had per capita incomes above the national average, and even those with 10–20 ha, with a per capita income averaging $387, were below the average. The great majority of smallholders were clearly well below that level. In fact the 'rural elite' was not only very small but not very rich. Nor was rural inequality as extreme as Amin and his followers have alleged. The lowest 40 per cent received 11.6 per cent of total smallholder incomes, while the top 10 per cent received 37.4 per cent. These figures were comparable to those for Tanzania and Zambia.

Indeed, the real Ivorian elite was not rural but urban, and was to be found among the bureaucrats, party officials and employees of foreign companies; their main sources of income were not from the land – even though many owned farms or plantations – but from offices, director-ships, or shares in manufacturing or plantation enterprises. High standing in the Parti Démocratique de Côte d'Ivoire (PDCI) – the single political party – was the key to opulence. M. A. Cohen, for example, found that 62 per cent of directors in eighty-eight state economic enterprises were members of the government.[54] In SCOA, one of the largest French-owned trading and investing companies, the presidents of the three largest subsidiaries were all members of the political bureau of PDCI.[55]

In fact, it was not in the traditional staples of cocoa and coffee, but in other more recently developed agricultural products, that a true capitalist bougeoisie could be found. From the mid-1950s European planters moved out of cocoa and coffee into plantation products – oil palms, rubber, bananas and pineapples; and in due course wealthy Ivorians followed them, either buying shares in existing enterprises or starting their own. These were areas of rapid growth. Between 1965 and 1975 production of palm oil increased from 10,000 to 162,000 tons, of rubber from 2,000 to 17,000 tons, of bananas from 10,000 to 170,000 tons, of pineapples for canning from 33,000 to 170,000 tons and fresh pineapples from 4,600 to 80,000 tons.[56] While these crops remained small as a proportion of the total value of exports – in 1975 exports of bananas were worth 3.0b. FCFA, fresh pineapples 3.1b., canned pineapples 6.2b., rubber 1.7b., and palm oil 10.5b. compared with coffee beans at 61.2b., cocoa beans at 47.6b., timber logs at 34.8b. and processed timber at 10.8b. – they offered potentially high profits, mainly because the prices were not controlled by the Caisse. The plantations were thus an attraction to those with money to invest, particularly members of the state bourgeoisie. It is alleged that Philippe Yacé, Secretary General of PDCI, owned a plantation of 400 ha producing 8,000 tons of pineapples, 10 per cent of the total export of fresh pineapples.[57] Such rural enterprises had ample access to credit and close relations with foreign trading companies and industrial firms.

For them diversification into new export crops was a means of converting political power into personal wealth.

There can be no serious doubt about the reality of the Ivorian agricultural 'miracle'; it had almost no parallel in modern Black Africa. The doubts arise as to its continuing momentum and its ability to fuel future economic development. First, on the supply side, could the growth of production be sustained? With good land in short supply, timber supplies seriously depleted, and so far very little increase in productivity in the staple exports or food industries, this was quite unpredictable. Certainly the government would have to plough a great deal more money back into the rural economy and avoid wasting resources on unrewarding areas such as state-organized sugar production, rice and palm plantations. Secondly, on the demand side, it was unclear whether the world market could absorb growing exports of these main crops without serious reduction in prices. After 1978 the whole Ivory Coast economy was shaken by the combined effects of the dramatic decline in cocoa and coffee prices (between 1977 and 1981 cocoa export prices dropped from 1,714 to 413 FCFA per kilo and coffee from 1,270 to 550), the rise of the petroleum prices and the decline of the franc in relation to the dollar. For the first time in 1980 Ivory Coast had an adverse trade balance and an adverse balance of payments. Between 1980 and 1983 the effects were felt in a 65 per cent drop in budget receipts, so that the investment budget had to be reduced substantially.

Table 7.1 *Ivory Coast's External Public Debt and Debt Service, 1967–1982 (US$m.)*

	A Debt outstanding	B Debt service	C EGS	A/C (%)	B/C (%)
1967	165.3	28.8	439.9	37.6	6.5
1970	256.1	38.6	563.9	45.4	6.8.
1973	578.1	72.1	987.4	58.5	7.3
1977	1,973.2	290.2	2,731.9	72.2	10.6
1979	3,942.7	737.1	3,293.2	119.7	22.4 [15.2[a]]
1982	4,537.3	996.7	2,960.2	153.3	33.7 [36.9[b]]

Note:

The ratios marked a and b are given in *Accelerated Development* and *Toward Sustained Development* respectively. In neither case is the basis of the calculation clear, since no total is given for EGS.

Sources:

1967: World Bank, *World Tables* (Washington DC, 1976).

1970–7: World Bank, *World Tables* (Washington DC, 1980).

1979: World Bank, *Accelerated Development*, App. 7, 17, 18.

1982: World Bank, *Toward Sustained Development*, App. 7, 13, 14.

1979 and 1982 column C: IMF, *International Financial Statistics Yearbook* (1984).

In the later 1970s, moreover, the volume and burden of external public debt increased very fast, as can be seen from Table 7.1. It seemed that the economic miracle was over and that Ivory Coast was as deep in crisis as the many other African states which had had no miracle.

The government responded positively with attempts to check inflation, reduce government spending, control the transfer of overseas profits, increase food production and revise foreign contracts.[58] But the doubt remained whether an export-oriented economy of this kind could adapt sufficiently quickly to a crisis which was essentially exogenous. This has always been the main danger to countries whose economy is based on commodity exports for which demand is relatively inelastic. It is the chief ground on which those who see Ivory Coast as a typical dependent economy on the periphery of the world system have predicted that it would eventually face the same stagnation or retrogression as most other Black African states.[59] It was too early by 1985 to be certain whether Ivory Coast could escape this dead end.

Notes

1 World Bank, *Accelerated Development in Sub-Saharan Africa* (*AD*) (Washington DC, 1981), App.1.
2 *AD* App. 33.
3 *AD* App. 2, 3.
4 *AD* App. 7.
5 *AD* App. 13.
6 ibid.
7 B. A. Tuinder, *Ivory Coast. The Challenge of Success* (Baltimore and London, 1978), tables 5.3, 5.4.
8 *AD* App. 17, 18; World Bank, *Toward Sustained Development in Sub-Saharan Africa* (*TSD*) (Washington DC, 1984), App. 2, 3.
9 Y. A. Fauré, 'Inversion d'une dynamique sociale. Le Cas Ivorien', unpub. paper given at a conference on 'The Fate of Post-Colonial Economies in West Africa', SOAS, July 1983, p. 12.
10 The concluding chapter, which summed up the argument, was later incorporated in Amin's *Neo-Colonialism in West Africa* (Paris, 1971; Eng. edn., New York and London, 1973; refs are to this edn.), p. 55.
11 Amin, *Neo-Colonialism*, p. 55.
12 *AD* App. 4.
13 *AD* App. 5.
14 Tuinder, tables 5.3, 5.4.
15 E. G. Bonnie Campbell, 'The Ivory Coast', in J. Dunn (ed.), *West African States* (Cambridge, 1978) who follows the line adopted by Amin.
16 Tuinder, pp. 65 f.
17 Robert M. Hecht, 'The Ivory Coast Economic "Miracle". What Benefit for the Peasant Farmers?' *JMAS*, vol. 21, no. 1 (1983), p. 30.

18 See Y.-A. Fauré, 'Le Complex politico-économique', in Y.-A. Fauré and J.-F. Médard (eds), *État et bourgeoisie en Côte d'Ivoire* (Paris, 1982), pp. 52 f.; Tuinder, pp. 41, 233 f., for details.
19 Tuinder, table 7.1.
20 This section is based mainly on Tuinder; J. Masini *et al.*, *Multinationals and Development in Black Africa. A Case Study in the Ivory Coast* (Farnborough, 1979).
21 Tuinder, table B.1.
22 *AD* App. 2, 3.
23 Tuinder, table B.2.
24 Masini, table 4.
25 Tuinder, table B.10.
26 ibid., pp. 231–2.
27 ibid., table B.6.
28 Masini *et al.*, p. 40.
29 ibid., table 5.
30 ibid., table B.
31 ibid.
32 Tuinder, table B.2.
33 ibid., table B.4.
34 Masini *et al.*, pp. 40–1, table 5.
35 ibid., p. 57.
36 Tuinder, tables SA 93, 94.
37 C. de Miras, 'L'Entrepreneur ivoirien: une bourgeoisie privée de son état', in Fauré and Médard (eds), table 2.
38 ibid., table 5.
39 ibid., table 7.
40 See de Miras; Tuinder, p. 154.
41 See Masini *et al.*, ch. 9, for details of these firms.
42 ibid., tables 29, 31.
43 ibid., p. 113 f., table 30.
44 Tuinder, table SA 37, pp. 369–71.
45 ibid., table 5.8.
46 ibid., table SA 68.
47 ibid.
48 ibid., table SA 69.
49 *AD* App. 1.
50 Tuinder, table 6.3.
51 ibid., p. 39.
52 Hecht, p. 39.
53 see Amin, *Développement du capitalisme*, p. 277, followed by Campbell, p. 104.
54 M. A. Cohen, *Urban Policy and Political Conflict in Africa. A Study of the Ivory Coast* (Chicago and London, 1974), p. 62 and table 8.
55 Hecht, p. 51; also J.-M. Gastellu and S. Affrou Yapi, 'Un myth à décomposer: la "bourgeoisie de planteurs" ' in Fauré and Médard (eds).
56 Tuinder, table SA 68.
57 Hecht, p. 52.
58 Fauré, 'Inversion'.

59 See the argument by E. J. Berg, 'Structural Transformation versus Gradualism. Recent Economic Development in Ghana and the Ivory Coast', in P. Foster and A. R. Zolberg (eds), *Ghana and the Ivory Coast. Perspectives in Modernization* (Chicago and London, 1971).

8

Francophone West Africa: Senegal

In the mythology of underdevelopment Senegal is commonly made to stand as a classic example of the penalties resulting from preserving the essentials of a 'colonial economy' – export-oriented monoculture, reliance on the one-time metropolis for capital, technicians and technology and very close economic and political relations with Europe. Much the same allegations have, of course, been made against Ivory Coast; the main differences are that Senegalese rhetoric proclaimed socialism not capitalism and that Senegal's strategy led to economic weakness almost as great as that of Ghana, not to the comparative affluence of Ivory Coast before the late 1970s. These are the facts which any study of Senegal after 1960 must attempt to explain.

The crude statistics demonstrate this relative failure. In 1950 GNP per capita in Senegal was among the highest in Black Africa: according to Morawetz (though his list is incomplete), only the Republic of Congo, Ghana, Ivory Coast and Zambia were then more affluent; and with a $238 average income Senegal stood well above the all-African average of $170. By 1979, according to the Berg Report, there were twelve Black African countries with higher per capita incomes. Between 1950 and 1960 Senegal's GNP per capita grew by an average of 4.4 per cent; from 1960 to 1970 it declined by an average of − 1.6 per cent, increasing between 1970 and 1975 by 1.1 per cent. For the whole period 1960–79 average incomes declined by −0.2 per cent.[1] Ignoring population growth, GDP grew at 2.5 per cent from 1960 to 1979, but the average annual growth of population was 2.4 per cent in the 1960s and 2.6 per cent in the 1970s, almost exactly cancelling this out.[2] The average growth rates of agriculture and industry kept ahead of population – agriculture growing at 2.9 per cent in 1960–70, 3.6 per cent in 1970–9, industry at 4.4 per cent and 3.5 per cent for the same years – while the value of services declined by − 1.7 and − 1.6 per cent respectively.[3] It is significant that, as a proportion of GDP, agriculture actually increased from 24 to 29 per cent between 1960 and 1979, and that the share of industry grew only from 17 to 24 per cent per cent. Conversely, the decline of services from 59 to 47 per cent

cent of GDP was against the general trend in Black Africa, reflecting the very high initial cost of the French federal bureaucracy in Dakar before independence; even so, the absolute size of the public service remained very large and continued to grow fast.[4]

Most other indicators reflected a virtually stagnant or declining economy. The average growth rate of exports by volume was only 1.2 per cent in the 1960s and −0.8 per cent from 1970 to 1978.[5] Imports of machinery and transport equipment represented 19 per cent of total merchandise imports by value in 1960, 18 per cent in 1978. In the same two years imports of non-fuel and non-food primary commodities were 2 and 21 per cent of the total, implying greatly increased dependence on foreign raw materials; but the proportion of 'other manufactures' in imports declined from 44 to 26 per cent of total imports as local protected consumer industries grew.[6] On the other hand, between 1960 and 1979 Senegal went some way towards diversifying away from her traditional market in Europe, which in 1960 had taken 89 per cent of her exports. By 1979 this had decreased to 59 per cent, while exports to other sub-Saharan states, mostly of manufactures, had risen from 4 to 27 per cent and to other developing countries from 7 to 14 per cent. The percentage share of the three principal exports declined from 79.9 to 49.7 per cent between 1961 and the average for 1976–8.[7] It must be said, however, that Senegal was affected by adverse trends in her terms of trade. With 1975 = 100, the net barter terms of trade in 1960, 1970 and 1979 were 71, 79 and 76. For the same years the income terms of trade were 52, 77, and 46.[8] This was much worse than the average for all middle-income oil-importing countries in Black Africa, and reflected both the adverse market for the main Senegalese export crops, groundnuts and groundnut oil, and, from the early 1970s, reduced export production caused by other factors.

Indeed it was the fluctuating and generally poor performance of the agricultural sector that was at the heart of the Senegalese problem and is inevitably central to any analysis of it. The growth rate of exports of groundnuts in shell in 1960–70 was −5.5 per cent, in 1970–9 −8.4 per cent. For the same periods exports of groundnut oil increased by an average of 4.4 per cent and then decreased by −3.5 per cent, while the average growth rate of prices for groundnuts was 0.1 and −3.5 per cent and −0.1 and −3.1 per cent for groundnut oil.[9] Food did no better. Between 1969/71 and 1977/9 the average growth rate of food production per capita was −1.6 per cent; and, although non-food production grew by an average of 8.7 per cent in these years, the total annual growth per capita of agriculture was −1.5 per cent.[10] Although there were wide fluctuations in production levels from year to year, there was an overall downward trend in the main exports, groundnuts and groundnut products. In 1960–2 average exports of these were 557,000 tons; in 1979–81 they were 265,000 tons.[11]

These generally adverse trends were reflected in the balance of payment and debt service positions. Between 1970 and 1979 the current account balance, before interest payment on external debt, deteriorated from − $14m. to − $394m. As can be seen from Table 8.1, external debts rose from $97.7m. to $738.5m., debt service from $6.7m. to $130m., and debt service as a percentage of exports of goods and service from 2.8 to 13.7 per cent.[12] By 1979 Senegal was very heavily dependent on official aid: in that year net official assistance represented $56.2 a head (more than 12.5 per cent of total per capita incomes), 13.1 per cent of GNP and 59.3 per cent of gross domestic investment.[13]

Such figures are merely a skeleton, suggesting a generally depressing experience without in any way explaining it. Here again, as with Ivory Coast, the standard explanation, against which subsequent assessments must be measured, is that of Samir Amin, originally put forward in his *L'Afrique de L'Ouest bloquée* and repeated in *Neo-Colonialism in West Africa*. His analysis forms part of his general denunciation of specialization by less developed countries in production of export commodities. Groundnut production in Senegal provides the classic example of over-specialization in a single cash crop, monoculture taken to extremes. He argues that the expansion of groundnut production was dominated by three main factors: availability of suitable land, sufficient labour supply and modern transport, whose decreasing real cost made possible the huge expansion of profitable cultivation. The size of this crop grew irregularly: by an average of 8.8 per cent a year from 1885 to 1914 to about 200,000 tons before 1914, and by an average of 2.7 per cent from 1918 to 1940, reaching a peak of 600,000 tons in 1936/7. After stagnating from 1945 to 1950, the growth rate accelerated to 7.7 per cent in 1950–6 and dropped to 4.0 per cent in 1960–9, producing a record sale of 1,011,000 tons in 1965/6. Thereafter, partly due to poor rainfall, production decreased; but it was over 1.4m. tons in 1975/6 and over 1m. tons in 1976/7 and 1978/9, though these last two years were after Amin's book was published.

Amin argues that in the earlier stages of this expansion it was possible to keep production increasing by bringing new land under cultivation and attracting an additional labour force. Once no suitable new land was available and the labour supply had reached a maximum, given variable ratios of land/labour in areas of different rainfall, only higher productivity could have kept expansion going. This point had been reached in most areas by the 1960s, and thereafter the state made efforts to increase productivity by the use of animal power and better quality seeds. This had some success; but the increased cost of modernization was only justified in areas of adequate rainfall − the centre and south, but not the north; and, given greater demand on labour from the higher intensity of farming, and relatively low prices

Table 8.1 *Senegal's External Public Debt*
and Debt Service, 1967–1982 (US$m.)

	A Debt out- standing	B Debt service	C EGS	A/C (%)	B/C (%)
1967	62.1	3.8	199.7	31.1	1.9
1970	101.8	6.8	237.8	42.8	2.8
1973	203.2	29.4	358.0	56.7	8.2
1976	352.9	42.9	695.9	50.7	6.1
1979	738.5	130.0	627.0	117.8	20.7 [13.7[a]]
1982	1,328.5	101.9	458.0	290.0	22.2 [n/a]

Note:
The ratios given in *Accelerated Development*. The basis of the calculation is not clear, since
   no total is given for EGS.
Sources:
1967: World Bank, *World Tables* (Washington DC, 1976).
1970–7: World Bank, *World Tables* (Washington DC, 1980).
1979: World Bank, *Accelerated Development*, App. 7, 17, 18.
1982: World Bank, *Toward Sustained Development*, Apps. 7, 13, 14.
1979 and 1982 column C: IMF, *International Financial Statistics Yearbook* (1984).

paid by the government, it became very doubtful whether the peasant
producer would receive an adequate return for his additonal effort and
risk. Thus, given exogenous determinants of the value of the crop,
there was a natural limit to the profitable expansion of groundnut
production. Since Senegal was one of the first West African states to
develop this type of export crop on a very large scale, it reached this
point earlier than states such as Ivory Coast, which began much later.
Hence the virtual stagnation of the Senegal economy after 1960 and the
need to adopt a totally different economic strategy.

   Amin, of course, did not believe that commodity production has
normally been to the best advantage of the producers because of
adverse secular trends in the terms of trade. In *Neo-Colonialism* he
argues that, while the overall relative price of groundnuts in relation
to the cost of foreign imports remained more or less constant between
1880 and 1960 (though with major short-term variations), 'the double
factoral terms of trade' (which take into account the relative labour
productivity of France, as the main market and source of imports, and
Senegal) implied a large-scale transfer of labour value from Senegal to
France. Hence groundnut production was not in the best interests of the
Senegalese producer at the price for his product set by the world market.
At this price he would do better to grow food grains such as millet and
also – if other parts of the country were provided with equipment,

transport and irrigation – rice, sugar cane and high-quality foods such as vegetables, fruit and palm oil. Such policies were incompatible with colonial rule, since France needed cheap vegetable oil; but independent Senegal could and should have attempted to diversify out of so unrewarding and inexpandable a commodity as groundnuts.

The new state should also have gone for industrial diversification. Although the Cape Verde region, centring on Dakar, was the leading industrial complex in West Africa in 1960, the breakup of the Federation left these import-substituting consumer industries with an inadequate market; hence slow industrial growth combined with a rapid increase in the unemployed urban population and predominantly foreign ownership of the existing industrial system. Again, the government should have gone for a much more ambitious industrialization programme to make use of the considerable stock of skills available. The Dakar complex should have been expanded to include a heavy iron and steel industry, using ores from neighbouring Mauritania and leading possibly to shipbuilding, and an integrated chemical industry and other related industries, which made use of Africa's natural endowment.

Amin's analysis and condemnation of post-independence Senegal's economic development, therefore, boils down to the proposition that independence made very little difference to the 'dependent' nature of the colonial economy. Senegal continued to be a trading economy tied to the European market, even though the rewards to both state and producer were small and the scope for further development along these lines very limited. At the centre of this analysis, as of almost every study of Senegalese economic development, lies the production and handling of groundnuts, and it seems impossible in this study to avoid following suit. To bring the study into line with that of other countries, however, it is proposed first to examine the nature and role of the post-independence Senegalese government before concentrating on the inescapable problem of groundnuts.

State, Party and the Economy

According to E. J. Schumacher, whose study remains the dominant interpretation of the relationship between government, policies and economic development in Senegal to the early 1970s,[14] the key to the nature of the post-colonial state in Senegal lies in the genesis and constituent elements of what became the sole official party before 1976, the Union Progressiste Sénégalaise (UPS). The UPS evolved from the original Senegalese party, Section Française de l'Internationale Ouvrière (SFIO), dominated by Lamine Gueye, associated with the French Socialist Party, and based mainly on clan alliances within the

four communes of the coastal region. In 1948 Léopold Senghor and
Mamadou Dia split the party to form the Bloc Démocratique
Sénégalais (BDS). They found support from inland areas outside the
communes and from other groups not benefiting from the narrow
politics of the communes. From 1951 they built their electoral strength
on an expanding rural electorate, exploiting the system of list voting
which gave exclusive control over candidates to the central party. Most
important, they made alliances with the three great Islamic
brotherhoods – Tijaniyya, Quadriyya and Mourides – who
dominated large sections of the predominately Islamic population and
much of the production of groundnuts, either on their own estates or
through control over peasant producers. As the dominant party in the
post-1957 territorial assembly, the BDS (which fused with SFIO in
1958 to form the UPS) made full use of state patronage to secure its
position, necessarily rewarding the clan membership for its support.
In this sense UPS was a 'machine party' which took over the assets of
the colonial state to secure its own position, so that after independence
the distinction between state and party became virtually meaningless.

Nevertheless UPS aimed to be a party of national consensus which
represented and provided rewards to all sections of the population. In
this it was spectacularly successful. Despite the existence of the radical
Parti du Regroupement Africain in 1958, which came into existence to
oppose de Gaulle's referendum of that year and to work for a genuine
socialist society not tied to the French economy, by the early 1960s
some 92.5 per cent of the voters were supporting UPS, even though
buyers of party cards in 1963 were only 22 per cent of the
electorate.[15] In the 1960s other parties were discouraged and officially
ceased to exist after 1963. From 1962, when Senghor broke with Dia,
hitherto president of the council, he established a presidential regime
of the type characteristic of most one-party African states.

It is important to this analysis, however, that Senghor did not have
unqualified power or control of policy. He was at all times constrained
by those forces which had brought him to power and whose interests
had been symbolized in the alignments of 1958. In that year Senghor
and Dia had compaigned for a 'yes' vote to join the French Community
and against those on the left who wanted to follow the example of
Guinea and vote 'no'. That decision, coupled with the breakup of the
Federation with Mali in 1960, reflected the essential conservatism of
those who supported UPS. It indicated that the dominant interests of
Senegal – the groundnut producers who provided more than 80 per
cent of exports, the largely French-owned industries of Cape Verde,
and the mass of salaried and self-employed middle class of the urban
areas – were not prepared to risk any radical change in the orientation
of the economy towards France. Independence, yes; but provided only

that it did not entail risk. Hence the arrangements made with France for Senegal to remain within the franc zone, to retain a preferential French market and to obtain other benefits, including massive aid and military support. Such arrangements may be labelled 'neo-colonialist' and critics have alleged that they prevented Senegal from adopting a true socialist policy. But the critical fact is that at the birth of the new state there was no politically possible alternative, given the structure of interests which were represented in UPS. The socialist, non-aligned alternative put forward by radicals was unacceptable to the vast majority.

The fact that Senghor and UPS maintained in most essentials an open economy based on preserving the traditional system of production and trade did not, however, imply a liberal political or economic structure. At the political level UPS monopolized power, with Senghor, as president, the sole focus of decision-making. The party took control of all organs of government, politicizing the bureaucracy at all levels. The bureaucracy, already excessively large as a hangover from the Federation, grew from some 10,000 in 1960 to 34,900 in 1965 and 61,000 in 1973; at that time there were only an additional 63,000 wage-earners (as distinct from self-employed or unemployed) in the whole country. On average civil servants had seven times the income of peasant households and twice the wage of skilled industrial workers.[16] Thus one of the main problems of Senegal was that a substantial proportion of state revenues went to support a political and administrative elite, particularly in the four communes, which had grown up to expect a French standard of living, together with the network of party affiliates who had grown up in the rural areas since 1956. The available statistics do not make it possible to measure the growth of public consumption or the proportion of revenues and GDP devoted to public salaries by the later 1970s; but World Bank figures for 1978 suggest that, as a proportion of total public expenditure, 'general public services' (24.1 per cent), education (19.0 per cent) and 'other services' (17.2 per cent) were all well above the average for middle-income oil-importing African countries.[17]

Senegal was not, however, an extreme example of direct state involvement in economic life. As will be seen, the state's main economic function consisted in controlling credit and banking – for example, by establishing the Banque Nationale de Développement and the Union Sénégalaise de Banque in the 1960s, and in taking shares in a number of joint banking ventures with foreign capital in the 1970s. In that decade also the state invested in new industrial ventures, such as the industrial free zone, the naval repair base, a petro-chemical complex and tourist facilities. Conversely, there were few purely state industrial enterprises of the type common in Ghana and elsewhere; the bulk of the industrial sector was left to French and later other foreign firms. It was in agriculture, and particularly in the dominant groundnut sector, that the state was most directly involved in production; and it is hardly too much to say that the key to Senegal's economic performance after 1960 lies in the effects state control had on this sector.

Agriculture: the Tyranny of Groundnuts

Although the record of groundnut production in Senegal after 1960 is in many ways depressing, both for the individual producers and for the country as a whole, the story is substantially different from that of export commodities in other African states, such as cocoa in Ghana or palm oil in Nigeria.[18] Here we do not find the same almost cynical readiness to squeeze the peasantry to pay for urban development and industrialization. It is true that, for much of the period, groundnut producers suffered from state control, but their suffering stemmed less from a deliberate policy of transferring the rural surplus than from a variety of factors which ranged from administrative incompetence to drought and fluctuations in the world market. One central fact ensured that exploitation would not be excessive or overt: UPS, as has been seen, was based on an alliance between urban politicians and an extended network of rural interest groups, dominated by the powerful Islamic brotherhoods, whose fortunes were closely tied up in groundnuts.

There was, therefore, no scope for Senghor to isolate and exploit his rural producers as Nkrumah could and did in Ghana. Indeed, the starting-point of the system of state intervention in the groundnut economy seems to have been a generally felt need to free the peasant producer from domination by the largely French trading companies which had previously marketed some 50 per cent of the crop, distributed over 75 per cent of the imported food and manufactures sold to peasants and provided, along with foreign banks and through the agency of Lebanese or African middlemen, much of the credit on which the whole productive system had always depended, but which resulted in chronic peasant indebtedness. In common with other French territories, colonial Senegal had no marketing boards on the pattern of British West Africa, but in 1958 a stabilization fund was set up to even out fluctuations in market prices; and since 1933 there had been Sociétés de Prévoyance as an alternative co-operative means of marketing produce, which had been extended considerably after 1945.

The aim of the post-1960 planners was to create a system of rural co-operatives which would not only control the buying of the groundnut crop but also dispense credit and disseminate technical knowledge. In this way the peasant would be liberated from capitalist exploitation and rural socialism would be created. The strategy was undoubtedly radical, imaginative and nationalistic, far from the neo-colonialism alleged by critics. But to carry it out a very complex bureaucratic machinery was set up, presumably largely on the advice of the still-dominant French advisers in Dakar. Control of all sales of groundnuts was vested in an Office de Commercialisation Agricole (OCA), which had a monopoly of buying from the co-operatives and at first the remaining private buyers. OCA would then sell either to the processing companies in Senegal or to importers of groundnuts in France. To promote agricultural improvement, Centres Régionaux de l'Assistance au Développement (CRADs) were established, provided with finance for credit by the new Banque Sénégalaise de Développement (BSD, later Banque Nationale de Développement Sénégalaise (BNDS)). The co-operatives were supervised by the Service de la Coopération (SC), part of the Ministry of Rural Economy. The structure was thus highly bureaucratic and centralized, but the intention was that most parts of it would gradually wither away as the co-operatives acquired competence. It was also intended that private buyers, mostly Lebanese, should eventually be eliminated and that retailing of trade goods, still largely left in private hands, should be taken over by the co-operatives.

This imaginative construct, in its own way as radical an attempt to restructure rural production as that of Nyerere in Tanzania later, lasted in its original planned form only for a couple of years, during which the system was tried out in full only in the major producing area of Thiès. By 1962 the co-operatives there were beginning not only to market groundnuts but also, along with five consortiums of French and Senegalese private traders, to distribute imported food and trade goods. But this early momentum towards a genuinely socialist system was checked by the fall of Marmadou Dia in 1962, and this marked the end of the early radical phase of development strategy. The shift away from idealistic socialism was not merely opportunistic. These first two years of experiment had shown up the incompetence of both state bureaucracy and local co-operatives in almost every respect, resulting, where the full system was in operation, in shortages of agricultural inputs, food and trade goods, in wide variations in selling and buying prices, in embezzlement and financial chaos. Clearly it had been unwise to exclude private enterprise so quickly and Senghor's rural allies were not prepared to allow dogma to destroy their economy. In the following years a compromise was therefore reached. Private buyers were given a temporary reprieve, though by 1967 no authorized private buying survived: all groundnuts had to be sold through the co-operatives. On the other hand, private firms continued to import and sell trade goods; and, although the import of the main food staples, rice and millet, remained in the hands of OCA, the distribution of these things was divided between foreign and local private traders. Thus in

1968 some 45 per cent of the 177,000 tons of imported food was distributed by the eight largest Senegalese and foreign companies, 25 per cent by 50 Senegalese traders organized in co-operatives, and 30 per cent by 200 small traders.[19]

But the main trend after 1962 was not towards greater freedom for private enterprise but towards bureaucratic centralism. In 1964 the SCs were taken over by the CRADs, who in turn were abolished in 1966 and their functions transferred to a new central authority, Office Nationale de Coopération et d'Assistance au Développement (ONCAD). In 1967 the OCA in turn was abolished and its functions taken over by a new Office de Commercialisation de Sénégal. This in turn only lasted until 1971, when it was also absorbed into ONCAD. Thus ONCAD had become the central government's single agency for running the whole rural sector. Its powers included supervision of the co-operatives, control of the agricultural modernization programme (in collaboration with BDS), marketing all the co-operatives' products (mainly groundnuts, but also some millet and other crops), transporting both inputs and the products, importing, storing and distributing rice and exporting of all products. With modifications (mostly suggested by Italian consultants Italconsult in 1971) this system survived until 1980, when ONCAD was dissolved and other state agencies took over its functions.

The evolution of ONCAD may at first sight look like a typical example of bureaucratic aggrandizement which destroyed an imaginative plan for rural development based on decentralization of responsibility. But in fact the experience of the 1960s made change essential.[20] The co-operative system was extremely complicated, involving the many government agencies mentioned above, and its efficiency depended on a high level of co-ordination and honesty in each organization, from the co-operatives upwards. In general this was not forthcoming. The key post of weigher and treasurer of the co-operatives, whose function was to weigh peasant crops on delivery to the co-operative, to give a receipt, to pay out cash and finally to distribute the rebate paid by BNDS at the end of the production and marketing circuit, seems to have been very widely abused for personal profit. CRAD agents, responsible for arranging the evacuation of the crop to central OCA depots, were misappropriating funds. Transport was often delayed. The whole structure was riddled with political patronage: as Schumacher wrote, 'patronage-oriented class politics embedded within the UPS sapped the cohesion, discipline and authority of the Senegalese public service'.[21] The result was that marketing agency profits in the mid-1960s were very much smaller than the profits previously made by private traders, while the producers did no better, suffering from low prices fixed by OCA and by inadequate end-of-season rebates, which reflected official incompetence and corruption.

The mid-1960s, in fact, were the crisis period of the groundnut economy, as it affected both state and producer. Its profitability had depended heavily on bulk-purchase of the crop (through the trading companies) by the French government at prices well above current world levels. From 1962, following France's entry into EEC, this system was gradually run down; and from 1967/8 all French subsidies ended and Senegal had to sell at world market prices that were substantially lower. Coincidentally, 1967/8 proved to be the beginning of a cycle of recurrent drought which hit production during five of the next nine years and reduced total marketed production from nearly 1.2m. tons in 1965/6 to under 600,000 tons in 1970/1 and 1972/3. The result was a serious decline in public revenues, and this shortfall was passed on to the peasant producer. Until 1967/8 the price he received was based on the subsidized Marseilles price, less all the costs, including administration, resulting for the 1966/7 campaign in prices ranging from 17 FCFA/kg to 22.75 FCFA/kg, according to the cost of inland transport: that is, the more distant producers suffered from their isolation.[22] The total cash revenue received by producers (FCFA) was 18.7b. in 1964/5, 21.2b. in 1965/6, and 17.4b. in 1966/7. From 1967/8 the government, to meet reduced selling prices, lowered producers' prices by 15 per cent (also reducing the margin between different regions). Simultaneously it withheld payment of 5 per cent of the price and paid in chits instead of money in order to improve its cashflow position.

This seems the explanation of the virtual destruction of the initial scheme for agricultural regeneration. Faced by an economic crisis and growing peasant dissatisfaction with both the new system and the reduced prices, the government put its faith in a more centralized bureaucratic structure which might stimulate higher levels of production and efficiency. To put it another way, Dakar lost faith in the ability of peasants, even if politically activated by the *animation rurale* programme and by the co-operatives, to become the main engine of economic and social development. ONCAD was intended to run the whole groundnut economy along centralized lines, using the co-operatives merely as subordinate agencies. Virtually the only element not controlled by ONCAD was production itself. Few African states established so comprehensive a system for regulating an export-oriented peasant economy.

This leads to the main question: how efficient was the new centralized system for both the producer and the economy as a whole? It cannot be answered with certainty, since many factors other than this state system influenced the outcome, among them fluctuating world prices and climatic conditions. Yet an answer must be attempted since this lies at the root of the debate over not only the value of export-oriented commodity production by also the role of the African state and its agencies.

First, the effect on the producers. On the face of it, the peasants seem not to have benefited from either groundnuts or the new state system. In constant prices the price they received was below the 1965/7 average in every subsequent year to 1980, except for 1974/5, and total payments received were below the 1965/6 level except for the years of bumper crops between 1974/5 and 1976/7. According to the World Bank, the price paid to producers as a percentage of the international f.o.b. price was 45–8 per cent in 1962–9; 36 per cent in 1969/70; 40 per cent in 1971/2; 30 per cent in 1972/3.[23]

This was the outcome of many factors, not all resulting from state expropriation of part of the value of the crop. The low prices of 1967/8 and payment by chit resulted in so much peasant resentment and reduced production – the *malaise paysan* – that cash payments were restored in 1969/70 and producer prices increased in the following two years. The establishment of the stabilization fund (CPSP) in 1973 resulted in a substantial levy on producers; but in several subsequent years there was a net subsidy to producers through debt cancellation and subsidies on seeds, etc.[24] The effect was that until 1973/4 groundnut producers indirectly subsidized urban consumers of rice and millet, since their earnings, held back by ONCAD, were used in part to keep down the selling price of imported foodstuffs; but thereafter, although ONCAD accounts showed a transfer to the stabilization fund in every year except 1979/80, when account is taken of payments from the fund to rural development funds and of debt cancellations, there was a net subsidy to producers of some 5b. FCFA between 1974/5 and 1979. By contrast consumers contributed 11.1b. FCFA to the fund in the same years.[25]

This suggests an important paradox. As Caswell puts it, groundnut producers did not benefit from the ending of private marketing or the creation of a state monopoly with related development services: their real incomes were probably reduced. Since one main reason for this was that producer prices were kept a long way below the world marketing price, even allowing for marketing costs, one would, therefore, have expected that a substantial surplus was being taken over by the state, on the model of other African state marketing organizations. Until the mid-1970s this transfer certainly did take place, though it is uncertain how large the sum available for public use actually was; but during the later 1970s the groundnut sector was a net consumer of resources, subsidized by the state. Yet the *malaise paysan* continued, with peasants again after 1975/6 moving out of groundnut production into millet and selling their groundnuts illicitly in The Gambia or to private buyers; and the state was receiving no apparent benefit from its monopoly. How does one explain this paradox of both producer and public poverty? Above all, what bearing does it have on the fundamental question of Senegal's adoption of a development strategy based on continued specialization in commodity production?

Exogenous factors were important. Drought again reduced production in several years, notably 1977/8 and 1980/1. International prices fluctuated, with a big reduction after the end of the subsidized French market in 1967, though prices were generally good in the mid-1970s. But ultimately the main reason must lie in the nature of the state system of management. Put simply, ONCAD and other agencies absorbed most of the profit which might otherwise have accrued either to the state or to the primary producer. The incompetence and dishonesty of many of its officials beggars description. The co-operative weighers were often dishonest: in 1976, 269 out of 1,734 of them were dismissed for mismanagement.[26] ONCAD made deductions from the price paid on the assumption that there would be loss of weight and impurities, but usually did not refund this. ONCAD itself probably suffered considerably from theft, loss and fraud during the process of evacuation of the crops by private firms under contract.

Dishonesty apart, however, it is clear that ONCAD was itself a major consumer of surplus. From the start it was grossly overmanned, yet short of competent officials. Italconsult pointed this out in 1970, but their recommendations were largely ignored. By 1977 ONCAD had 2,127 full-time staff; by 1980 estimates put the total at between 5,500 and 7,400.[27] It grew because it was a means of providing political patronage, and its running costs were disproportionate to its functions or profits. In 1980 it had debts of 90b. FCFA – more than three times the total public sector investment budget for 1979/80;[28] and, in 1973, 11.4b. FCFA of the nominal 12.6b. reserves of ONCAD's stabilization fund had to be written off before the new fund was established, having been used for other unspecified purposes. Where all this money went remains a mystery; but, apart from frauds committed by officials, the most likely answer is that it was dissipated in the many forms of political patronage. The great clan leaders of the brotherhoods were probably major beneficiaries, as were members of the ruling UPS. From top to bottom of the system, party members held key posts in ONCAD and the co-operatives. Since most of these men were protected from dismissal or control by their political affiliation, it was virtually impossible for ONCAD to run its affairs efficiently or honestly. It had become primarily a mechanism whereby the political and administrative bourgeoisie extracted value from the groundnut economy.

This makes it the more surprising that ONCAD was wound up in 1980 and its functions redistributed within the state system. Caswell suggests two possible explanations: that it had become too autonomous and difficult for the state to control; and, more important, that by the late 1970s the peasants, backed by their Islamic leaders, were increasingly refusing to sell their groundnut crop through the state system: in 1980/1 only about 30 per cent of the drought-reduced harvest went through ONCAD.

The failure of ONCAD does not, however, imply that all similar state enterprises were equally incompetent. In non-groundnut areas SUDEFITEX, controlling cotton production, paid producers a reasonable price (the world price less costs) and did quite well; and SAED, which was responsible for all development in the River Region, was also quite successful in improving irrigation and producing a range of other crops. Barker attributes the relative success of these and other state organizations to the absence in these areas of the type of 'rural aristocracy where patron–client ties penetrate the state bureaucracy as well as the party' in the groundnut areas.[29] On the other hand, some parastatals did proportionately as badly as ONCAD: by 1980 SOSAP (for fisheries) had debts of 12b. FCFA; the debts of BUD Senegal (for market gardening) were 10b. FCFA, and those of SAED (rice) also 10b. FCFA.[30]

The record of comparative failure in Senegal's major staple crop brings us back to the fundamental question posed by Amin: would or could independent Senegal have done better by diversifying out of groundnuts and from an open, export-oriented economy still closely tied to Europe through membership of the franc zone and adherence to the Yaoundé and Lomé agreements, to some form of autonomy? There are various ways in which this question can be approached. One is to take the stance adopted by the World Bank and IMF and to consider Senegal's relative efficiency in the production of groundnuts as compared with other crops. Rimmer's table for the domestic resource costs of the various crops produced in Senegal suggests that the domestic resource cost coefficient of groundnuts was very low: 0.36, lower than either of the two main alternative food crops – millet at 0.62 and sorghum also at 0.62 – and much lower than rice, which, at 1.02, could be imported at a slightly lower resource cost.[31] On this basis Senegal wisely clung to the principle of comparative advantage, even though the benefits were reduced by the ending of French subsidies and fluctuation both in the size of the crop and international prices. Moreover, since about 30 per cent of the total turnover of the manufacturing sector[32] consisted in processing groundnuts, and most of the oil was exported, this crop was critical both for industrialization and for export earnings. While it was clearly wise, especially after the crisis of the later 1960s, to concentrate on growing more food and to develop fisheries further, it would have been economic nonsense to do so at the cost of running down this main economic staple.

But from a quite different standpoint it would clearly have been politically and socially impracticable for any government after 1960 to make major changes in the groundnut economy. As has so often been emphasized, the political power of the Islamic marabouts in the Wolof states, the homeland of groundnuts, was basic to the strength of UPS. The early nationalist leaders, having allied with these, had to pay the price by preserving the interest of their complex networks of supporters. As Barker has put it, 'The "neo-colonial solution" was no ready-made recipe but rather the outcome of a trial of strength and a jockeying for position'.[33] Conversely, the pressures of groundnut producers and the rural aristocracy seems to have been decisive in forcing an increase in producer prices in 1973/4 and, through the reduced volume of production and sales to ONCAD, to the abolition of ONCAD in 1980. In short, Senegal's strategy was the only one open to the sort of government and state that inherited power in 1960. If the options open to it were limited by the colonial inheritance, it was the realities of local politics rather than the pressure of French neo-colonialism that determined that this pattern would largely be retained.

If, then, failure resulted from exaggerated monoculture, this can be attributed not so much to the strategy as to the way in which it was executed and the agencies used. The original plan for rural self-determination through the co-operatives was imaginative and offered the possibility of development based on the self-interested enterprise of producers, backed by public provision of what was needed to increase productivity and efficiency. The weakness of the system adopted lay partly in its complexity, but still more in the lack of people at every level competent to run it efficiently and honestly. To put it another way, too rapid a break was made with the very long-established structure of private trade and provision of goods on credit. From 1962 the trend was towards centralized bureaucratic control, which proved increasingly expensive and inefficient. The result was that neither the state nor the peasant obtained the benefits expected to result from specialization in groundnuts. Moreover, it is not enough to say that adverse weather and market conditions destroyed the potential surplus: as has been seen, the value of the crop, at constant prices, reached an all-time peak in the mid-1970s, and Senegal's terms of trade (groundnuts and cotton, 1970 = 100) were favourable throughout the 1970s, except for 1971 (97.3) and 1979 (91.3).[34]

Clearly, then, there was profit to be made from groundnuts, but it was going to third parties within Senegal rather than to the peasant producers or the state. Who obtained it is unclear. Possibly it was diffused among the rural aristocracy, the marabouts, who were able to evade many of the restrictions imposed on peasants, among the private transporters, private merchants who provided additional credit, and the bureaucracy and politicians, who controlled and exploited the system. In principle these funds might provide resources for private investment and so benefit the economy as a whole; Caswell concludes that 'certain of those benefiting from the Office's [sc. ONCAD] operations are now engaged in commercial and even industrial activity, representing points of dynamism in an overall stagnant economy'.[35] How far this actually occurred may to some extent be tested by looking at the development of industry and other sectors of the economy.

Industry and Manufacturing

The main problem concerning the industrial sector is not whether it grew – which it did quite successfully after 1960 – but whether and to what extent indigenous Senegalese capital and entrepreneurship developed, possibly benefiting from resources extracted from the primary sector. The growth statistics of industry are quite impressive. In the 1960s industrial production grew at an average of 4.4 per cent, in the 1970s at 3.5 per cent; and it increased its share of GDP from 17 to 24 per cent over the whole period. Between 1962 and 1978 manufacturing increased as a percentage of merchandise exports from 4 to 7 per cent and manufactures decreased from 44 to 26 per cent of total merchandise imports, reflecting a substantial degree of import substitution.[36] On the other hand, imports of machinery and transport equipment did not maintain their initial momentum. They increased from 19 per cent in 1960 to 25 per cent in 1970, but fell back to 18 per cent in 1978.[37]

The 1960s, however, were a period of relatively successful industrial growth. Starting from a strong base in the Dakar region and with a stock of urban industrial workers unique in West Africa, Senegal looked set to become an important regional manufacturing centre, with the opportunity to replace French imports, hitherto duty free, with local products. Its main problem was the market. The domestic market was limited by the low level of incomes and small population and fluctuated with the size of the crop. The potential overseas market, apart from that of Europe for processed vegetable oil and other commodities, lay in West Africa. But the component parts of the previous free trade zone of French West Africa were now free to develop their own industries behind protective walls, as has been seen in the case of Ivory Coast, which had previously had almost no industry. Thus Senegal's best hope of export-led industrial growth lay in negotiating a free trade area. Early attempts at such a union – the Union Douanière de l'Afrique Occidentale (UDAO), which lasted from 1959 to 1966, and its successor, UDEAO, during 1966–72, had limited success. UDAO's aim of a common external tariff proved too difficult to achieve, since all the Francophone countries relied very heavily on import duties as a source of public revenue: the proportion ranged from 33 to 60 per cent. In 1966 UDEAO accepted that a looser system was inevitable and it was agreed that member states might impose duties, ranging from 50 to 70 per cent of those on external imports, on goods from member states.[38] The formation of the Communauté Economique de l'Afrique de l'Ouest in 1973 aimed to solve the problems faced by earlier agreements by moving over a period of years to a partial free-trade area between the six signatories, with a common external tariff and preferential treatment for intra-regional industrial products, the rates to be determined on an industry-by-industry basis.

The benefits for Senegal of these attempts to find a market for exports was limited. Thus in 1966 exports (mostly industrial) to the other five West African customs union states were 2.6 per cent of total Senegalese exports. By 1970 they had risen to an encouraging 15 per cent, and in 1973 to 19.7 per cent, but then fell back in 1975 to 13.1 per cent. On the other hand, Senegal always had a large favourable balance of merchandise trade with these states: in 1966 her imports from them were only 1.4 per cent of total imports; in 1970, 5.9 per cent, in 1973, 5.2 per cent; in 1975, 4.4 per cent.[39] Thus, while Francophone West Africa provided a useful extension of the market, with Ivory Coast always among the top four of Senegal's foreign markets, in the early 1970s economic nationalism in the other states, duplication of the same basic consumer goods industries (particularly in the more dynamic Ivory Coast) and generally low consumer capacity restricted the potential value of the region as a source of economies of scale for Senegalese manufacturing.

The result was to limit industrial growth. By one measure, in 1967 there were only 204 industrial establishments, employing 13,400 workers;[40] by another, 230 enterprises in 1969 (of which 70 had been started after 1960);[41] by a third about 239 enterprises in 1974.[42] Processing primary commodities, mainly for export, was the most important industrial activity. Of total industrial production of 223.6b. FCFA in 1976, vegetable-oil production was worth 64b. (of which 41.9b. was exported); mining (mainly phosphates) 16.3b., down from 27.8b. in 1975; the petro-chemical industry, 38.5b.; and fish products 13b. Industrial textiles also came high on the list, at 14b. FCFA in 1976, as did mechanical, metallic and electrical goods at 11.3b., though both these were mainly for domestic consumption.[43] This was the characteristic pattern of African industrial development, a combination of processing for export and manufacturing consumer goods for domestic consumption behind relatively high protective barriers.

But, by West African standards, Senegalese industry was relatively efficient. Output per worker in the major industries for which comparable information is available was relatively high, though the comparison is weakened by slightly different dates being given for different countries. In most cases Senegal was second only to Ivory Coast. Thus, in food, beverages and tobacco, Senegal (1967) produced US$27,000 per worker, as against $21,000 for Nigeria (1971) and $18,903 for Ivory Coast (1971); in textiles, clothing and leather,

$10,084 against $10,328 and $12,484 respectively; in chemicals and chemical products, $24,083 as compared with $22,580 and $27,460; and in fabricated metal products and machinery, $16,939 against $12,096 and $22,341. In every case Senegalese productivity was more than three times that in Ghana and well above that for Benin, the other two states compared in this table.[44] Measured in value added per worker, Senegal (1967) was very much more efficient than Ghana (1970): for example, in food, beverages and tobacco, $8,640 as against $4,942; in fabricated metal products, $7,314 compared with $1,223.[45]

This relative efficiency may have been closely related to the fact that in Senegal, as in Ivory Coast, the bulk of the major industries were foreign owned and managed, a point which has drawn adverse criticism from Amin and others. Thus, of an estimated total share capital of 37.8b. FCFA in 1976, only 24.5 per cent was held by Senegalese, most, 21.5 per cent, by the state. Foreign firms owned 75.5 per cent, of which 70 per cent was French. The Senegalese share varied considerably from one branch of activity to another. In extractive industries it was 49.6 per cent in 1976; in processing sea foods, 21 per cent; in vegetable-oil production, only 3.7 per cent; in agro-industry, 20.6 per cent ; in foodstuffs, 4.5 per cent; in timber products, 9.7 per cent; in tobacco, none; in textiles, 17.6 per cent; in the petro-chemical industry, 7 per cent. Only in electricity and water supply was the national ownership 100 per cent.[46]

More striking still was the small share of private Senegalese capital in the domestic ownership of industry – only 3.0 per cent of total capital; and, on the other side, the preponderance of French capital, amounting to 70 per cent. Historically the reasons were the same as for other African countries: industry had been developed almost entirely by French capital and Senegal lacked both capital and entrepreneurial experience. In terms of policy, Senghor's government accepted the situation it inherited and aimed, in the words of Louis Alexandrenne, minister for industrial development, 'to develop in the interstices of foreign capital a network of small and middle-sized complementary national enterprises'.[47] At the extraordinary congress of UPS in December 1978, Senghor himself justified this Fabian approach as follows:

Il faut nationaliser ce qui est nationalisable sans dommage pour la Nation . . . Si, dans un premier temps, nous préférons les s[ocié]tés [sic] d'économie mixte dans les branches rentables, c'est parce que nous ne sommes pas encore en mesure d'assurer cette gestion efficace . . . La nationalisation sans limite présente plus d'inconvenients que d'avantages.

Grâce à l'Etat, qui par la création des stés d'éonomie mixte, poursuit une politique de participation au capital dans les grandes entreprises motrices, les capitaux sénégalais son plus présents qu'on ne le dit dans l'industrie de notre pays. Le problème, ici, c'est l'insertion de chefs d'entreprises sénégalais dans le secteur secondaire.

Le problème de la sénégalisation est au centre un débat sur l'industrie . . . Sans exclure jamais les étrangers, il est question que, progressivement, en avançant pas à pas, nous sénégalisions une industrie qui, par définition, est sénégalaise: par ses capitaux, ses directions et ses technostructures comme elle l'est déjà par ses ouvriers et ses employés.

Again, in April 1977, Senghor repeated his theme.

La place du secteur privé doit être confortée dans le cadre d'une participation plus active au processus de développement. L'existence d'un secteur privé dynamique n'est nullement contradictoire avec notre option du socialisme démocratique. Le secteur privé, c'est bien sûr la logique du profit, mais aussi la capacité d'initiative et l'acceptation du risque.[48]

This was a somewhat bland defence of a situation which, after some sixteen years of independence had hardly increased Senegalese participation in industrial ownership and it adds weight to the charge that Senghor was prepared to preserve the predominance of foreigners, mostly French and Lebanese, in business as well as at the higher levels of the civil service. French capital owned most of the industrial sector in 1960; and thereafter the big trading firms which had previously refused to invest on a large scale outside their import–export business – CFAO, SCOA and the Unilever subsidiary, NOSOCO – moved from trade into manufacture and other parts of the modern sector, as they were doing in other parts of West Africa. For their part the Lebanese, forced out of the groundnut circuit, moved into wholesale and retail trade and into small-scale industry. Thus they were occupying precisely those gaps between the big capitalist firms which the government hoped would be filled by Senegalese.

Their activities were undoubtedly valuable to the economy, given the absence of equally experienced Senegalese; but the government was forced to take positive action. In 1967 it set up a parastatal organization, SONEPI, whose capital was 20 per cent state and 80 per cent privately owned, to help Senegalese to invest in industry by providing cheap surveys of possible opportunities and lending investment funds for up to six years on the security of land, buildings, etc. The effects were very limited: by 1979 only 23 out of the 144 largest enterprises were either wholly or partly owned by Senegalese capitalists, and of these 13 were part public, part private. In 1972 a revised version of the investment code aimed to give

Senegalese an advantage as capitalists and employers by providing them with five-year exemption from profit tax and patent laws, provided they invested at least 5m. FCFA ($23,000) over a two-year period, and offered five years' exemption from all taxes and import licence controls to all companies with an initial capital of 40m. FCFA ($182,550) and employing at least forty Africans.

The results were very small, because the conditions for obtaining the necessary credit were very tough and few Africans could put up so large an initial capital without borrowing.[49] In employment also the French remained exceptionally important. Uniquely in West Africa, Senegal had a substantial influx of French workers in industrial, commercial and clerical jobs after 1945, and many of these remained. In the later 1960s, while Senegal's rate of replacement of foreign employees was one of the highest in West Africa, resulting in less than 7 per cent of foreigners in industry and 10 per cent in commerce, more then 75 per cent of technical and managerial positions were held by foreigners. Conversely, only about 27 per cent of employers and upper management and 18 per cent of technicians and officials were Senegalese.[50] In the early 1970s a technical college was set up at Dakar to train technicians and middle management, but in the short term its products met with some resistance from foreign firms on the ground that they did not meet their needs and that they expected excessively high salaries and the same conditions of employment as expatriates.[51] At the highest level of government there were still a large number of French officials, seconded under 'technical assistance', especially in the key ministries of Finance, Infrastructure, and Rural Development and Industry. At the beginning of 1975 there were some 1,125 French technical assistants, 816 of them in education. Collectively they enabled the state to carry on much as before independence, but they also acted as a block to the advancement of Senegalese to responsibility.[52]

The French and Lebanese dominance made it difficult for even the most enterprising Senegalese to find a niche in industry, except in the 'informal' sector. Gerry has estimated that the artisanal population of Dakar in the 1970s was between 30,000 and 50,000, and that there were some 6,365 urban artisan enterprises, though the definition of these is vague. These provided a wide range of cheap goods and services. They received little formal help from the capitalist sector, but depended heavily on it for initial training in skills and also for cheap raw materials. Gerry gives as an example the dominant position of the BATA subsidiary in footwear production, which inhibited the evolution of small indigenous shoe factories but also stimulated a large number of very small producers, who used cheaper raw materials such as vinyl. Such enterprises had such low rates of return that capital accumulation was very difficult. Most of the Senegalese who managed to buy into foreign and state enterprises accumulated their capital from their role in the public service, from state contracts, sub-contracting to foreign firms or their access to credit based on political networks. There was little or no evidence that indigenous capitalism had the capacity to grow on its own momentum.[53]

How, then, should one assess Senegal's economic performance after 1960? A recent paper by Boubabar Barry, a historian at Dakar University, appears to express a current Senegalese consensus. Senghor, for all his rhetoric concerning negritude and national independence, was 'the incarnation of the last French Proconsul' who believed in the value of French civilization and accepted the necessity of maintaining close economic and political links with France. His economic policy consisted in preserving the essentials of the old trading economy, which rested on groundnut production and export, though now under indigenous control, while also encouraging the expansion of the export-oriented processing industry and import-substituting consumer industries through alliance with foreign capital. Politically he aimed at consensus; but, as the economic crisis developed from the later 1960s, he depended increasingly on presidential power and the machinery of the police state to contain discontent, particularly among the urban intelligentsia and proletariat. To defuse growing hostility he notionally ended the political monopoly of UPS in 1976; then, in 1980, resigned the presidency and left his successor, Abdou Diouf, to complete the transition to nominal democracy while in practice strengthening presidential power. By the 1980s the Senegalese economy was virtually stagnant and debt-ridden; and Diouf was left with the problem of how to sustain a politico-economic system which was beyond the country's resources.[54]

How acceptable is this hostile diagnosis? Its main weakness, like that of Amin, is that it assumes a far greater freedom of choice and action on the part of Senghor and the post-colonial state than in fact they possessed. The key fact to emerge from the literature is that both the political and economic systems were dictated very largely by the realities of the social structure. The immense power of the Islamic brotherhoods as a rural aristocracy in the Wolof states, the vested interests of the large urban bureaucratic elite, and the huge commitment of the peasantry to cash-crop farming, made it virtually impossible for any nationalist leader to make a radical or rapid departure from the fundamentals of the status quo. In this respect the heavy rural dependence of UPS from the start excluded the sort of policies adopted by Nkrumah in Ghana, based as they were essentially on the towns and against the interests of the cocoa farmers. For much the same reasons the Senegalese state had to respond to the *malaise paysan* of the later 1960s by increasing payments to producers, even at the price of reducing or eliminating the state's share of the surplus and, in the later 1970s, providing a net subsidy to the groundnut sector.

If it was politically impossible to follow Amin's prescription and run down the groundnut economy, it would from the start have been quite impractical – or at least extremely difficult – to make radical changes in the foreign ownership of much of the modern sector. Here the very fact that Senegal had so comparatively well-developed an industrial base constituted a problem. With virtually no industry, Ghana's options were open: the state could fill gaps with state, parastatal, or mixed enterprises. In Senegal few such gaps existed: foreign firms were already there. Senghor could, in principle, have nationalized them outright or insisted on rapid dilution of their capital by sale to the state or Senegalese nationals. He knew, however, that this would have involved high economic costs. New foreign investment would have been inhibited and Senegal lacked both entrepreneurs and corporate managers to take over these firms or to establish new enterprises in the short term. Foreign ownership involved high economic and social costs, but for Senegal the danger of losing what it had was reasonably thought to outweigh these. As a result Senegal avoided the disasters of Ghana's industrializing policy and its industrial sector did reasonably well within the limits set by the market and by the global strategies of the foreign firms.

If Senegal's policies were, as has been suggested, almost inevitable, cautious and basically rational, why, then, did she face recurrent and intensifying economic, social and political crises from about 1967?

There is no single or simple answer. Of exogenous factors, the end of the preferential market for commodities in 1967 put a serious strain on foreign exchange, as did the oil price increases of 1973 and 1979: as a proportion of total imports, fuel increased from 5 to 12 per cent between 1970 and 1978.[55] Yet the rate of increase of the net barter terms of trade was 1.3 in 1961–70 and 1.4 in 1970–9; significantly that of the net income terms of trade in 1970–9 was only 0.2 per cent, reflecting the declining quantity of commodity exports.[56] Official foreign aid came in increasing quantities: $43m. in 1970, $309m. in 1979.[57] A key to underlying weakness in the economy can be seen in the low figures for domestic saving – 15 per cent of GDP in 1960, only 2 per cent in 1978,[58] with low rates of growth for gross domestic investment – 1.1 per cent in 1960–70, 1.8 per cent in 1970–9.[59] Even this was increasingly dependent on foreign official and private capital flows. Fundamentally the stagnation of the Senegalese economy can best be explained in terms of four main factors: exogenous constraints on an export-oriented commodity-producing economy; the limited market for industrial products; failure to make significant improvements in agriculture productivity; and the inefficiency of a political and administrative system which seems to have absorbed and dissipated most of the surplus that should have been available for investment in modernization in all sectors. In the last resort, and even taking account of the effects of drought, Senegal's limited development can best be attributed to weakness of policy and administration, which itself stemmed from fundamental characteristics of the society. If this, in Amin's phrase, was 'blocked development', the main blockage lay within rather than outside Senegal.

Notes

1 D. Morawetz, *Twenty-Five Years of Economic Development, 1950–1975*, (Washington DC, 1977), Statistical Appendix, table A1; World Bank, *Accelerated Development in Tropical Africa (AD)* (Washington DC, 1981), App. 1.
2 *AD* App. 2, 33.
3 *AD* App. 2.
4 *AD* App. 3.
5 *AD* App. 7.
6 *AD* App. 9.
7 *AD* App. 12, 14.
8 *AD* App. 13.
9 *AD* App. 15.
10 *AD* App. 25.
11 D. Rimmer, *The Economies of West Africa* (London, 1984), table 28.
12 *AD* App. 17, 18.
13 *AD* App. 22.
14 *Politics, Bureaucracy and Rural Development in Senegal* (Berkeley, Los Angeles and London, 1975); see also B. Barry, 'Arachide, bourgeoisie bureaucratique et sechéresse', draft paper given at a conference on 'African Independence', University of Zimbabwe, Harare, January 1985.
15 Schumacher, table 2.1.
16 D. C. O'Brien, 'Ruling Class and Peasantry in Senegal, 1960–76', in R. C. O'Brien (ed.), *The Political Economy of Underdevelopment* (London, 1979).
17 *AD* App. 41.
18 The following account is based mainly on Schumacher; Nim Caswell, 'Peasants, Peanuts and Politics: State Marketing in Senegal, 1966–80', unpub. paper given at a conference on 'The Fate of Post-Colonial Economies in West Africa', SOAS, July 1983; Barry; World Bank, *Senegal. Tradition, Diversification and Economic Development* (Washington DC, 1974); H. D. Nelson (ed.), *Area Handbook for Senegal* (2nd edn, Washington DC, 1974).
19 Schumacher, p. 146.
20 ibid., ch. 8, *passim*.
21 ibid., p. 168.
22 Caswell, p. 18.

23 ibid., fig. 11.
24 ibid., table 2.
25 ibid., p. 26.
26 ibid., p. 27.
27 ibid., p. 21.
28 ibid., pp. 28, 32.
29 J. Barker, 'Stability and Stagnation in the State of Senegal', *CJAS*, Vol. 11, no. 1 (1977), p. 39.
30 Barry, p. 28.
31 Rimmer, *The Economies of West Africa*, table 27.
32 *Area Handbook*, p. 298.
33 J. Barker, 'Stability', p. 35.
34 *AD* App. 31.
35 Caswell, p. 36.
36 *AD* App. 2, 3, 8, 9.
37 Rimmer, table 18.
38 *Area Handbook*, pp. 298–9.
39 ibid., p. 318, table 14; *L'Economie Sénégalaise* (*ES*) (4th ed, Paris, 1977), 'Commerce extérieur', p. 6.
40 J. O. C. Onyemelukwe, *Industrialization in West Africa* (London, 1984), table 4.1.
41 *Area Handbook*, table 11.
42 *ES*, 'Données générales', p. 3.
43 ibid., 'Industrie', p. 3.
44 Onyemelukwe, table 4.4.
45 ibid., table 4.8.
46 *ES*, 'Industrie', p. 3.
47 ibid., p. 2.
48 ibid., p. 3.
49 R. C. O'Brien, 'Foreign Ascendance in the Economy and State: The French and Lebanese', in R. C. O'Brien (ed.), *Political Economy*, pp. 105–10.
50 *Area Handbook*, p. 251.
51 R. C. O'Brien, 'Foreign Ascendance', p. 117.
52 ibid., p. 122 f.
53 Chris Gerry, 'The Crisis of the Self-employed. Petty Production and Capitalist Production in Dakar', in R. C. O'Brien, *Political Economy*.
54 Barry, *passim*.
55 Rimmer, *The Economies of West Africa*, table 18.
56 *AD* App. 13.
57 *AD* App. 23.
58 *AD* App. 5.
59 *AD* App. 4.

9

Summary and Conclusions: Economic Decolonization and 'Arrested Development'

The title of this book suggests that it investigates two themes: economic elements in the process of decolonization and the reasons for subsequent 'arrested' or alternatively (as was explained in the Preface), limited, decelerating or checked development in Black Africa. The title also implies that there may have been a link between them. Part One examined the economic dimensions of the transfer of power by the imperial states and some features of the economic and political systems inherited from them by the new states of Black Africa. Part Two surveyed broad economic trends during the first two decades of African independence and Part Three investigated in rather more detail what happened in six of the more important Anglophone and Francophone states. But so far no systematic attempt has been made to discover possible links between decolonization and what happened afterwards. This concluding chapter will first summarize the evidence and arguments on each of the two basic problems and then sketch an answer to the most difficult of all questions: what were the economic consequences of economic decolonization?

The Economic Dimensions of Decolonization and the Colonial Inheritance

The argument of Part One can be recapitulated quite briefly. There was little or no economic rationality or calculation behind the liberating of Black Africa. From the imperial standpoint the colonies were set free at a time when they were economically more dynamic than at any period since 1920. Carried along by the long world boom that started about 1942, and fuelled by an unprecedented inflow of foreign capital, most colonial economies were expanding fast at the time of independence: they were appreciating assets. As markets they were now, for the first time, beginning to buy the more sophisticated products of European industry, not merely its low-grade consumer goods. In 1956, for example, British West Africa imported nearly twice the value of goods (at current prices) it had done in 1950 and about four times that of 1920, the great boom year after the First World War. In 1956 total British exports to British Africa (including South Africa) were £406.3m. – 12.8 per cent of total British exports and again some four times the value of total British exports to the same region in 1920, though these had then constituted 22.2 per cent of total British exports. Conversely, never had British African exports been larger nor, except in 1920, had a greater proportion of them been sent to Britain than in the period after 1945. In 1956 all British African exports were worth £381.2m. – nearly ten times their 1937 value at current prices and more than four times their 1920 value. Although the proportion sent to Britain in 1956 was down from the very high 58.4 per cent of 1950, its absolute value was steadily increasing; and Britain benefited from African goods sent elsewhere because, as colonies, their foreign currency earnings were held by the Bank of England.

Clearly, then, in the decade and a half after 1945 the unfulfilled dream of pre-war years that African colonies might become a support for the metropolitan economy had at last become a reality. Why, then, did the imperial powers decolonize? The answer suggested in Chapter 1 was complex. The main motive was in the broadest sense political: by transferring power the metropolises could escape from a multiplicity of growing responsibilities and liabilities. Given the actual or potential force of nationalist feeling in many colonies, it would have been politically and militarily expensive to attempt indefinitely to keep the cork on so many genies. Public opinion at home would, or did, eventually rebel against repression on both financial and moral grounds. The potential burden of aid seemed intolerable to metropolitan taxpayers.

But it is critical that such incentives to transfer political power did not operate in an economic vacuum. Two main economic considerations gave the politicians freedom of manoeuvre. On the one hand, the economic recovery of Western Europe in the early 1950s made the colonies very much less important than they had been between 1945 and *c.*1951. On the other, it was generally assumed that, if the colonies were liberated quickly and good relations established with the succesor regimes, there would be little or no economic loss to the metropolises. African markets would remain open; colonial exports would continue to flow to their traditional European terminals or entrepôts; once the colonies were independent, foreign, particularly American, capital would flow into them and this would not only reduce the strain on metropolitan investment funds but would increase the consumer capacity of Black Africa. There were, of course, many uncertainties involved in decolonization. Previously closed imperial markets might be lost to other, more competitive Western states;

African exports might go to other destinations; nationalist governments might put obstacles in the way of foreign capital or even expropriate foreign assets. But the odds seemed reasonable and by about 1960 all the imperial powers except Portugal had decided to gamble on general decolonization.

What significance had the timing of decolonization for the future economic development of Black Africa? At the time it seems generally to have been believed that the sooner they were liberated the quicker and more effective their development would be because they were considered to be ready for and capable of self-government. This can now be seen, as it was by many of the more informed and cautious European observers at the time, to have been fallacious. Chapter 2 pointed to some of the many grounds for thinking that none of these Black African countries was in fact well equipped for independence as 'modern' economies when they acquired political sovereignty. They were very short on the human skills essential in any Western-style economic system. Their infrastructures could not carry the weight of large-scale modern industry or agriculture. Their welfare services were inadequate for an increasingly urbanized society. Few had accepted or had even been seriously exposed to the work ethic of Western capitalism or socialism. Manufacturing was a very small, though growing, part of the domestic product and agriculture, by far the largest sector measured by output or the numbers engaged in it, was still predominantly a peasant activity and was only partly integrated with the market economy.

But almost certainly the area in which the new African states were least well equipped for independence lay in politics and administration. In the later 1940s even the more liberal thinkers on the British left believed that it would require a generation or more for African colonies to learn the arts of government to the point at which independent regimes could run nation-wide democratic electoral and party systems and maintain an efficient and disinterested bureaucracy. Under pressure from the rapidly increasing support aroused by the proto-nationalist African politicians, these men quickly changed their minds: there was now no time for a prolonged apprenticeship.

In retrospect it is clear that their first thoughts were right, even if impracticable. The apparent unity of conglomerate African societies under the banners of front organizations calling themselves political parties soon proved illusory. They had no real cement, and multi-party democratic systems soon turned into ethnic or regional power struggles which in turn led to one-party states or military regimes. Equally the apparent competence and probity of the few first-generation Africans trained to replace European bureaucrats at the highest levels either did not survive the post-independence politicization of almost all civil services, or failed to permeate down to the party supporters quickly recruited to fill the lower levels of these organizations. It is hardly too much to say that, however well endowed any African country might have been in economic terms, political weakness and administrative incompetence of these kinds were almost certain to retard or even destroy the prospects of sustained development. The fact that power was transferred when African societies were still quite unprepared for the difficulties ahead must be seen as a major economic consequence of decolonization and a possible link between decolonization and later 'arrested development'.

The Causes of 'Arrested', Decelerating, Limited or Checked Development

The argument in Parts Two and Three turned on a single basic question: if Black Africa's rate of economic growth after independence was not as satisfactory or as sustained as many had projected, nor sufficient to raise living standards to levels comparable with those in more affluent countries, what were the reasons? Before recapitulating the evidence, it is necessary to decide which of the various terms used in the Preface and the text – 'arrested', decelerating, limited or checked development – seems best to fit the facts. In other words, what have we to explain?

The evidence suggests that all three of these non-dogmatic terms have validity at different times and in different ways. Although there was very considerable growth in most countries during the 1950s and down to the mid-1970s, development in its broadest meaning was indeed limited in that no Black African country overcame the structural problems it faced at independence. For most (though not all) the rate of growth also declined significantly in the 1970s as compared with the previous two decades, though for some (notably Ghana) deceleration began in the mid-1960s while for others it did not start until the later 1970s. Deceleration was thus a general experience. But a check (or conceivably 'arrest'), if it occurred at all, came only at the end of the period, from about 1979 and into the crisis period of the early 1980s. World Bank figures for 1981–3 show negative growth of per capita GDP in sub-Saharan African as a whole and very low growth of GDP. This suggests at least a temporary check to development, without the necessary implication that it had come to a final halt. Yet, because there were such wide variations between the experience of different countries over time and in the intensity of these experiences, it is wise not to be too specific. It would be better to adopt neutral terminology which can apply to almost all states: things did not go consistently well, certainly not as well as had been and might have been hoped for. Let us now simply call this failure, even if in fact it was relative. How best can it be explained?

A wide range of possible explanations were surveyed in Part Two and then tested out against individual states in Part Three; but essentially all these can be reduced to two broad alternative propositions: failure was not the responsibility of African governments because the decisive factors lay outside their control; alternatively, failure was the result of their incompetence. The first of these, the 'non-policy' interpretation, takes account of such things as 'the colonial inheritance', the exigencies of the international capitalist economy and endogenous African obstacles such as climate, geology and sociological conditions. The second, the 'policy' approach, is concerned with the actions of African governments, which are taken to be the prime determinants of economic success and failure. On which side does the evidence fall?

The basis of any assessment must be the proposition that almost everyone expected far too much at the start: they were as over-optimistic about Africa's potential then, because they took the booming 1950s as their model, as people had been over-pessimistic twenty-five years earlier because they judged by the depressed 1930s.[1] Such expectations were fostered by highly theoretical models constructed by economists whose intellectual coherence was rendered irrelevant by their ignorance of real African conditions. It is significant that S. H. Frankel, with direct experience of African peasant production, always held that rapid development was impossible and that sustained growth must be built on slowly improving agricultural productivity.[2] At the time he and other gradualists were regarded as anachronisms, but time has proved them right. The obstacles they pointed to were real. Climate, recurrent drought, poor soils and limited factor endowment had retarded growth in the past and remained unaltered. Plant and human disease and limited human resources were other obstacles which might respond to human action; but the cost was bound to be very high and the results slow to come. Thus limited development has nothing to do with failure to achieve the impossible: it should mean only failure to maintain whatever rate of growth was compatible with Black Africa's limited potential during two short decades after independence.

In fact is has been seen that for most of this time the majority of Black African states had respectable rates of growth: it was their greatest period of economic expansion. In this achievement the international economy proved, on the whole, helpful until at least the mid-1970s. Although African states remained heavily dependent on foreign countries for markets, supplies of capital and technology, the nature of their dependence changed as they slowly detached themselves from the leading strings of their former imperial masters and, in most cases, diversified the range of their commodity exports.[3] For most countries, the barter terms of trade improved significantly in the 1960s,

dropping slightly in the mid-1970s and only deteriorated sharply to
below their 1960 level with the international recession of 1979–82.[4]
Foreign markets remained open to all main commodities and to most
processed goods, though there were some restrictions on manufactures.
EEC provided a more valuable European partner for all African states
which chose to become associate members through the Yaoundé and
Lomé agreements than their individual metropolises had been
previously. Investment capital was in very good supply, coming now
from many parts of the capitalist world and from multilateral agencies:
the flow of public and private loans in 1980, in US dollars, was more
than nine times that in 1970.[5] The costs of debt service were, of
course, critical; but the evidence suggests that, while interest rates rose
with world inflation from the early 1970s, they did not do so
dramatically until 1979. Then, indeed, the combined effects of very
large borrowing on the commercial market coupled with the decision
of foreign banks to raise their interest charges to match inflation and
high domestic rates of interest hit many of the more profligate African
states very seriously. It is significant, however, that those hit worst
were not the poorest but some of the richest; and the fact of their heavy
borrowing falls within the range of 'policy' rather than 'non-policy'
considerations.

This is, of course, to reject the argument of those who use the
international capitalist economy as proxy for most of the disappointing
aspects of African development, with the corollary that African states
should opt out and become 'autonomous'. It is certainly true that
African economies remained 'peripheral' in the sense that their health
depended largely on the well-being of an economic system whose core
was in North America, Western Europe and Japan; and in this sense
their destinies were beyond their own control. It is, therefore, within
the margins set by the international economy that one must judge
Black Africa's performance. Yet it is precisely because this economy
was more continuously favourable to growth in Third World countries
between *c*.1950 and *c*.1975 than at any known previous period, and also
because most African states did less well than countries in other parts
of the Third World, that one has to turn to the alternative possible
source of limited or 'arrested' development, to the policies adopted by
African states and the manner in which they were carried out.

On this at least left and right of the political spectrum agree: Africa's
economic development was in general not well served by its new rulers.
The evidence suggests that they are right. Governments committed
most of the errors in the book. They gave excessive support to import-
substituting industries which were mostly condemned to be inefficient
by the limited size of the market. They spent more than their
economies could afford on prestigious public buildings, state-owned
enterprises, the armed forces and the civil service. Many maintained

currencies at artificially high rates of exchange in order to offset excessive public spending, and so encouraged imports and discouraged domestic producers. They paid such low prices to farmers that output and exports of commodities often declined sharply, using the surplus extracted from the land to finance public expenditures which mainly benefited the towns. To meet accelerating deficits on both domestic budgets and the balance to payments they borrowed recklessly abroad, in the 1970s increasingly at very high cost from private sources; so that by the end of that decade many states carried an intolerable burden of external debt. Above all, perhaps, most governments refused to tackle the most difficult of all the problems they inherited – the low productivity of peasant agriculture and its causes.

This list of 'policy' weaknesses could be extended indefinitely: there was almost no field – except the improved provision of public goods such as education and health services – in which government policies seem to have been based on a balanced appreciation of national needs. Such serious and almost universal inadequacy obviously demands explanation, and it has been seen that many explanations are on offer. These can, in fact, be reduced to two broad propositions: that Africans lacked the experience and competence to do better; and that the politics of survival forced all African politicians to consider their own interests and those of their supporters before all else.

That government should lack the competence expected and necessary in a 'modern' state should cause no surprise. No new African state had sufficient experience in the politics of self-government, nor an adequate supply of able administrators, to run an intensely managed modern economic system. The alternative proposition requires more careful examination. The underlying truth is that the key to political survival in any state during its early stages of development lies in maintaining a flow of resources sufficient to lubricate the political system. If enough funds are available to pay for large-scale projects in the public sector, the beneficiaries, who range from contractors to party politicians and the urban work force, will support the government as the main source of patronage. If the flow dries up, the whole system will collapse. Deficit financing was thus essential to political survival as well as to economic expansion.

This was in no sense peculiar to modern African states: the same can be seen, for example, in earlier societies of white settlement, such as British North America, Australia and New Zealand during the later nineteenth century. Their governments, lacking an ideological basis for party support, quickly learned to rely on the power of the purse. Since poor societies lack sufficient capacity to save, capital had to be borrowed abroad. During the international recessions of the 1880s and 1890s, and again in the early 1930s, the weight of fixed interest public debt regularly destroyed ministries and caused widespread economic hardship. African states after 1960 were, therefore, following a well-trodden path. Their main difference from these settler societies lay not in the morality of the politicians but in the use made of foreign borrowing. Despite much waste, nineteenth-century colonial borrowing created an invaluable infrastructure and these economies proved able to respond to the stimulus of large injections of foreign capital. In mid-twentieth-century Black Africa foreign loans seem largely to have disappeared into the sand and the inflow of funds resulted in inflation rather than growth of productive capacity.

It is on these general grounds that economic failure can reasonably be explained in terms of government policies. By itself, however, this is clearly not enough: policies must be seen in conjunction with other non-policy influences on economic development. During the boom years before the mid-1970s most African states did as well as could reasonably be expected, given their existing capacities. The effects of poor government only became fully evident when international conditions changed. Some states were hit by short-term fluctuations in the price of particular commodities: for instance, Ghana in the mid-1960s, Zaire and Zambia when copper prices plunged in the early 1970s. But for most states it was the recession of the later 1970s that really threw serious doubt on the expansionist policies they, in common with most Western as well as Third World governments, had been operating for the past couple of decades. It was only at this point that the concept of 'arrested development' could be taken seriously, even though pessimists such as Samir Amin had been writing of 'blocked development' for more than a decade.

The effects of 'policy' were, therefore, marginal, but they were nevertheless very important. During the boom years poor policy-making ensured that development was less real and growth more limited than they might have been; when recession came, its effects were that much more severe because locusts had eaten the seed corn. Black Africa would undoubtedly have been better developed if it had been more wisely governed; but in a recessionary world even the best-run state was bound to lose momentum.

Economic Decolonization and 'Arrested Development'

We must now face the most controversial and difficult of all these questions: the connection or link, causal or merely sequential, between economic decolonization in Black Africa and the economic failure of the following two decades. There are several ways in which this problem can be formulated. The simplest question is a counterfactual: how much difference might it have made if Europe had been able and willing to maintain political control for another two decades? This is, in fact, impossible to answer because it involves too many unknown variables; above all, whether colonial economic policy would have continued unchanged under changing world and African conditions. An alternative and more manageable approach might be to compare salient features of the colonial system with that adopted by independent African states: for example, methods of promoting industry and agriculture, fiscal policy, attitudes towards public indebtedness and the nature of government. Or, to put the same question more simply, and assuming that the exogenous variables were the same in both cases, how much continuity was there between colonial and post-colonial economic policies and what discontinuities? Even if this question cannot be answered with any confidence, it is worth attempting to do so, using mainly evidence from the six states considered individually here, because it pinpoints some of the basic characteristics of modern African economic development.

There are many ways in which continuities and discontinuities might be measured. Figure 9.1 takes nine aspects of economic and social policy and provides a very crude indication of how far these six African states maintained or broke with past colonial practice. It is, of course, crude because it allows for no qualifications; and in practice neither continuities nor discontinuities were total. Nevertheless, it offers a methodological way into the problem.

The figure can be read in two ways: by state or by subject area. Consider first individual states according to how completely they broke with colonial policies. Ghana did so in all but three areas: preservation of 'communal' (used here merely to indicate non-individualized) land tenures, dependence on cash crops and use of marketing boards. Nigeria broke the pattern under all heads except over land tenures and marketing boards. Kenya was marginally more conservative in that it maintained a stable externally tied currency (first to the pound, then the dollar, and finally to IMF drawing rights). Its land policy of individualization of tenures was in fact a continuation of that of the late-colonial state. Tanzania was more radical than any of these: its only conservative elements were marketing boards and, until the economic disasters of the later 1970s, an attempt to keep down foreign indebtedness. By contrast, Ivory Coast and Senegal, in common with most other Francophone states, carried on colonial practices in four main areas, innovating primarily on industrial protection, indebtedness, the civil service and levels of public expenditure.

Reading the figure the other way, by subject area, probably provides a more useful general approach to economic continuities and discontinuities. Only two of these states – Nigeria and Tanzania, and for very different reasons – did not continue to rely on export-oriented cash-crop production as their economic staple, though Ghana practically destroyed its main cash crop by ill-advised pricing and other policies. All used state marketing boards to control producer prices and

Figure 9.1　*Continuities and Discontinuities between Colonial and Post-*
Colonial Practice

Field of Policy	Country					
	Gna	*Niga*	*Kena*	*Tana*	*I.C.*	*Sen*
1. Peasant agric. & land tenures	+	+	+	−	+	+
2. Cash crops	+	−	+	−	+	+
3. Close links with metropolis	−	−	−	−	+	+
4. Marketing boards	+	+	+	+	n/a	n/a
5. Stable realistic currency	−	−	+	−	+	+
6. Moderate protectionism	−	−	−	−	−	−
7. Low indebtedness	−	−	−/+	−/+	−	−
8. Non-political civil service	−	−	−	−	−	−
9. Low public consumption	−	−	−	−	−	−

Notes:
+ indicates substantial continuity, − = substantial discontinuity, −/+ a middle position.
n/a is used against marketing boards for Ivory Coast and Senegal because these did not
　　exist during the colonial period. Comparable institutions were established in both
　　places soon after independence.

extract a surplus for the state, though Kenya did so more moderately
than the other Anglophone states. Ivory Coast and Senegal only
introduced comparable monopolistic organizations after independence
and Ivory Coast gave producers a better return than most African
countries. All these states adopted much higher levels of protection or
other means of promoting import-substituting industry. All, by 1980,
had very large foreign debts, politicized public services, much
expanded welfare services and high levels of public consumption. The
main contrasts were in currency matters: only the Francophone states
and Kenya maintained stable and realistic exchange rates; and over
land tenures, on which Kenya and Tanzania stand our as distinctive,
the first by individualizing tenures on a capitalist principle, the latter
by partially collectivizing them through the villagization policy.

　　What does this imply about the relationship between decolonization
and later development? Much depends on whether one regards
continuation of colonial practices as good or bad. The left, typified by
Samir Amin and Suret-Canale, has maintained that continuity was a

main cause of 'arrested development'; the right that the most successful economies were those which innovated least. But not all continuities are bad nor all novelties good: the economic consequences depend on whether particular policies do or do not meet changing needs and circumstances. Everything, therefore, depended on whether the new states chose the best or worst elements of colonial practice to preserve or replace.

The key fact is that, on the whole, the new states tended to maintain what one may reasonably regard as the least progressive or economically most unrewarding elements in the colonial legacy but did not preserve those which had kept the colonial economies in equilibrium, even though this was a low-level equilibrium. That is, they chose the worst of all possible worlds: their economies remained in most respects unreconstructed and poor, yet their governments acted as if they were new-modelled and rich. Let us examine this proposition in more detail.

First, what were the most non-progressive elements of colonial practice and to what extent were these retained? Perhaps the most obvious weakness of all colonial economic systems in Africa was dependence on a peasant-based agriculture as the only significant earner of foreign exchange, the source of food for local consumption, the mine from which enforced savings could be extracted for domestic capital formation, and the main market for nascent local industries. Integrally related to peasant agriculture were the many forms of collective (rather than individualized) landownership and, as has been strongly emphasized above, very low levels of technology and productivity. This dependence and these characteristics remained almost unchanged throughout the colonial period. They survived because it would have required too great an effort to change agricultural practices and would have been politically too dangerous to challenge collective landownership; Kenya was a special case where the example of white settlers and the emergence of capitalist elements among the Kikuyu and some other groups made individualized tenures politically popular with the emergent African elite.

Precisely the same considerations seem to have influenced most later African governments: twenty years after independence the only significant changes were in Kenya and Tanzania. Most other states, unwilling to tackle a problem that had baffled colonial administrators despite the fact that their indigenous rulers could claim far greater legitimacy for making changes, simply left things as they were or (as in most of the states studied here except Tanzania) tried to bypass the 'peasant problem' by encouraging large-scale capitalist or state-owned modern farms on the side. The results were almost universally disastrous. World Bank statistics suggest that, in aggregate, the weighted average growth rate of the volume of agricultural production for all Black Africa was 2.5 per cent from 1960 to 1970 and only 1.4 per cent from 1970 to 1982; on a per capita basis the growth rates for the same periods were 0.2 and −1.1 per cent.[6]

Heavy dependence on cash crops was another characteristic feature of colonial economies, which has been criticized on the left on the ground that fluctuating commodity prices and adverse trends in the terms of trade made comparative advantage irrelevant to Black African conditions. It was continued by most Black African states because there was no other way, at least in the short term, in which they could earn foreign exchange, though Tanzania showed little concern for its staple sisal industry. The economic consequences are difficult to define. As has been seen above, the barter terms of trade were generally favourable for African commodity exports until the early 1970s, less good but not disastrous from then until 1979, and only seriously (and probably temporarily) adverse for most states during the international recession from 1979 onwards. Possibly the most serious aspect of this continuing policy was that some states (for example, Senegal) attempted to sustain cash-crop production under adverse circumstances when greater emphasis on food crops at a time of low commodity prices and drought might have been more sensible.

A far more injurious carry-over from the late-colonial period was the use of the marketing board as a monopolistic price setter for commodities. In its colonial context this had not been seen or used as a means of extracting a surplus for general public use, rather as a buffer against commodity price fluctuations. But the very existence of accumulated marketing board funds in the British colonies proved too attractive to capital-hungry new independent governments, and their French neighbours quickly copied the institution. The results, except in the case of Kenya and to a lesser extent Ivory Coast, were almost universally bad in that peasants were deprived of the means of improving or even maintaining production and of acting as a sufficient market for new urban industries.

It is at this point that the important continuities between public policy in the colonial period and thereafter end. For the rest decolonization meant radical new departures in almost all fields. Without going over the ground again in detail, the new economic course involved a huge increase in public consumption and in the levels of taxation and foreign borrowing necessary to finance it. For all Black Africa the average public consumption of GDP rose from 10 to 14 per cent between 1960 and 1982, growing at a median rate of 5.9 per cent in the 1960s and 6.4 per cent in 1970–82.[7] Between 1972 and 1981 the weighted average of total central government expenditure (omitting the very substantial additional expenditure at other levels of government) rose from 17.3 to 21.1 per cent of GNP.[8] The ratio of taxation to GDP rose considerably. For example, in Nigeria it increased from 8 per cent in 1959 to 23.9 per cent in 1977; in Tanzania from 9 per cent in 1959 to 16.4 per cent in 1978; in Kenya from 14 per cent in 1959 to 19.4 per cent in 1978; in Ivory Coast from 17 per cent in 1963 to 21.8 per cent in 1978; and in Senegal from 15 per cent in 1962 to 21.8 per cent in 1978.[9] Even so very greatly increased levels of public expenditure could not fully be paid for by increased taxation: in 1972 the average recorded deficit on public expenditure was −3.3 per cent of GNP; in 1981 it was −5.9 per cent.[10] In 1977 the median ratio of taxes to expenditure for Black Africa was 66.1 per cent.[11] Nor could domestic saving match domestic investment. In 1960 gross domestic investment was 16 per cent of GDP, gross domestic saving 13 per cent of GDP; by 1982 the figures were 19 and 12 per cent, leaving resource gaps of −3 per cent and −7 per cent of GDP.[12]

This persistent and growing overspending, both on current and capital account, is at once a reflection of the expansionist economic policies followed by most new African states and a measure of the discontinuity caused by decolonization. Colonial accounting had been severely orthodox, conservative even by contemporary European practice after 1945. African governments rejected such conservatism as anachronistic. Encouraged by their European economic advisers, they put needs and wants first, paying the cost second. Budget deficits on current account quickly grew as a result of greatly increased spending on welfare services, education, a greatly enlarged public service, much larger military forces, prestige buildings and functions and a variety of economic services. They were increased by deficits run by state and parastatal enterprises. Deficits on capital account were inevitable, given the inability of poor societies to raise their rate of savings above a relatively low proportion of GDP. They were made worse in Africa by the failure of much of the new state investment to make any contribution to new capital formation from profits. The result, on both current and capital accounts, was that most African countries were left with a growing shortfall of resources, which meant that they had to depend on foreign grants and loans.

This dependence, of course, was not entirely a post-independence novelty: it was born during the last two decades of colonial rule and encouraged by the reformist late-imperial states. Before about 1940 colonies were expected to live within their incomes and service their own borrowing: in British colonies the only 'aid' on offer consisted of grants under the 1929 Colonial Development Act to meet the cost of servicing loans approved for capital projects. French colonies had comparable help, the Belgian Congo none. From 1940, however, the CD&W Acts promised far wider subsidies for current as well as capital expenditure in British colonies and after 1945 France, through FIDES, made a very substantial contribution to colonial costs. Precise figures for this early aid are very difficult to come by, but some idea of their scale can be gained from official British figures for the early 1960s. In 1959, for example, British East Africa (Kenya, Uganda and Tanganyika) received £5m. in official grants; by 1962 that had risen to £23m. Nigeria received an official donation of £5m. in 1960.[13] These, of course, were in addition to commercial loans raised on the London money market. But these were still quite modest. Nigeria, for example, raised only £6.8m. in new loans between 1946 and 1955, Tanganyika £6.69m. Kenya was a heavier borrower, as was reflected in Table 2.6 above: in these years it borrowed £18.7m.; and in addition the East African High Commission borrowed £31.5m., whose burden was spread between the three colonies.[14]

From such small beginnings grew increasing dependence on external finance. The difficulty in measuring the growth of this dependence stems from the fact that the distinction between normal capital loans and grants is unclear. World Bank statistics distinguish between 'the total flow of resources' (the amount needed to meet balance of payments deficits) and 'net official development assistance', defining the latter as 'loans and grants made at concessional financial terms by official agencies' and grants as 'gifts of money or in kind for which no payment is required'.[15] In 1982 the total recorded 'flow of resources' to Black Africa was some $12,768m., or $33 a head of population, of which $7,183.5m. consisted of 'net disbursements of official development assistance'. Official development assistance then represented 3.8 per cent of Black Africa's GDP and 13.1 per cent of its gross domestic investment. Of the one-time British colonies mentioned above, in 1982 Nigeria, though oil-rich, received $36.7m. in official development assistance, Kenya $485.4m., Tanzania $695.5m., Uganda $133.0m.[16]

Thus, while the seeds of Africa dependence on foreign concessionary loans and grants were sown in the late-colonial period, the most important single consequence of decolonization was its grotesque flowering into unmanageable overspending and indebtedness. Colonialism, for most of its course, had kept colonial public expenditure, investment and borrowing in line with a colony's capacity to pay; and this capacity was closely related to the health of the international economy, since this determined a colony's balance of payments position and the size of government revenues. After independence these constraints were gradually thrown off: need and ambition rather than ability to meet the costs became the criteria of policy-making. During the first decade and a half after 1960 international conditions generally concealed the dangers. Commodity prices remained generally good, interest rates and repayment terms on foreign borrowing low, the flow of foreign equity capital high. By the later 1970s most of this had changed. Black Africa found itself in a position no colonial government would ever have permitted, heavily indebted, deeply committed to continuing large expenditure, but facing greatly increased interest charges, lower commodity prices and a virtual stoppage of fresh equity capital as a consequence of the compulsory indigenization of foreign private capital.

It is at this point that the economic consequences of decolonization became for the first time really obvious. Colonial economic policy had been cautious to the point of inertia; but caution had at least provided insurance against disaster. Most new African states preferred to gamble. The superficially impressive achievements of the first two decades after independence, which had made colonialism appear to have achieved so little, were built on sand. Growth resulted from booming exports, unexploited domestic tax potential and huge injections of foreign capital; it did not reflect structural development in Black Africa. When it was no longer possible to extract so large a surplus from the peasants and foreign borrowing became prohibitively expensive at a time when the commodity markets were depressed, most African states found themselves virtually bankrupt.

This, then, is the main link between decolonization and economic failure in Black Africa. Colonial rulers, afraid of the political and social consequences of economic recession, were probably too reluctant to innovate at the cost of indebtedness. Their successors, impelled rather by the political need to demonstrate progress, to reward supporters and to employ growing urban populations, went to the other extreme. Because the development they planned was, in many cases, ill-conceived and based on wildly over-optimistic assessments of what was possible, it was bound sooner or later to slow up or be checked. But that is not to say that it was 'arrested' and therefore could not be resumed: merely that development in Black Africa was at all times bound to be slow and that it could only be sustained when governments tackled the underlying weaknesses which neither colonial nor post-colonial regimes had been able to remove by the mid-1980s.

Notes

1 See, for example, the assumptions in (Sir) Keith Hancock's *Survey of British Commonwealth Affairs*, Vol. II, *Problems of Economic Policy, 1918–1939* (two parts, London, 1942), which reflect the experience of the 1930s in the same way that the development economics of the later 1950s and early 1960s reflected the boom period after *c.*1950.

2 As a South African, Frankel had studied peasant food production at first hand and his first major book, published in the 1930s, was on maize marketing. He was attached to Lord Hailey's team which produced the *African Survey* in 1938 and his later book, *The Economic Impact on Under-Developed Societies* (Oxford, 1953) was a testament to his then very unpopular belief in the need for a gradualist approach to economic development in Africa.

3   P. J. McGowan, 'Economic Dependence and Economic Performance in Black Africa', *JMAS*, Vol. 14, no. 1 (1976).
4   World Bank, *Accelerated Development in Sub-Saharan Africa* (*AD*) (Washington DC, 1981), App. 13; *Toward Sustained Development in Sub-Saharan Africa* (*TSD*) (Washington DC, 1984), App. 11.
5   *TSD* App. 16.
6   *TSD* App. 21.
7   *TSD* App. 4, 5.
8   *TSD* App. 31.
9   UN, *A Survey of Economic Conditions in Africa, 1960–1964* (New York, 1968); *AD* App. 40.
10 *TSD* App. 31.
11 *AD* App. 40.
12 *TSD* App. 5.
13 *Commonwealth and Sterling Area, Statistical Abstract No. 85* (London, 1964).
14 See D. J. Morgan, *The Official History of Colonial Development* (5 vols., London, 1980), Vol. III, table 2.2 for a list of all colonial loans raised in London between 1946 and 1955.
15 *AD* p. 192.
16 *TSD* App. 18, 19.

Bibliography of Works Cited in the Text

Amin, S., *Le Développement du capitalisme en Côte d'Ivoire* (Paris, 1967).

Amin, S., *L'Afrique de l'Ouest bloquée* (Paris, 1971).

Amin, S., *Neo-Colonialism in West Africa* (New York and London, 1973).

Amin, S., *Unequal Development* (Hassocks, Sussex, 1976).

Annuaire statistique de la France (Paris).

Anstey, R., *The Atlantic Slave Trade and British Abolition, 1760–1810* (London, 1975).

Arrighi, G. and Saul, J., *Essays on the Political Economy of Africa* (New York, 1973).

Bairoch, P., *The Economic Development of The Third World Since 1900* (London, 1975).

Bairoch, P., 'The Main Trends in National Economic Disparities since the Industrial Revolution', in P. Bairoch and M. Levy-Leboyer (eds), *Disparities in Economic Development since the Industrial Revolution* (London, 1981).

Bairoch, P. and Levy-Leboyer, M. (eds), *Disparities in Economic Development since the Industrial Revolution* (London, 1981).

Baran, P. A., 'On the Political Economy of Backwardness', *Manchester School of Economic and Social Studies* (January 1952).

Baran, P. A., *The Political Economy of Growth* (New York, 1957).

Barker, C. *et al.*, 'Industrial Production and Transfer of Technology in Tanzania: The Political Economy of Tanzanian Industrial Enterprises', Mimeo, Institute of Development Studies, Dar es Salaam, 1976.

Barker, J., 'Stability and Stagnation in the State of Senegal', *Canadian Journal of African Studies (CJAS)* vol. 11, no. (1), 1977.

Barry, B., 'Arachide, bourgeoisie bureaucratique et sechéresse', draft paper given at a conference on 'African Independence', University of Zimbabwe, Harare, January 1985.

Bates, R. H., *Markets and States in Tropical Africa* (Berkeley and Los Angeles, 1981).

Bates, R. H., *Essays on the Political Economy of Rural Africa* (Cambridge, 1983).

Bauer, P. T., *West African Trade* (Cambridge, 1954).

Bauer, P. T. and Yamey, B. S., *The Economics of Under-Developed Countries* (Cambridge, 1957).

Bauer, P. T., *Dissent on Development* (Cambridge, Mass., 1973).

Beckman, B., *Organizing the Farmers: Cocoa Politics and National Development in Ghana* (Upsala, 1976).

Beckman, B., 'Imperialism and Capitalist Transformation: A Critique of a Kenyan Debate', *Review of African Political Economy (RAPE)*, vol. 19 (1980).

Beckman, B., 'Ghana 1951–78', in J. Heyer, P. Roberts and G. Williams (eds), *Rural Development in Tropical Africa* (London, 1981).

Berg, E. J., 'Structural Transformation versus Gradualism. Recent Economic

Development in Ghana and the Ivory Coast', in P. Foster and A. R. Zolberg (eds), *Ghana and the Ivory Coast. Perspectives in Modernization* (Chicago and London, 1971).

Bernstein, H. (ed.), *Underdevelopment and Development* (Harmondsworth, 1973).

Bienefeld, M., 'Evaluating Tanzanian Industrial Development', in M. Fransman (ed.), *Industry and Accumulation in Africa* (London, 1982).

Bissell, R. E. and Radu, M. S. (eds), *Africa in the Post-Decolonization Era* (New Brunswick, US and London, 1984).

Bloch-Lainé, F., *La Zone franc* (Paris, 1956).

Board of Trade Jounal (London).

Campbell, E. G. Bonnie, 'The Ivory Coast', in J. Dunn (ed.), *West African States* (Cambridge, 1978).

Caswell, N., 'Peasants, Peanuts and Politics: State Marketing in Senegal, 1966–80', unpub. paper given at a conference on 'The Fate of Post-Colonial Economies in West Africa' at the School of Oriental and African Studies, London University (SOAS), July 1983.

Cell, J. W., 'On the Eve of Decolonization', *Journal of Imperial and Commonwealth History*, vol. 7 (1980).

Central Statistical Office, *United Kingdom Balance of Payments, 1965* (London, 1965).

Central Statistical Office, *Statistical Abstract for the British Commonwealth* (London).

Clark, W. E., *Socialist Development and Public Investment in Tanzania, 1964–73* (Toronto, 1978).

Cohen, M. A., *Urban Policy and Political Conflict in Africa. A Case Study of the Ivory Coast* (Chicago and London, 1974).

Commonwealth and Sterling Area, Statistical Abstract No. 85 (London, 1964).

Cooper, F., 'Africa and The World Economy', *The African Studies Review*, vol. 24, nos 2/3 (1981).

Coquery-Vidrovitch, C., 'SCOA et CFAO dans l'Ouest Africain, 1910–1965', *Journal of African History*, vol. 16, no. 4 (1975).

Coquery-Vidrovitch, C., 'Economic Decolonization in French Africa', draft paper given at a conference on 'African Independence', University of Zimbabwe, Harare, January 1985.

Coulson, A., *Tanzania. A Political Economy* (Oxford, 1982).

Crowder, M. (ed.), *The Cambridge History of Africa*, Vol. 8, *c.1940–c.1975* (Cambridge, 1984).

Dalby, D. and Church, R. J. H. (eds), *Drought in Africa* (London, 1973).

Dalby, D., Church, R. J. H. and Bezzaz, F. (eds), *Drought in Africa II* (London 1977).

Derrick, J., 'The Great West African Drought 1972–74', *African Affairs*, vol. 76, no. 305 (October 1977).

Dobb, M., *Economic Growth and Underdeveloped Countries* (London, 1963).

Duignan, P. and Gann, L. H. (eds), *Colonialism in Africa*, Vol. 4, *The Economics of Colonialism* (Cambridge, 1975).

L'Economie Séngalaise (4th edn, Paris, 1977).

Emmanuel, A., *Unequal Exchange* (London, 1971).

Fauré, Y.-A., 'Le Complex politico-économique', in Y.-A. Fauré and J.-F. Médard (eds), *Etat et bourgeoisie en Côte d'Ivoire* (Paris, 1982).

Fauré Y.-A., 'Inversion d'une dynamique sociale. Le Cas Ivorien', unpub. paper given at a conference on 'The Fate of Post-Colonial Economies in West Africa', SOAS, July 1983.

Fieldhouse, D. K., 'The Economic Exploitation of Africa', in P. Gifford and W. R. Louis (eds), *France and Britain in Africa* (New Haven, 1971).

Fieldhouse, D. K., *Unilever Overseas. The Anatomy of a Multinational, 1895–1965* (London, 1978).

Fieldhouse, D. K., 'Decolonization, Development and Dependence: A Survey of Changing Attitudes', in P. Gifford and W. R. Louis (eds), *The Transfer of Power in Africa* (New Haven, 1982).

Fieldhouse, D. K., 'The Labour Governments and the Empire–Commonwealth, 1945–1951', in R. Ovendale (ed.), *The Foreign Policy of the Labour Governments, 1945–1951* (London, 1984).

Forrest, T., 'Recent Developments in Nigerian Industrialization', in M. Fransman (ed.), *Industry and Accumulation in Africa* (London, 1982).

Foster, P. and Zolberg, A. R. (eds), *Ghana and the Ivory Coast. Perspectives in Modernization* (Chicago and London, 1971).

Frankel, S. H., *Capital Investment in Africa* (London, 1938).

Frankel, S. H., *The Economic Impact on Under-Developed Societies* (Oxford, 1953).

Freeman, L., 'CIDA, Wheat and Rural Develpment in Tanzania', *CJAS*, vol. 16, no. 3 (1982).

Freyhold, M. von, 'The Post-Colonial State and its Tanzanian Version', *RAPE*, vol. 8 (1977).

Gastellu, J.-M. and Affrou Yapi, S., 'Un myth à décomposer: la "bourgeoisie de planteurs" ', in Y.-A. Fauré and J.-F. Médard (eds), *Etat et bourgeoisie en Côte d'Ivoire* (Paris, 1982).

Gerry, Chris, 'The Crisis of the Self-employed. Petty Production and Capitalist Production in Dakar', in R. C. O'Brien (ed.), *The Political Economy of Underdevelopment* (London, 1979).

Gifford, P. and Louis, W. R. (eds), *France and Britain in Africa* (New Haven, 1971).

Gifford, P. and Louis, W. R. (eds), *The Transfer of Power in Africa. Decolonization, 1940–1960* (New Haven and London 1982).

Graham, E. with Floering, I., *The Modern Plantation in the Third World* (London, 1984).

Gutkind, P. and Wallerstein, I. (eds), *The Political Economy of Contemporary Africa* (London, 1976).

Hancock, W. K., *Survey of British Commonwealth Affairs*, Vol. II *Problems of Economic Policy, 1918–1939* (2 parts, London, 1942).

Hart, K., *The Political Economy of West African Agriculture* (Cambridge, 1982).

Hazlewood, A., *The Economy of Kenya. The Kenyatta Era* (Oxford, 1979).

Hecht, R. M., 'The Ivory Coast Economic "Miracle". What Benefit for the Peasant Farmers?', *Journal of Modern African Studies (JMAS)*, vol. 21, no. 1 (1983).

Heyer, J., Roberts, P. and Williams, G. (eds), *Rural Development in Tropical Africa* (London, 1981).

Hirschman, A. O., *The Strategy of Economic Development* (New Haven, 1958).

Hopkins, A. G., *An Economic History of West Africa* (London, 1973).

Hopkins, R. F., 'Food, Agricultural Policies and Famine: Implications for African International Relations', in R. E. Bissell and M. S. Radu (eds), *Africa in the Post-Decolonization Era* (New Brunswick, US and London, 1984).

Hyden, G., *Beyond Ujamaa in Tanzania* (London, 1980).

Iliffe, J. *The Emergence of African Capitalism* (London, 1983).

International Monetary Fund (IMF), *International Financial Statistics Yearbook* (New York, 1984).

Joseph, R. A., 'Affluence and Underdevelopment: the Nigerian Experience', *JMAS*, vol. 16, no. 2 (1978).

Kahler, M. *Decolonization in Britain and France* (Princeton, NJ, 1984).

Kamarck, A. M., *The Economics of African Development* (New York, 1971).

Kamarck, A. M., *The Tropics and Economic Development* (Washington DC, 1976).

Kaplinsky, R., 'Capital Accumulation in the Periphery: Kenya' in M. Fransman (ed.), *Industry and Accumulation in Africa* (London, 1982).

Kay, G., *Development and Underdevelopment: A Marxist Analysis* (London, 1975).

Kennedy, P., 'Indigenous Capitalism in Ghana', *RAPE*, vol. 8 (1977).

Kilby, P., *Industrialization in an Open Economy* (Cambridge, 1969).

Kilby, P., 'Manufacturing in Colonial Africa' in P. Duignan and L. H. Gann (eds), *Colonialism in Africa*, Vol. 4, *The Economics of Colonialism* (Cambridge, 1975).

Killick, T., *Development Economics in Action* (London, 1978).

Killick, T., 'Trends in Development Economics and their Relevance to Africa', *JMAS*, vol. 18, no. 3 (1980).

Kirk-Greene, A. and Rimmer, D. *Nigeria Since 1970* (London, 1981).

Kitching, G., *Class and Economic Change in Kenya* (New Haven, 1975).

Koehn, P., 'The Role of Public Administrators in Public Policy Making: Practice and Prospects in Nigeria', *Public Administration and Development*, vol. 3, no. 1 (1983).

Kuznets, S., *Post-War Economic Growth* (Cambridge, Mass., 1964).

Langdon, S. W., 'Multinational Corporations, Taste Transfer and Underdevelopment: A Case Study from Kenya', *RAPE*, vol. 2 (1975).

Langdon, S. W., *Multinational Corporations in the Political Economy of Kenya* (London, 1980).

Lee, J. M., *Colonial Development and Good Government, 1939–64* (Oxford, 1967).

Lee, J. M. and Petter, M., *The Colonial Office, War and Development Policy* (London, 1982).

Leibenstein, H., *Economic Backwardness and Economic Growth* (New York, 1957).

Leo, C., 'The Failure of the "Progressive Farmer" in Kenya's Million-Acre Settlement Scheme', *JMAS*, vol. 16, no. 4 (1978).

Leo, C., 'Who benefited from the Million-Acre Scheme? Towards a Class Analysis of Kenya's Transition to Independence', *CJAS*, vol. 15, no. 2 (1981).

Leo, C., *Land and Class in Kenya* (Toronto, 1984).

Lewis, W. A., 'World Production, Prices and Trade 1870–1960', *The*

Manchester School of Economics and Social Studies, vol. 20 (1951).

Lewis, W. A., *Report on Industrialization and the Gold Coast* (Accra, 1953).

Leys, C., *Underdevelopment in Kenya* (London, 1975).

Leys, C., 'Accumulation, Class Formation and Dependency in Kenya', in M. Fransman (ed.), *Industry and Accumulation in Africa* (London, 1982)

Lipson, C., *Standing Guard. Protecting Foreign Capital in the Nineteenth and Twentieth Centuries* (Berkeley, Los Angeles and London, 1985).

Little, I. M. D., *Economic Development. Theory, Policy and International Relations* (New York, 1982).

Lonsdale, J., 'States and Social Processes in Africa: An Historiographical Survey', *The African Studies Review*, vol. 24, nos 2/3 (1981).

Louis, W. R., *Imperialism at Bay* (Oxford, 1977).

Marseille, J., *Empire colonial et capitalisme français. Histoire d'un divorce* (Paris, 1984).

Masini, J. et al., *Multinationals and Development in Black Africa. A Case Study in the Ivory Coast* (Farnborough, 1979).

McGowan, P. J., 'Economic Dependence and Economic Performance in Black Africa', *JMAS*, vol. 14, no. 1 (1976).

Milburn, J. E., *British Business and Ghanaian Independence* (London, 1977).

Miras, C. de., 'L'Entrepreneur ivoirien: une bourgeoisie privée de son état', in Y.-A. Fauré and J.-F. Médard (eds), *Etat et bourgeoisie en Côte d'Ivoire* (Paris, 1982).

Morawetz, D., *Twenty-Five Years of Economic Development, 1950–1975* (Washington DC, 1977).

Morgan, D. J., *The Official History of Colonial Development* (5 vols, London, 1980).

Morris-Jones, W. H. and Fischer, G. (eds), *Decolonization and After: The British and French Experience* (London, 1978).

Mueller, S. D., 'The Historical Origins of Tanzania's Ruling Class', *CJAS*, vol. 15, no. 3 (1981).

Myint, H., 'An Interpretation of Economic Backwardness', *Oxford Economic Papers* (June 1954).

Myrdal, G., *An International Economy* (New York, 1957).

Myrdal, G., *Economic Theory and Under-Developed Regions* (London, 1957)

Nelson, H. D. (ed.), *Area Handbook for Senegal* (2nd edn, Washington DC, 1974).

Nixson, F., 'Import-Substituting Industrialization', in M. Fransman (ed.), *Industry and Accumulation in Africa* (London, 1982).

Nurkse, R., *Problems of Capital Formation in Underdeveloped Countries* (Oxford, 1953).

Nurkse, R., *Patterns of Trade and Development* (Stockholm, 1959).

O'Brien, D. C., 'Ruling Class and Peasantry in Senegal, 1960–76' in R. C. O'Brien (ed.), *The Political Economy of Underdevelopment* (London, 1979).

O'Brien, R. C., 'Foreign Ascendance in the Economy and State: The French and Lebanese' in R. C. O'Brien (ed.), *The Political Economy of Under-development* (London, 1979).

Organization for European Economic Co-operation (OEEC), *Foreign Trade Statistical Bulletin*, Series 1 (Paris, 1954).

Onyemelukwe, J. O. C., *Industrialization in West Africa* (London, 1984).

Ovendale, R. (ed.), *The Foreign Policy of the Labour Governments, 1945–1951* (Leicester, 1984).

Pearce, R. D., *The Turning Point in Africa* (London, 1982).

Peemans, J.-P., 'Capital Accumulation in the Congo under Colonialism: The Role of the State', in P. Duignan and L. H. Gann (eds), *Colonialism in Africa*, Vol. 4 (Cambridge, 1975).

Phillips, A., 'The Concept of Development', *RAPE*, vol. 8 (1977).

Poquin, J.-J., *Les Relations économiques exterieures des Pays d'Afrique de l'Union française, 1925–1955* (Paris, 1957).

Prebisch, R., *The Economic Development of Latin America and its Principal Problems* (New York, 1950).

Rimmer, D., 'The Crisis of the Ghanaian Economy', *JMAS*, vol. 4 (1966).

Rimmer, D., 'The Abstraction from Politics', *Journal of Development Studies* (April 1969).

Rimmer, D., *The Economies of West Africa* (London, 1984).

Robinson, R. E., 'Andrew Cohen and the Transfer of Power in Tropical Africa, 1940–1951', in W. J. Morris-Jones and G. Fischer (eds), *Decolonization and After: The British and French Experience* (London, 1978).

Rodney, W., *How Europe Underdeveloped Africa* (London, 1972).

Rostow, W. W., *Stages of Economic Growth* (Cambridge, 1960).

Rweyemamu, J., 'The Political Economy of Foreign Investment in the Underdeveloped Countries', *African Review*, vol. 1, no. 1 (1971).

Rweyemamu, J., *Underdevelopment and Industrialization in Tanzania. A Study of Perverse Capitalist Industrialist Development* (Nairobi, 1973, 2nd edn, 1978).

Schatz, S. P., *Nigerian Capitalism* (Berkeley and Los Angeles, 1977).

Schatz, S. P., 'Pirate Capitalism and the Inert Economy of Nigeria', *JMAS*, vol. 22, no. 1 (1984).

Schumacher, E. J., *Politics, Bureaucracy and Rural Development in Senegal* (Berkeley, Los Angeles and London, 1975).

Scitovsky, T., 'Two Concepts of External Economies', *Journal of Political Economy* (April 1954).

Scott, E. (ed.), *Life Before the Drought* (Boston, 1984).

Sík, E., *The History of Black Africa* (2 vols, Budapest, 1966).

Singer, H. W., 'The Distribution of Gains between Investing and Borrowing Countries', *America Economic Review Papers and Proceedings* (May 1950).

Singh, A., 'Industrialization in Africa: A Structuralist View', in M. Fransman (ed.), *Industry and Accumulation in Africa* (London, 1982).

Smith, A., *Wealth of Nations* (1776; London, 1966).

Steel, W. F., 'Import Substitution Policy in Ghana in the 1960s', PhD dissertation, MIT, 1970.

Suret-Canale, J., 'From Colonization to Independence in French Tropical Africa: The Economic Background', in P. Gifford and W. R. Louis (eds), *The Transfer of Power in Africa. Decolonization, 1940–1960* (New Haven and London, 1982).

Swainson, N., 'The Rise of a National Bourgeoisie in Kenya', *RAPE*, vol. 8 (1977).

Swainson, N., 'State and Economy in Post-Colonial Kenya 1963–78', *CJAS*, vol. 12, no. 3 (1978).

Teal, F., 'The Objectives of Development Policy in Nigeria and the Growth of the Economy since 1950', unpub. paper given at a conference on 'The Fate of Post-Colonial Economies in West Africa', SOAS, July 1983.

Tomlinson, B. R., *The Political Economy of the Raj, 1914–47* (Cambridge, 1979).

Tuinder, B. A., *Ivory Coast. The Challenge of Success* (Baltimore and London, 1978).

United Nations (UN), *Statistical Yearbook* (New York).

UN, *A Survey of Economic Conditions in Africa, 1960–1964* (New York, 1968).

UN, *Survey of Economic Conditions in Africa, 1973* (New York, 1974).

Viner, J., *Studies in the Theory of International Trade* (New York, 1937).

Wallace, T., 'The Challenge of Food: Nigeria's Approach to Agriculture 1975–80', *CJAS*, vol. 15, no. 2 (1981).

Westcott, N. J., 'Sterling and Empire: The British Imperial Economy 1939–1951', unpub. paper.

Westcott, N. J. 'The Politics of Planning and the Planning of Politics: Colonialism and Development in British Africa, 1930–1960', unpub. paper.

Westcott, N. J. with Cowen, M. P. 'British Imperial Economic Policy During the War', unpub. paper.

Williams, E., *Capitalism and Slavery* (Chapel Hill, 1944).

World Bank, *The Economic Development of Kenya* (Baltimore, 1963).

World Bank, *Senegal. Tradition, Diversification and Economic Development* (Washington DC, 1974).

World Bank, *World Tables* (Washington DC, 1976 and 1980).

World Bank, *Accelerated Development in Sub-Saharan Africa* (Washington DC, 1981).

World Bank, *Developments in and Prospects for the External Debt of the Developing Countries: 1970–80 and Beyond* (Washington DC, 1981).

World Bank, *Toward Sustained Development in Sub-Saharan Africa* (Washington DC, 1984).

World Bank, *Development Report, 1984* (Washington DC, 1984).

Young, C., 'The Colonial State and its Connection to Current Political Crises in Africa', draft paper given at a conference on 'African independence', University of Zimbabwe, Harare, January 1985.

Index

administrative controls
  and exploitation 6–7
agriculture
  and drought 125–7
  colonialism and low productivity 36–7
  post-colonial decline 84
  post-colonial strategies 93, 241–2
    expansion in Ivory Coast 200–3
    in Ghana 144–7
    in Kenya 168–71
    in Nigeria 157–9
    in Tanzania 178–82
    mono-culture problems in Senegal
      208, 209–11, 214–22
  see also peasantry; state farming
aid programmes 7, 23, 59, 107, 209,
  228, 243–4
Algeria
  independence 17, 18
  war costs 22
Angola 5
'arrested' development 85
  explanations of 93, 97, 234–8
  links with economic decolonization
    238–45

banking
  effects of French decolonization 19–20,
    61
  in Senegal 213
  restrictions on loans 120
Barclays 9
Belgian Congo
  growth of manufacturing 42, 44–5, 47
Black Africa
  attitudes to economic development
    127–31
  food imports 36
  manufacturing outputs 43
  post-colonial economic performance
    71–85
  see also individual countries
British Commonwealth 58–9
bureaucracy
  in Senegal 213, 215, 216, 219

business enterprise
  agro-business parastatols in Ivory
    Coast 193
  and decolonization 9–12, 17–21
  and socio-cultural factors 127–9
  in Ghana 144
  in Nigeria 154–5

Cadburys 9
Cameroon
  private debt 120
capital formation 38–9
capital investment
  French public policies 12–14, 39
  obstacles to 41–2
  post-colonial 106–8
    Ivory Coast state policies 191–2
    Senegal strategies 225–6
  post-war 39–40
  sources of 37
capitalism
  impact on African economies 11, 31–2
  in Kenya 166–8
  'nurture' 155
  'pirate' 157
class structure
  in the post-colonial state 91, 95–6, 97,
    182, 202, 227
climatic conditions
  as obstacles to economic efficiency
    123–4
  see also drought
cocoa production
  and Ghanaian economy 145
  and Ivory Coast economy 188, 200
colonial development 27
  and human resources 34–5
  and infrastructure 35–6
  and transfer of power 4–5, 56–7
  see also colonial economic development
Colonial Development & Welfare Acts 6,
  7, 23, 58, 243
colonial economic development 23, 29,
  54–5
  and agricultural productivity 36–7, 242

and manufacturing outputs 42–8
and public indebtedness 48–54
and saving and capital formation 37–42
French government post-war
    investment 12–14
limitations on 28, 30, 34
see also growth rates
'colonial economy' 207
colonial state (the)
    characteristics of 55–6
    transitional political structures 57
colonialism
    and conflict 22
    function of 4, 29
    impact of 27–32
Compagnie Francaise de l'Afrique
    Occidentale
    effects of decolonization 18–19
competition 47
cooperative system
    and rural socialism in Senegal 214–16,
        221
currency
    in post-colonial economic relations 59,
        61
    reserves 49–50

debt
    at independence 49–53
    post-colonial 106–8, 111, 147–50,
        159–60, 172, 182–3, 187–8, 203–4,
        209, 210
        problems 119–21
        ratio between public and private
            108, 112–18
debt service ratio 51–2, 54, 108–10, 120,
    121, 148, 160, 172, 183, 203, 209,
    210
decolonization 4–6, 21–2
    and private business interests 9–12,
        17–21
    and relations with metropolitan states
        58–61
    economic influences on 22–4, 231–2
    factors supporting 7–9, 232
    international influences on 22
    see also economic decolonization
dependency theory 101–3
'development economics' 87–90
drought
    economic significance of 124–7, 219
'dual economies' 102–3

East African Common Market 45

economic decolonization
    and economic problems 238–45
economic development *see* colonial
    economic development; post-colonial
    economic development
economic management
    in post-colonial states 92–3, 242–5
    Ghanaian failure 139–50
    Ivory Coast success 182–204
    Kenyan success 163–73
    links with metropolitan states 58–63
    Nigerian problems 150–60
    Senegal failure 207–29
    Tanzanian socialism 173–83
economic planning
    and development economics 87–90
    and theories of poverty 85–7
    effects of incompetent governments
        236–7
economic policy
    and French colonial policies 14–17
    continuities and discontinuities of
        colonial policies 239–41
    in Ghana 139–40
    post–colonial expansionism 242–3
economic problems
    and colonial exploitation 6–7, 12–13
    and decolonization 7–8
    and effects of the international
        economy 104–21, 132–3, 236
    post-colonial 84–5, 102–3, 207–11, 243
    see also 'arrested' development
education 34–5
environmental factors
    as obstacles to economic development
        123–4, 235
European Economic Community
    protectionism and African exports 105
    relations with ex-French colonies 60–1,
        191
exploitation 6–7, 12–13, 21, 28, 29
export decline
    post-colonial 84, 108, 121, 157–8, 174,
        180, 187, 188, 208
export of goods and services
    and public debt 51–2, 54, 110, 121,
        159, 172, 183, 203, 209

federalism *see* Nigeria
foreign direct investment 106, 107, 236
    and dependency theory 87
    and industrialization in Ivory Coast
        195–6, 197–9
    decline in 118–19

in Kenya 165
in Nigeria 154–5
France
  colonial development 4, 12–14
  economic factors and decolonization
    policy 14–17
  post-colonial economic and political
    relations 60–1, 190–1, 213, 224
free trade areas 222–3
French colonies *see* Ivory Coast; Senegal
French Community 58–60

Gabon 120, 187
Ghana
  agricultural policies 144–7
  capital formation 38, 39
  centralized economic system 139–40
    failure of 150
  debts 120, 147–50
  discontinuity of colonial policies 239,
    240
  industrialization policies 140–4
  political and class influences on
    economic development 95, 96–7
  political changes and British business
    firms 10, 11
  population 150
Gold Coast 4, 29
  cocoa exports 36
  decolonization process 9–10
  industrialization report 141–2
  see also Ghana
government
  control of economy in Tanzania 174–5
  inefficiency and economic performance
    90–2, 97, 233–4, 236–7
  maintenance of power 94
Great Britain
  decolonization policies
    and business enterprise 9–12
    economic factors 6–9
  economic relations with ex-colonies
    58–9
  post-war investment in Black Africa
    39–40
Gross Domestic Product 32
  and domestic savings 38–9
  and taxation 242–3
Gross National product 33, 38,
  107–8
  and public debt 51
  growth and decline in Senegal 207
  stagnation in Ghana 140
groundnut production
  and exports 208

and 'monoculture' in Senegal 209–10,
  214–22
growth rates
  post-colonial 70–1, 234–5
  in Ghana 139
  in Kenya 163–4
  in Senegal 207–8
  post-war 32–3, 38
Guinea 5

health hazards
  as obstacles to economic efficiency 124
human resources
  and economic development 34–5,
    127–31

imports
  basic food 36, 146, 158
independence
  and public indebtedness 48–55, 108–10
India 22
Indo-China 17, 22
industrialization policies
  in Ghana 140–4
  in Kenya 165–8
  in Nigeria 152–7
  in Senegal 211, 213, 222–5, 228
  in Tanzania 175–8
interest rates
  and colonial demands 7
  and debt repayment 108–21
international economy
  and colonies 31
  and post-colonial economic difficulties
    104–21, 236, 238, 244–5
  favourable conditions and African
    development 122, 235–6, 244
  problems 132
investment *see* capital investment;
  foreign direct investment
Ivory Coast
  agricultural growth and expansion
    200–3
  continuation of colonial policies 239,
    240
  debt 120, 187–8, 203
  economic policy 188–9
    economic liberalism and relations
      with France 190–1
    public investment policies 191–2
  industrialization and foreign
    investment 195–6, 197–9
  post-independence economic
    performance 187, 204
  state intervention policies 192–4

Kenya
  agricultural policies 168–9, 171, 241
    land transfer schemes and farming
      169–71
  centralized economic system 164–5
  continuity of colonial policies 239, 240
  debt 120, 172
  industrialization and manufacturing
    strategies 45–6, 165–8
  population 150
  post-independence economic
    performance 163–4, 171–3

labour
  employment of foreigners in Senegal
    226
  public employment levels in Ghana
    139
land transfer programmes 169
loans 106–7, 120, 237–8, 244
  switch to private 118
  to Ghana after independence 147–9
  see also debt

Macmillan, H. 7
Malawi 39
manufacturing development
  and colonial economic development
    42–6
  early obstacles to 46–7
  in Ghana 142–3
  in Ivory Coast 194, 196, 197
  in Kenya 165–6
  in Nigeria 153–5, 156
  in Tanzania 176–8
  post-war 47–8
market forces
  and overseas protectionism 105–6
  and post-war competition 47
marketing boards 242
  and prices 151
minerals 124
  and market fluctuations 104–5
monetary controls 91
Morocco
  and French business interests 17, 18
Mozambique 5
multinational corporations
  and investment in Africa 5, 58, 119,
    165

nationalism
  and 'development economics' 89, 90,
    94

neo-colonialism 62, 213
Nigeria 4, 38
  agricultural exports 36
  business development
    and socio-cultural factors 128–9
    incentives 48, 154–5
    political influences on 10–11
  debt 121, 159–60
  discontinuity of colonial policies 239,
    240
  export commodity production 157–8
  food-grain imports 125, 158
  food production strategies 158–9
  industrialization strategies 152–7
  population 150
  post-independence economic strategy
    150–2, 159
    effects of ail revenues 150–1, 155–6,
      159–60

oil prices
  and economic problems 51, 103, 132,
    228
  and revenues effects on Nigerian
    economy 150–1, 155–6, 159–60

peasantry
  as economic development constraint
    129–31, 241–2
  in Ghanaian economy 145–7
  in Ivory Coast agricultural production
    200–1
  Tanzanian ujamaa system 180–1
  Tanzanian compulsory 'villagization'
    130, 181–2
political influences
  affecting decolonization 5, 8, 10–11,
    232
  affecting economic development 70,
    85, 94–5, 211–14, 237, 245
political structures
  economic consequences of 57
  establishment of 56–7
  weak 233–4
post-colonial state (the) 233
  'classes against masses' policies 95–6
  continuity and discontinuities of
    colonial policies 239–40
  need for economic management 92–3,
    242–5
  political weakness 233–4
  poor economic performance 90–2, 97,
    107–8
post-colonial economic development
  71–85

and development economics 87–90, 94
and discontinuity of colonial policies
    239–40
'classes against masses' analysis of 91,
    95–6, 97
effects of political weakness 62, 233–4
non-policy analysis of 69–70, 101–4,
    235
    effects of the international economy
        104–21, 132–3
    objectives 91–2
    obstacles to 122–31
    open economies 164–5
    policy analysis of 69, 90–4, 235
    state intervention strategies 94–5,
        139–40, 174–5
poverty theories
    and economic planning 85–7
power
    in the colonial state 55
    in the post-colonial state 94
    see also transfer of power
production
    agricultural 36–7, 241–2
        in Ivory Coast 200–3
        in Tanzania 130, 180–2
    agro-business parastatals in Ivory Coast
        193
    growth rates 74–7
    see also manufacturing development

railways system 35
risk
    and increased capital accumulation 42
roads system 35

Senegal
    agricultural problems 208, 209–11,
        214–22
    debt 209, 210
    foreign labour 226
    industrialization strategies 211, 222–5,
        228
    investment strategies 225–6
    political structure 211–13, 227
    post-independence economic weakness
        207–8, 211, 228–9
    post-independence relations with
        France 213, 227
        continuation of colonial policies 239,
            240
slavery 3–4

social structure
    influence on political and economic
        systems 227
    see also class structure
socialism
    in Senegal 211–13, 214–15
    in Tanzania 173, 174–5, 176, 178–82
Société Commerciale de l'Ouest Africain
    effects of decolonization 18–19
Southern Rhodesia 39
    manufacturing development 45
state farming
    bureaucratic centralism in Senegal
        216–20
    in Ghana 145–6
    in Tanzania 130, 180–2
    see also cooperative system
supply and demand
    and economic performance 70, 80–4
'syncretic articulation' 31

Tanganyika 175
    capital formation 38, 39
    see also Tanzania
Tanzania
    agricultural policies 130, 178–82
    debt 183
    industrialization 175–8
    population 150
    post-independence economic
        performance 173–4, 239, 240
    socialism 173, 174
    state control of economy 174–5
        weaknesses of 182
    worker participation policy 131
Togo 38, 39
trade agreements
    post-colonial 59, 60, 104–5
transfer of power
    and political structures 56–7, 232–3
    process of 4–5, 8, 56
transport costs
    and manufacturing 44

ujamaa system 173
    and Tanzanian agricultural policies
        180–1
Unilever
    colonial political change and business
        policies 10–11
United Africa Company 9
United States of America
    disapproval of colonial regimes 22

wages
    in post-colonial Nigeria 152
    post-war rises 44, 46
welfare services
    in Tanzania 173
white settlers 5, 11–12
    in Kenya 163, 167
    in Southern Rhodesia 45

workers' councils
    in Tanzania 176

Zaire 35, 58
    capital formation 39
    debt 120
Zambia 39